November 2015   ch
9/17
P—

To Jen,

Enjoy my

ONE GOOD TREE

ONE WOMAN'S JOURNEY THROUGH
THE TURBULENT SIXTIES, VIETNAM AND
THE COUNTER CULTURE

Time Capsule
Peace on Earth

Irene

ONE GOOD TREE

*One Woman's Journey through
the Turbulent Sixties, Vietnam and
the Counter Culture*

IRENE ISOBEL CARVER

LUMINARE PRESS

WWW.LUMINAREPRESS.COM

Luminare Press
467 W 17th Ave
Eugene, OR 97401
www.luminarepress.com

LCCN: 2015955697
ISBN: 978-1-937303-66-2

I would like to dedicate this book to my son Paulie

Thank you, son, for having the courage to be my firstborn. You truly were the side kick sent from God to keep me from falling off life's edge and it was no easy job.

Eternal love, Mum

ACKNOWLEDGMENTS

I would like to thank my Siskiyou County Writers Group without whom this book, would just not be this book. First, great gratitude to our teacher, the ever wise and cool Jacalyn McNamara.

Secondly, to the amazing group of astute listeners Melinda Field, Donna May, Sally Landaker, Madeleine DeAndreis-Ayres, Catherine Barash, Leslie Berkhart, and Roberta Van de Water. Thanks Gals, I couldn't have done it without you.

Prologue

TO BEGIN THIS BOOK, I WILL PARAPHRASE THE MUCH admired Dylan Thomas, "I write for the love of Man and in praise of God"—my feelings exactly.

I am sixty-six years old now and for fifteen years I have wanted to be able to identify what it is I need to write and why; I hope I am finally there. Much time has lapsed as I waited for inspiration; I am tired of waiting. I have determined that writing, for me, will take strategy and perseverance, not merely inspiration. But I will not rule out divine assistance. Maybe if I finally and consistently show up, the divine will as well.

I say *need* to write, but it is probably more accurate to say that I need to communicate something. I have generally attributed this to astrology, as five planets were in the sign of Gemini at the time of my birth, and in the grand scheme of things Gemini's planetary job is to communicate. I surely hope it is astrological and not ego or narcissism that drives the words to this page. I guess I will find out as I go along. In the meantime, I will tell the stories of who we were and allow myself to emerge into who I am.

Chapter One

Woodstock

WE WERE THE UNCOMMON ONES, THE ONES WITH the tickets to Woodstock and a babysitter, to say nothing of the bra I wore there! Okay, so I just wasn't naturally hip, but Woodstock was one hell of a crash course, I'll tell you that. People traveled from as far as Texas and California for this event in New York and there were lots of children there. To this day I say one of the best decisions I ever made in my life was to leave my son, Paulie, at home with his grandparents.

We had been living in apartment 9N for five months and almost immediately met the people in 8N, Gwen and Randy. They were another young couple with a one-year-old son, so before we knew it we were at each other's apartments in the evenings, smoking joints and listening to music. As soon as we heard the advertisements for Woodstock we began making our plans to go together. We planned to leave on Thursday evening as soon as Paul and Randy got home from work. The concert was Friday, Saturday, and Sunday so we figured we'd get there and get our camp spot the night before. On Thursday afternoon Gwen and I took our sons to their grandparents' so our cars would be all packed when our husbands got home. Gwen and I were quite the pair planning for Woodstock; it sounds like an oxymoron in retrospect, but plan we did.

"What are you bringing for clothes?" Gwen asked me.

"An extra pair of jeans, three tops, four pairs of underwear, and a night shirt, and you?" "Sounds good to me," Gwen agreed.

We decided we needed two cars in case we had to sleep in them and also, as I found out, so Gwen could pack her kitchen sink. Did I tell you Gwen is full-blooded Italian? She packed a cast iron pan, a 12" spaghetti pot, sausage, pepperoni, capers, cheese, crackers, and everything else a stoned person could want to munch on. I packed a tent, sleeping bags, potatoes, eggs, juice, Kraft macaroni and cheese in boxes, and chocolate chip cookies. Paul and Randy were in charge of the pot! Off we went on a beautiful August night heading for the Massachusetts Turnpike to New York. Woodstock was about a four-hour drive from our house on a normal day but nothing normal was about to happen. Somewhere on the New York State Thruway the traffic began to get very slow, eventually stopping. When we began to realize that we weren't going to move for a while, people began getting out of their cars. People were sitting on the hoods of their cars and music was blasting from car radios. Woodstock had begun; we just didn't know it. By early morning we had inched our way off the freeway and into the town of Woodstock. Eventually we realized that this was as close as we were going to get so we pulled into the first place that looked like a good spot to camp and we set up housekeeping. Paul, Randy and I put up the tent while Gwen set up her kitchen.

We thought we were going to be the early birds with our campsite all set up, but when we walked the fifteen minutes from our campsite to the concert grounds, we were completely blown away to find that there was no gate, no

Irene Isobel Carver

collecting of tickets, and thousands of people were already camping on the festival grounds. No kitchen sinks here— this was a sleeping bag and crackers world. People were too high to eat. LSD was surely afoot; it was time to feed your head, not your stomach. I will never forget the feeling I had as I stood at the top of the hill by the outhouses and looked down to the stage over a sea of heads. I felt it physically in my chest. It wasn't the tightness of fear but the opposite, my whole being expanded in awe. I now knew what the saying, "it blew my mind" actually felt like. I was carrying a blanket and Paul was wearing the backpack. We stopped, held one another's hands and both audibly gasped at the sea of people before us. Gwen was next to me and she suddenly yelled out, "Mikey, hey, Mikey," and there, twenty feet from us, was Gwen's brother. What are the odds? Well, we went no further. We set our blankets down next to him and prepared for the unpreparable.

We assumed we were going to Woodstock to hear all these incredible bands, but when we got there, the music became the background to an experience with its own momentum. I can't remember when the rain began because all that was going on around me totally overrode the weather, but begin it did; I mean the monsoons began, I mean we became the rain. A mudslide began about ten people over to our left. Wild-haired, barely-dressed, and tattooed people began to slide in the mud on purpose. Soon there was a line of people running, sliding, rolling, reveling, and becoming very much one with the mud. I watched people sliding in the mud to the music of Ten Years After; it was incredible, we were making rain fun instead of annoying. Who needed to be clean anyway? We had been clean all our lives. Becoming one with mud was about equal to two years of therapy for those sliding, and one year for those watching. I could just feel the pent up anger and confinement draining away. The people sliding must have been the people on the "good acid." Over the speaker system it was being announced that there was some "bad acid" going around. "Don't take the brown acid," they announced over and over. Apparently people were having some very bad trips. Then they asked if there were any nurses in the crowd and if they would please come to a tent up front by the stage. We all looked at Gwen who said, "Hey, I may be a nurse but there is no way I'm going into a tent with a bunch of people on bad acid." Her brother looked at her and said, "And I wouldn't even let you, you haven't even tried acid yet, you're not qualified," and we all laughed.

It was while watching these people that I realized I had on a bra. I looked down at my breasts. Since the age of twelve they had been safely held in their white uniform protected from gravity. Without a word, I took down the shoulder straps, unsnapped my bra, and quietly put it in the bottom of my backpack. I didn't put one on again for three years.

When Richie Havens came onstage and sang "Freedom" every cell in my body vibrated with the new meaning of this word. But the real energy changing event happened for me when Country Joe and the Fish came on stage and began to yell, "Give me an F, Give me a U, Give me a C, Give me a K, what's that spell?" And 500,000 people yelled, "FUCK." Oh my God, we yelled "FUCK" three times and the unblocking of repressed emotion I felt was better than any high. It was lift-off for me and I have never really come down. You see, when I was thirteen years old, I was punished for a week for saying the word "fart" out loud; it was not ladylike. Gum chewing was considered cheap and walking with more than two friends was not allowed; it was too much like a gang. So as I yelled the work "FUCK" with the other half-million people, the words "well- bred" were cast from my psyche. My soul was escaping the restrictions of all that had meant and I was soaring with my wild woman self that had been waiting for me to learn to fly. County Joe kept singing, "One, two, three what are we fighting for?" I looked over at Paul and I could see his hand beginning to shake, so I scooted over next to him and took hold of his hand.

PAUL

I slipped my hand out of Irene's as I could feel myself crashing down from my high space. The sound of the helicopters that were bringing musicians and supplies into the concert were opening up the fear and tension in my body that I had been trying to ignore. I stood up, thinking, I've got to get out of here. Country Joe sang on, "don't ask me I don't give a damn, next stop is Vietnam." I ducked behind an outhouse as the whirling sounds of the helicopters catapulted me back to the scene where I held a fallen soldier whose leg had been blown off. My arms were waving wildly to the copter alerting him to my position while I found my tourniquet and wrapped it with as much pressure as I could around the soldier's thigh. I saw the medic and another soldier lift him into the copter. I was startled when I felt someone touch my shoulder and I looked up into the eyes of a girl with a multicolored peace sign painted on her forehead. She asked, "Are you alright, did you take the bad acid?"

"Yea, I took the bad acid alright, it's called war," I said

as I stood up looking around, remembering where I was. "Here, have this," she said as she handed me a small hemp braided wristband. "I made it." She gave me a kiss on my cheek and walked away. I shoved the wrist band into my jeans pocket and walked back to our blanket and sat down feeling drained, exhausted.

I took hold of Paul's hand as he sat close to me and I could feel his pain as it moved from his hand to mine. Out of the corner of my eye I could see that his chest looked caved in and his macramé cross hung suspended in the void. His shoulder length strawberry blonde hair hung in his eyes and I was unable to make eye contact with him, but at least his hand wasn't shaking now.

I closed my eyes and a memory of Paul waking in the night a few months back came to me. He had been shaking and sweating as he dove under our bed and screamed at me to get down. He would have shoved me out of bed with him except that I slapped him really hard across the face to wake him up. I shook my head, not wanting to go back to that scene. I looked to the stage; Arlo Guthrie was singing "Coming into Los Angeles, bringing in a couple of keys . . ." Someone helped me get back to the present by passing me a joint. I let go of Paul's hand and sucked in a hit. I passed it to Paul and I could feel his desperation as he sucked in hit after hit before he passed it on. *Could the smoke hold back his memories*, I wondered?

It was then that I felt someone tap me on the shoulder and ask, "Hey, you want to cop a bead of opium?" Randy, sitting next to me whispered in my ear, "It's probably a ball of tar he got off the street corner." "How much?" I asked. "Ten bucks." I pulled a ten-dollar bill out of my jeans pocket,

Irene Isobel Carver

put the little black tar ball into my pipe, and suddenly I was all cool and savvy; it wasn't tar. I lay back on the blanket and looked up; there was actually some blue sky and white clouds as I drifted away from the past. "I like your vibe," said the dude lying behind me on our little spot of claimed earth. "I'm married," I said as I passed him my pipe. Smiling, I sunk into the word vibe. *You're on my wavelength,* I thought to myself, and I felt like I was picking up words from the air; some cosmic vibration that was happening, a gift of the magical moment.

From then on I seemed to stay on a wavelength of calmness. I didn't own any of Paul's experience and when Gwen went back to our campsite and didn't come back all day, I had no fear wondering about her. I was somehow, amidst the thousands of people, encapsulated in my own vibration. I didn't stray far from our little group physically but I did stray quite far in my mind. Imbedded in my soul is the memory of when Joe Cocker came on stage and with one twang from his guitar he began singing, "I get high with a little help from my friends," which silenced half-a-million people. With his spastic movements and intense shrieking, everything else stopped, and after his performance the rain started. Apparently the sky Gods had come to hear him as well and with them came the rain. Nothing was ever the same.

The rain sent Paul, Randy, and I back to our campsite where Gwen was busy protecting her kitchen from the attack of the elements. We huddled in our tent eating pepperoni and cheese and waited for the rain to stop. It didn't. A mini soup kitchen formed around our tent because Gwen had brought a beef bone of course, just in case. Others brought over a carrot, an onion, a piece of kale here and there, and she just kept adding water. Someone pulled out a deck of cards. From inside our tent we could hear Crosby Stills, Nash, and Young singing "Wooden Ships." The speaker system was amazing.

We made the grand decision to leave early Sunday morning knowing we would miss Jimi Hendrix, but we just didn't have it in us to stay. We were, after all, still the ones with jobs to go to on Monday morning; same jobs—different heads.

Chapter Two

Official Maniac, I Mean Mainer

I FELT LIKE I WAS "BORN AGAIN" AT WOODSTOCK; at least that's the opinion of one of my Gemini twin selves. Now I'll let the other half give you *her* story.

I came to earth with a bang on July 4, 1948. My mother was Mary Macalister Adams. She and her doctor planned my arrival. You see, I was due to be born on July fourteenth, but the doctor wanted to go on vacation, so he and my mother decided that the Fourth of July would make a lovely birthday; he could just "start my mother up," as Mummy always said. I never did get the story about how a doctor started a women's labor back in 1948, but I kept a copy of my birth announcement, which read:

Goodness gracious sakes alive,
here's little Adams number five.
Seven pounds three ounces of dynamite,
this little girl is more than alright.

When I first began to learn about astrology, I wondered if my mother and doctor had disturbed my life's rhythm with this early start, but with time I have come to believe that God set the time of my birth and the people involved fell into step with the divine plan. The perfection of the universe set up my five Gemini planets, which move in their orbits as I move in mine, living a story that I feel destined to tell. It was a beautiful morning in South Portland, Maine when I joined the world stage. My dad always kidded that I came in screaming and haven't shut up since. Apparently, I'm not about to either!

Early one spring morning, when I was about six years old, I was sitting near the forsythia bush when my two brothers began to trap bees in a glass jar and then threw lit matches in the jar. I ran screaming to my mother who said, "Oh my, boys, go wash your hands. Renie, it's time for lunch." As I looked into my mother's calm face, I felt myself go numb as I realized that no one was going to protect the bees, butterflies, insects, or me. I ran to my apple tree, where I always felt protected, with tears streaming down my face.

My mother was the matriarch of our home. Before marriage she had been Mary MacAllister, a beautiful and classy, one hundred percent Scottish lassie. She was born on May 11, 1906. She loved her Catholic faith, but in marriage her dignity and pride would not allow any of the hard truths of our family to be looked at; denial was her ally.

My dad, John James Bushbee Adams, was born September 28, 1904 to Margaret 0'Riley, a beautiful sixteen-year-old girl who landed in Boston fresh off the boat from Ireland. She was alone in a new country, young and naïve, before birth control was common. My father was fortunate to be the oldest of the seven children that Margaret gave birth to. Margaret's husband died young in a street brawl and she had no means to support her children. There was no public assistance in those days. The children were all taken from her and put into foster care, except for my dad, who went to live with his German grandmother, Emma Koch. Margaret begged the Catholic Church to help her keep her children but she failed to get their sympathy or their money. Maggie had become an alcoholic and at that time this was seen as a "moral weakness" instead of a disease. The church and society judged her harshly as an unfit mother and took her children away.

My dad's paternal grandmother, Emma, lived with her sister Jenny in a poor but happy multi-ethnic neighborhood on Columbia Street in Cambridge, Massachusetts. My dad was seven when his family was split apart and Emma and Jenny felt they could take care of their Johnny together. My dad received two blessings early in his life: first, he was born with a natural kinesthetic ability and played all sports with excellence. Secondly, the local librarian took an interest in my dad and encouraged him to read a wide variety of books; not just the sports books he had come to the library to borrow. She became a mentor to him during his elementary school years, requiring him to give her book reports on the classics like Huck Finn and Moby Dick, which she would steer him to.

When my dad missed his siblings and asked his grandmother where they were and what happened, she told him the truth—that after his father's death his mother's drinking became quite bad and she could not care for the children. So at a very young age my father vowed never to touch a drop of alcohol. He kept that vow until he was thirty-three years old. During those years he went from Cambridge High and Latin School to Exeter Academy in New Hampshire, then to Harvard University on a sports scholarship, where he was the captain of the baseball team. He was also on the hockey team. I always felt that my father's intense ambition was due to the shame that he felt around his mother's life; he couldn't be proud of his family but he would be proud of himself. My dad was a wonderful and loving man. It is so very sad that he ever had that first drink, as alcohol would continue to be a heavy cross to bear. My father found out the hard way that alcoholism is cunning, baffling, and powerful.

After college in 1930, my dad went to work for the New England Telephone and Telegraph Company, AT&T. Even though dad had a degree from Harvard, the telephone company had a policy that every employee needed to start at the foundation of the company and learn all the ropes to get to the top. Being an agile man, my dad climbed those poles as a lineman, connecting telephone cables, mastering the physical jobs, and then literally climbing his way quickly to Public Affairs Manager.

If you read Tip O'Neill's memoir, in it he refers to his friend, whom he calls Mr. Telephone; yup, that was my dad. Tip and my dad grew up together in the North Cambridge neighborhood where the famous Barry's Corner group originated. They used to belt out that old song "Heart of my heart, old friends were dearer then." What a great old ballad that was. To this day, when I miss my parents, I stand out under the night sky and sing those words and it brings back precious memories. I also owe the Telephone Company a moment of thanks for setting up the meeting of my parents in 1934. I love the story of how my parents met; it was so romantic and divinely orchestrated.

At age twenty-eight, Mary Macalister had also risen from an order clerk at AT&T to the supervisor of all the service representatives. That job had always been held by a man, but times were changing, and when the position became available for a woman, Mary slipped right into that place. It was September, and in an effort to sign up the Harvard students with their own telephones, the phone company set up a booth outside the Harvard Coop, manned by two people, John Adams and Mary Macalister; shall I say the rest is history? Yes, and a painfully shocking history, I must say, as the hand of God moved in.

My parents had this job for two weeks. As the days passed, John began to walk Mary home and soon they planned dates. Mary began to fall in love with this handsome and majorly cool catch, but there was one glitch—John already had another girlfriend named Eleanor McGowen. Mary wasn't happy about this, but for about six months she accepted that he was dating them both, hoping he would fall in love with her and drop Eleanor. These were innocent times, when dating went on for years without too much physical connection and John and Mary were still in the romantic deep kissing stage. It was during that time that Mary's younger sister, Irene, was in a sanatorium in New Hampshire with tuberculosis. John and Mary would take Saturday drives up from Boston to visit her. When my sisters and I were teenagers, mum would tell us this very private story. She would capture our attention anytime we brought up a dating issue by retelling how she and my dad had been driving home from New Hampshire one Saturday when she realized she was falling in love too deeply. She told him it was time for him to choose between her and Eleanor. We would sit mesmerized as mum told us how her heart broke when dad told her he wasn't ready to make that choice, but mum stuck by her guns and stop dating him.

That story has been a role model for me all my life. My mother respected herself too much to let a man two-time her. She said that if he couldn't grow up and make a choice, then she didn't really want him. Then came the hard part as she had to let the man she loved go, and could only hope and pray that he would come back and choose her, which, of course did happen, or I would not be telling you this story.

Irene Isobel Carver

Chapter Three

$\mathcal{F}ate\ \mathcal{H}as\ \mathcal{I}ts\ \mathcal{W}ay$

MY PARENTS WERE MARRIED ON JUNE 16, 1937. They went on a ten-day honeymoon to Bermuda where they conceived their first child and nine months later, on March 26,1938, their son was born and died, only living for nine minutes due to brain damage. After two days of labor, the baby arrived feet first. If it had been modern times the doctors would have performed a caesarean section and saved the baby. Many times over the years, she would tell us how beautiful our first little brother was, with eyelashes so long they were down to the middle of his tiny cheek. She always ended by saying that we had an angel brother watching over us from heaven.

A couple of weeks after the baby's birth and death, the mailman came to the door and seeing mum was no longer pregnant, he asked her if she had a boy or a girl. Mum, who had been in shock, ran weeping to her room and remained there for days. The pain of that loss never went away. Over the years, when mum would tell me the story, she would squeeze my hand so hard that I thought it would break; I always let her squeeze. Forty-eight years later, when my dad died, the first thing mum said to me was, "Now he is with our little son in heaven." The connection of love to her first-born was so strong, it was as if those forty-eight years had not passed at all and she was comforted to know that dad would be with their baby. When mum went for her six-week check up after losing the baby, the doctor told her she was healthy as a horse and should go right home and get pregnant again, and that is what she did. Nine months later, on February 25, 1939, my sister Janet was born. In 1941 my brother Johnny was born, and Alex was born in 1943.

My dad was a hospital trustee in Cambridge, Massachusetts when Alex was due to be born, so the doctors offered my parents their 1943 high-tech medical knowledge. My mother, along with most people of those times, regarded doctors as gods and didn't think to question them. Feeling special, my mother decided to go ahead and try the gas they offered that would eliminate all birth pain. As the story goes, they gave my mother so much gas that she was groggy for three days. My brother was born with terrible eczema, which went into his ears, causing hearing loss. He was also mentally slow. If that wasn't bad enough, the pediatricians told my mother to tie Alex's hands to the crib so that he wouldn't scratch himself when he slept. I have had a hard time coming to terms with how a mother could actually tie a baby to a crib, no matter what the doctors advised. So began the karmic illusion busting of my parents' dreams for their children. They fantasized about Johnny going to Harvard, and Alex going to Yale; what a fun rivalry that would be.

Dad's grandmother, who raised him, now needed some caring, so she came to live with this growing family. The ninety-year-old Emma would sit in her mahogany rocker that had roses carved in the wood, offering to rock Alex when he was crying, but mum, trying to be a more modern mother, told Emma she didn't want the baby spoiled. Emma, disappointed at modern thinking, had to make do by knitting squares for the endless afghans she made, mumbling that you can never give a baby too much love. Emma died before I was born.

Daddy would occasionally bring home a can of sauerkraut and a jar of pig's feet he would buy at a delicatessen in Harvard Square. The entire house would smell of this new pungent odor when he heated them on the stove. It was the only time I ever saw my father cook, and tears would be running down his cheeks as he remembered his grandmother. He'd take a hanky out of his pocket, blow his nose hard and keep stirring. As children, we were very glad we weren't raised in Germany because we hated the smell of these delicacies, and the thought of pig's feet was downright scary! But dad's German blood did sneak in, as two of us five girls show our German heritage in our broad hips. Birthing hips, the doctors called them, and, actually, I now love sauerkraut and have even made my own.

My dad was promoted to District Sales Manager of AT&T and was transferred to Portland, Maine in 1946. Off the family went, and bought a beautiful house in South Portland, which had a view of the ocean and a screened in porch that circled the entire house—all for the whopping cost of $12,000! It was here that my older sister Clare and I were conceived and born. Therefore, we are official Mainers, or "Maniacs," as I call us. You could live in Maine all your life, but if you were not born there, you were not considered a Mainer. I, of course, did it backwards. I was born there but only lived there for four months of my life. I will forever be an official Mainer and I have lobster earrings to prove it.

My sister, Clare, was born a year-and-a-half before I was, and we are the only two in the family with my dad's brown eyes; the rest have our mother's green eyes. Dad told mum he wanted to name the first baby born there, and he wasn't going to tell my mother the name until she was born. He wanted to name her after County Clare, Ireland, where his ancestors were from, and he didn't want any disagreement from my Scottish mother. He got his wish and Clare actually looks the most like him.

When Clare was nine months old, Mum got pregnant with me and she was not happy about this since she had just gotten her figure back. But because of her faith, she pulled herself together pretty quickly and had just one request of God: Could the baby please be a girl so she could hand down all the baby clothes from Clare, and as we grew we could share the same bedroom and play together. As mum prayed for this during her pregnancy with me, she also realized that she wanted a girl so she could name her after her beloved sister Irene, who had died fourteen years earlier.

Did I say, "All The World's A Stage"?

On a July fourth morning in Maine, 1948, the next generation Irene entered the family scene. Yes, my mother got her prayer answered; I was a girl, which was convenient, if nothing else. Mum also got another wish, as my dad was transferred back to Boston where they bought a house in Bridgetown—just a stone's throw from their beloved Harvard Square. The ever-growing family of five children happily moved into our "Tara" in Bridgetown on Aunt Irene's birthday, October 28, 1948, when I was almost four months old. This house was my mother's fortress from loneliness; the loneliness she had experienced while in Maine, which she never wanted to experience again. I realized, over time, that if my mother was more than a half-hour from Harvard

Square, she was lonely, or as she put it, "I'd just feel out of the loop."

My mother and father once visited me in Seattle and I took them on a ferry to Vashon Island. As we drove around, my mother commented, "Oh they must be so lonely out here." That began a series of quotes from my mother on what loneliness is. Here's the kicker: "Hell itself is never-ending loneliness." In other words, if you weren't in the heart of the social action, then you surely must be lonely. Ma once said to me, "I hope when I die, I just go shopping and drop dead right next to Nini's Corner." That was a little newsstand right next to the Harvard Coop where she met my dad.

Our Bridgetown house qualified as "not lonely" because you could drive to Harvard Square in fifteen minutes and it was right on the bus line, should something happen to your car. We were also right on the town line of Larchmont, a slightly more exclusive area that gave me all three of my husbands. My mother was forty-two years old when we moved into that house, and we celebrated fifty years there, just one month after she died at the age of ninety-two. My mother loved her house and I knew she wanted to die right there, but it was not to be. I was blessed to be with her on her last day there, and as we drove down our beloved tree-lined street in an ambulance to the hospital, I watched as my mother's eyes turned sideways to look out the window at the neighbors' houses as we passed. I knew she was saying goodbye; she knew she wouldn't be back. But I'm skipping ahead. We have fifty years of gracious and grueling living to do and I have to introduce you to my apple tree.

Chapter four

My Giving Tree

"I will go back a little while and be with old untroubled things.
There was a hill where huckleberries grew and a tree no wind could harm."

—Author Unknown

THIS IS A QUOTE FROM A POEM I LOVE. IT SURELY speaks to my heart. I came and went through love and war, marriage and divorce, and I could always return home to my Tara and my apple tree, right where I left them. There stands my tree with all her gnarly roots, ready to absorb my pain or share my joy. I keep a tiny piece of her bark on my altar wherever I am living and occasionally I put it on my tongue, like communion, and I go back in time for a little while.

When we were growing up, this tree was our summer shade while we were playing dolls. My sisters and I would spread out a blanket and host a tea party for our baby dolls, which grew into playing with Barbie dolls. When I outgrew dolls, I would lie in the shade for hours reading book after book. I floated away one summer into *Judy's Journey*, as the author took me on an adventure with a migrant family to Georgia to pick peaches. Slowly our books grew into

Irene Isobel Carver

romance novels until one summer my sisters and I read the queen of all books, *Gone with the Wind*. When Clare finished it, she passed it to me, then I passed it to Teresa, and Teresa passed it to Brigette. On the last page, we each wrote of our eternal love for Scarlett and how sure or unsure we were that she would get Rhett back.

The gentle summer breeze would rustle the leaves of the apple tree overhead and lull me to sleep only to be awakened by rolling onto a gnarly root that was sticking through the sparse earth, or by one of my brothers picking up an apple and bopping me on the head with it. I would jump up, spill lemonade all over me, and the blissful tranquility of the summer's day would be broken. I would begin heaving apples back at my brother, wondering just why God found it necessary to create boys at all. It didn't take me long to figure it out.

I was fifteen when I met Paul "Tiger" O'Connell. The nickname "Tiger" was because of his beautiful strawberry blonde hair, but also because he was the one in his crowd always ready for a fight. Those were the days of high school rumbles, where gangs of boys from different parts of town would set up a Friday night street fight like it was a sport. No one really got hurt; it was just a way for teenage boys to release the testosterone taking over their bodies. In Paul's case, as I grew to know and love him and his family, I could see that he was also motivated to fight by his frustration with his father, Ed, and his anger at his mother. Paul did not respect his father, who was a mild-mannered man who read the gospel in church on Sundays. Paul found his mother, Dora, very irritating as she would begin drinking whiskey at dinnertime and then would annoy them all evening asking questions while they were trying to watch television. Paul would tell his mother to be quiet but Ed would not allow this. Ed just tolerated the constant interruptions and Paul judged his father to be complete wimp. Paul vowed not to be like his father, and thus the scrappy "Tiger" was born.

Paul was only five feet nine inches tall. He realized that if he was going to fight, he'd better begin lifting weights. So in the evenings, he retreated to the basement where he had set up a gym. Occasionally, he took some of his mother's whiskey and really got into smashing the punching bag. But I didn't fall in love with the Tiger part of Paul. What I saw was the gentle sadness buried deep in his sky blue eyes and the playful boy in his madras shirt who would drive me home from school on the handlebars of his bike on the side street so no one would see us stealing kisses. On a deeper level, I needed Paul. I needed an escape valve. Our house, which warded off my mother's loneliness, also kept buried the roots of my brother's mental illness, and masked the dysfunction of my dad's alcoholism.

It took me many years to admit to the word "molestation," but there it is finally, like it has the right to exist and be expressed. My friend Annie had to actually convince me to use that word. We were camping in the back of my pickup truck one hot summer night on the edge of the Trinity River in Northern California. As she, my sister Bridgette, and I lay there like three peas in a pod looking up at a million stars, our friend told us of her molestation. I told her about our brother Alex touching and fondling us sexually when we were growing up, saying that I could not relate to the word molestation, because to me that word brought up images of violence, fear, and pain, and my experience contained none of that. We lay there performing psychic surgery on our souls, with each of us taking turns telling our stories.

Irene Isobel Carver

We gave ourselves the theme of the first time we had sex. I was lying in the middle and said that I would go first. Both heads turned abruptly to me when I said that I was fifteen-and-a-half the first time that I went all the way. The quiet and pensive attitude suddenly changed as both of them began firing questions at me.

"Did you use birth control?"

"Weren't you afraid of getting pregnant?"

"What about burning in hell forever?"

"What if he told everybody?"

"Did you plan it?"

All of their own fears came rushing forward like shooting stars from the heavens. I didn't respond until Annie calmly said, "How did you make such a major decision so young?" I looked up at the endless stars above me and realized that none of these questions had even occurred to me. I had just let Paul follow and continue the path that my brother Alex began when I was seven. That path began one hot summer's day, while I was reading on the porch.

I loved to curl up on the upstairs screened porch under the shade of the apple tree. It was my tree house and was so quiet that I could hear the bees buzzing and the summer breeze moving through the leaves. Alex would sometimes join me and bring me some penny candy from the store down the street. He knew I loved the cherry-flavored red money, soft and chewy and shaped like quarters. Alex was twelve and I was seven. Alex would carefully begin to "tickle" my leg as I nibbled my candy slowly to make it last. We called this touch "tickling" because he would move his hand slowly over an area with the tips of his fingers, like a curtain blowing gently back and forth in the breeze. It felt wonderful and could have lulled me to sleep, but Alex's tickling would move gently from foot to knee, and then ever so gently move up my dress to my thigh. Alex would distract me, saying "read that part again," as he pretended interest in whatever book I was reading.

I remember I had a book called *The Like-To-Do Stories*. I loved this book because in all the stories there were fairies that followed the children around helping them make the right decisions. If a word was hard to pronounce, Alex would help me sound it out as he moved his hand ever closer to my underwear. If he got too close and I felt odd, I'd just get up and walk away. He would never force me to stay but sometimes he would try to coax me with more candy. I never felt scared of him. There were times when he could distract me enough to get me interested and I would let him move my underwear to the side and explore my little girl-ness. My cheeks would get hot and pink. I could have floated onto my favorite branch of the apple tree, except the crows would begin a major ruckus, causing us both to stop and be embarrassed.

Annie chimed in, "Your first moment of shame." But I had to disagree as I thought that shame would make you feel dirty and I didn't feel that. On the contrary, I remember feeling quite beautiful. What I experienced was true sensuality. A gentle touch, a summer's day, my tree and a brother whom I knew loved me, and whom I loved. It was society and the church that taught shame and I was not paying attention to their opinion. I was listening to the bees, the breeze rustling in the leaves, and the crows.

Now as I look back and analyze how this affected my life and why I can now call it molestation, I see that it broke down my personal and physical boundaries. I got used to being touched by a boy at an early age and it felt good. So

Irene Isobel Carver

when I met Paul at the age of fifteen and he made the same advances, it did not seem odd or unnatural to me. I'm not sure why my Catholic upbringing didn't fill me with the necessary fear and guilt to keep me from being sexually active at such a young age, but it didn't. I was standing at a fork in the road of life and I took the well-worn path to physical pleasure. Now it seems obvious to me that it was genetic. I already had the personality traits of an alcoholic, being careless, self-willed, and fearless. It was only by the grace of God and some caution on Paul's part that I didn't get pregnant until I was nineteen.

Chapter Five

Boys Will Be Boys

PAUL AND I GREW UP IN AN AMERICAN GRAFFITI world, and the movie about Ron Kovic (*Born on the Fourth of July*) depicted our world-view at the time. We were brainwashed, hometown USA kids. Joining the army was a way of growing up and becoming a man, as well as a way to see the world. It was 1965; I was naive, and my consciousness had not yet been cracked open. The horror of the Vietnam War was yet to hit us, ripping open millions of hearts; the pain of it forcing America awake.

Paul had been attending a junior college in downtown Boston for two months, when one evening his high school pal Teddy came over to his parents' house and told him of "the Buddy System" that the army was offering. If three people signed up to join the army together, then you would be kept together, and assigned to the same base. Teddy smuggled in a couple of beers in his jacket, and they went down to the basement to discuss this and figure out who the third friend should be. When the beer was gone, they hopped into Teddy's '59 black Impala and drove to Ralph Delbeanco's house. They stopped and bought a six-pack this time. They didn't want to go into Ralph's house with his parents there. Teddy knocked at the door and soon Ralph, aka, Del, was in the backseat with an open Budweiser. The

Irene Isobel Carver

three of them cruised through the Mount Auburn cemetery, where all big decisions can be made, drinking, planning, and laughing until the beer was all gone and they had a plan to go to the recruiters office the following Monday morning instead of going to school. When Paul told me I wasn't surprised. I had one more year of high school and I was sad that I wouldn't have a boyfriend around to make it more fun. I had no plans to find another boyfriend as I was in love with Paul and knew I would be at home waiting for him when he returned. Loyalty was in my heart and he assured me he felt the same.

In October, Paul and his buddies were sent to Fort Dix, New Jersey, for boot camp. Teddy egged them on to become paratroopers, so the three of them were placed in the 101st Airborne in Fort Bragg, North Carolina. Paul graduated from boot camp with leave to come home for Christmas. Then the three buddies went to Fort Bragg, North Carolina for their paratrooper training. After another leave home for a month, the 101st Airborne Division was sent to do their one-year-tour of duty in Vietnam. The one-year part was the only sane thing about this war, as it gave us a beginning and an end to the fear and separation that war causes, which is something our other major wars did not have. From June 1966 through June 1967, Paul was in Vietnam. We chanted, "We can do this" over and over as we bolstered one another up during our last goodbyes. "It's only one year and we've got angels to watch over us," we told each other; our Catholic training at last had a purpose.

I spent that year at Boston State College, but my heart was never in it; I was just waiting for Paul to come home. My friend Maryanne would meet me in the cafeteria for lunch and we would cram in the study hall, but I just didn't care. By year's end it showed and I flunked all my classes except English Literature and Psychology, in which I got A's. As I stood holding the letter saying that I had flunked out, I remembered when I was a sophomore in high school overhearing my parents having a conversation about me. I stood outside their bedroom door trying not to move a muscle or cause the floorboards to creek. Dad was saying "Let's start putting money aside to send Renie to Trinity College in Ireland." I realized how big my father's dreams were for me and how much he loved me. But at the time the word *Ireland* had made me shrink with fear. I had just started going steady with Paul and I didn't want to leave him or any of my friends.

My father read the letter that I handed him, crumpling it as he threw it in the trash next to his chair. I saw his jaw clenched in defeat. "I guess we should have enrolled you in the Katie Gibbs Secretarial School in the first place, like your mother had wanted." I took his hand and said, "I'm sorry I'm such a disappointment Dad; it's the damn war, I just can't concentrate on things that don't matter to me." "Are you saying I shouldn't waste my money on Katie Gibbs either?" Dad said as he stood angrily. "No, Paul will be home from Nam soon and I won't be so stressed, and I do want to learn to type. I think I'll make a good writer someday," I said as I threw my arms around his neck and whispered, "I promise I'll try hard at Katie Gibbs." I needed his forgiveness.

1967—THE SUMMER OF LOVE

Paul returned home after his one-year tour of duty in Nam in June of 1967. That summer, the radio played the song "San Francisco," about the transformation taking place all over the country. The media termed it "the summer of love." Paul and I didn't need to go to San Francisco to be swept into the love vibration; after a year separated by war we were now inseparable. At summer's end, before I went to the Katie Gibbs School, and before Paul's leave from the Army was over, we spent the weekend in a friend's cabin on Lake Winapasocci, New Hampshire. We had never slept overnight together and on that comfortable and magical weekend I conceived our son, Paulie. I was only nineteen.

September arrived and Boston was teaming with life. Not only were thousands of college students arriving from all over the country like they did every year, but the Boston Red Sox were playing in the World Series. Everyone had baseball fever. You couldn't help but catch it, it was in the very air we breathed and it was electric. When I took the trolley to school each morning, the intensity of war seemed to be lessened by the exquisite fall air and the joy of baseball throughout the streets. Baseball united perfect strangers on street corners as they recapped a pitch or a throw while waiting for a light to change. For three whole weeks, war was not the headlines; that was a gift.

In the midst of this I was beginning to feel the first queasy churnings of morning sickness. As I sat at my type-writer, listening and following instructions on how to hold my fingers on the keyboard, fear began to creep in as I waited anxiously each day for my period to arrive. It didn't. When my period was two weeks overdue and the Red Sox had lost the series, I told my unsuspecting mother that I was not going to school that day because I thought I could be pregnant. My mother asked me how late I was and when I told her ten days, she dried her hands on her apron, stopped her morning chores, and took me to a clinic in Cambridge where they took a urine sample called a rabbit test. We came back home after the test and my mother sent me to my room and told me to say the rosary. My penance had begun.

At 4:30 p.m. the phone rang. I sat up in bed and held my breath. When I heard my mother hang up the phone, I went downstairs and saw her stirring gravy in the pot on the stove. She looked up at me and said, "It's positive." As I began to walk by her, she took my hand and quoted a poem by John Greenleaf Whittier: "The saddest words of tongue or pen are these, my dear, it might have been." I went out to the backyard and climbed my apple tree. I sat way up high on the branch I called my airplane. My mind fought to find a balance as I tilted between childhood and motherhood while the evening sky turned a brilliant pink. When all the color had left the sky and only the rooftops were etched against the last edges of light, I climbed down from the tree, leaving childhood behind me forever.

My two younger sisters were in the kitchen dipping bread in the gravy when I walked back into the house. Mum gave me a "don't say a word" look, so I walked quickly past them to my bedroom. We had our own telephone line in our room. I sat there alone holding the phone in my lap, hugging it, waiting for the courage to call Paul and give him the news. Only my friend Maryanne knew my fear, so I called her first. When Maryanne answered the phone, I could hear her parents' record player blasting the sound track from the Music Man, "Trouble, oh we got trouble, right here in River City, with a capital "T" that rhymes with "P" and that stands for Pool." The music began to fade as Maryanne stretched the phone cord around the corner of the door for privacy.

"I'll say there is trouble in River City," I said.

"What did you say?" Maryanne yelled into the phone.

"The test was positive, I'm pregnant," I said, speaking softly.

"Shit, Oh God, are you sure?" she whispered automatically; I could feel her biting her already ragged fingernails. "Yes, I'm sure, my mother took me for the rabbit test today, so she knows. The thought of telling my dad is like hell, she'll have to do that." There was silence on the line and the phone felt heavy. There was life-changing information stuck in the atmosphere somewhere between Bridgetown and Arlington. I felt like saying something funny to break the tension, like, "So do you want to be a bridesmaid?' but instead I said, "Well, I better hang up and call Paul, he doesn't know yet, and don't tell anyone else, okay?"

I wished I had been Maryanne right then, going back to her homework thinking, *thank God, it's not me*. But it was me, and I had to call Paul fast, and get it over with before I missed him for the night. I didn't want to carry this burden all night long on my own. I dialed the number of the barracks at Fort Devens and the man who answered yelled down the hall, "Hey O'Connell, call." I could hear Paul jogging down the hall, his steps echoing against the bare walls; it felt like life was in slow motion.

"Hi, Honey," is what Paul said when he grabbed the phone.

"How'd you know it was me?" I asked.

"You're the only one who calls me here, that's why."

He waited for me to speak, and when I was silent he said, "So what's up?"

I couldn't speak, so Paul said, "Hey is something wrong?"

"I'm pregnant," I finally blurted into the phone.

I could actually hear the silence; I could hear air and electricity in the wires. I heard life going on as usual in the kitchen downstairs. I was suspended in time, hearing my thirteen and sixteen-year-old sisters doing homework around the kitchen table while my mother, cooking, held a huge secret in her heart. I saw myself with my pink princess phone, holding my life like a dream between my knees, and Paul saying nothing.

"Say something," I yelled at him.

"Are you sure?" he asked quietly.

"No, I'm kidding," I said as I slammed the receiver down on the phone. It rang within five seconds and Paul said, "I'm sorry."

"What, you're sorry I'm pregnant?"

"No, I'm just sorry, I'm an idiot, I can hardly talk, it feels like my throat has gone numb or something."

"Well, my life has gone numb and I can hardly think," I said beginning to cry softly to myself. I finally took a breath and said, "What are we supposed to do?"

"We're supposed to get married," Paul said, matter-of-factly. I loosened my grip on the receiver; this is what I needed to hear. There was a solution to my panic. Paul said, "Irene, we've been going together for four years; I guess this is what happens next." Paul sounded so calm. He was twenty-one years old, had seen some of the world, had seen war and death; I guess this wasn't all that shocking to him.

"So I should tell my parents we want to get married?" I asked

"Irene, your parents are going to tell us we HAVE to get married."

I, too, was suddenly awake and calm. "You're right Paul, thank you for being so calm; I'll call you tomorrow night after I've told my parents, I love you."

Irene Isobel Carver

"Hey, I love you, too, and don't worry; the Army has good benefits for wives."

Just as I hung up, Teresa walked into our bedroom. "Paul and I are getting married," I said with a new happiness. "This is a secret," I said, seeing amazement in her green eyes. "Don't say anything 'till I tell Mum and Dad tonight." I walked out of our room feeling a new strength.

After dinner my mother called me into her bedroom. I saw my dad sitting on the edge of his bed; he looked different, smaller. I had never seen him with his shoulders slumped. "I'm so sorry, daddy, I don't know how this happened, we…" I was cut off in mid-sentence as my father stood and with outstretched arms, he pulled me into his chest and held me as if he was trying to scoop up all my parts and hold them together. As he held me, I cried into his soft heart cavity and I could feel all his broken dreams for me in the tears flowing down his cheeks. Dad never said a word; he just stroked my hair and held me. At that moment I knew what unconditional love feels like. He wasn't holding me because I got great SAT scores or because I had just been accepted to college. He was holding me because he loved me no matter what life brought. I let myself sink deeper into his warm Aqua Velva scent, and I realized what a wonderful father he was.

Mummy finally broke up our hug by saying, "I'll call the monsignor in the morning and we'll get going on a date for the wedding." Dad turned to her and said, "I'll call the school and see what their policy is about dropping out early." I chimed in and said, "I'll go call Paul and let him know we've talked." I was so relieved this was over that I moved fast to the door, but mum caught my arm and said, "Dad and I would prefer that you keep this just between us;

no need to tell anyone our business, including your sisters." I already knew what she really meant: I'm a bad example. But I was glad that mum had given dad a good pep talk and calmed him. I could just hear her rationalizing that Paul is at least from a good family and we had been going together for four years, and so on. Mummy always found a way to make any situation positive, so I guess pregnancy and dropping out of school after the tuition had been paid, was no exception.

I sat on my bed trying to digest all of this, when the phone rang and it was Paul. I filled him in on all the details and he told me that they had just been told that day that his company was being transferred to the 82nd Airborne and they were to report to Fort Bragg, North Carolina, by October 20th. These new orders felt in tune with our situation. It would give us time to have a wedding and a reason to fib and tell everyone we wanted to get married before Paul left for his new assignment so that I could go with him. "Thank you, God," said my mother when I told her. "Now, I'll have a good reason to give to the monsignor for rushing the wedding instead of the undignified truth."

Irene Isobel Carver

Chapter Six

My Wedding

I FIRST WALKED DOWN THE LONG COOL AISLE OF OUR
Lady of Mercy church at age seven, to make my First Communion. I remember kneeling down, staring at the statue
of the Blessed Mother for hours waiting for her to move. I
would squint my eyes and try to hallucinate her into action.
I recall sitting alone on the hard bench during Lent, getting
angry with the apostles for falling asleep on Jesus when he
was trying to pray in the Garden of Gethsemane. I thought
to myself, *What kind of friends were they to fall asleep three
times when Jesus was just asking them to keep watch while
he prayed to his Father in Heaven? I would never do that to
my friends*, I vowed to the statue of Jesus.

I again walked down that aisle at age thirteen, when I
made Confirmation, the Sacrament that enlists you into
the army of Christ to be his soldier. At Confirmation you
were given a new middle name, a saint's name, someone
you could emulate. I chose the same middle name that my
Aunt Irene had—Isobel—spelled the Scottish way with an
"O" not an "A." My mother suggested this name but she did
not push it; it was my own soul that made that choice, and
I remember feeling a certain beauty as I said both names
together with the double I's, Irene Isobel. When my sisters
gave me questioning looks, I told them I felt like a queen.

Ten-year-old Teresa said, "Why not Karen?"

Clare said, "How about Laura?"

"It just doesn't mean anything special to me," I told them. I already loved the story of being named for my Aunt Irene who died so young. "It is so romantic" I said, and they just gave me more weird looks and walked away.

And now, on October 13, 1967 here I was walking down that same aisle again. It was a Friday evening at 7:00 p.m., the only time the monsignor had open with such short notice. "You're getting married on Friday the thirteenth, it's unlucky," my friends said. "Well, I'm changing that stupid superstition," I replied, "I say it's a lucky day from now on." I challenged their beliefs; at nineteen I already seemed to have a spiritual knowledge (or arrogance) that would bubble up throughout my life when I needed it. One time I told a priest in Seattle I was my own church. This was my attitude as I walked down the isle in my white-heeled shoes that holy day in October. I wore a simple white brocade dress that came to my knees and a small white veil on top of my head, which cascaded down to my chin like a puffy halo. I felt beautiful as I walked down that isle into my new life, with my black hair flipped up at the ends, bangs meeting my eyebrows perfectly, and eyes deeply outlined with black liner. The ceremony was short and to the point; there was no time for a Mass. Clare, who was just one year older than I, was my maid of honor. She was the only one we told that I was pregnant, just to shut her up so she would stop asking questions. We swore her to secrecy.

After the ceremony, our two immediate families went for a dinner reception at IGO's Restaurant in Cambridge. We did the traditional things, like feeding each other cake, and the best man, Paul's brother in law, made a toast. He said something cheery about the purity of young love and optimism, and we all clicked glasses of champagne together. That night Paul and I stayed in a hotel room overlooking the Charles River. I think we were both quite nervous to have permission to spend the night alone in such a luxurious hotel room. Paul was twenty-one, so he bought us a bottle of wine to bring back to our room. This helped with the transition into my new world, but it was probably why I woke up with morning sickness for the first time since I found out I was pregnant.

In the morning, after checking out of our hotel, we went to my parents' house to say goodbye, because we had to leave right away for Fort Bragg, North Carolina; this would be our honeymoon. I felt my heart being torn in two directions as I closed the door to our white 1964 Dodge Dart, and looked up to wave a final time to my parents and my two little sisters, who stood squished together in the doorway of the only house I had ever known. Mummy and daddy had big smiles of relief on their faces; but my baby sister Brigette, only thirteen-years-old, looked so very sad that I got out of the car to give her one last hug. Her curly blonde hair tickled my face as I held her to me.

"You will come home for Christmas, Renie?" she demanded.

"Of course I will," I answered, having no clue if I could or not.

And then Teresa, whom I had fought with every day throughout high school over whose clothes were whose, said, in a having-to-be-strong sixteen-year-old way, " I kept your green paisley shirt, do you want it back?"

"Nah, you keep it, it looks better on you with your green eyes," I answered, never knowing until that moment how very much I loved her and how beautiful she was.

What I remember most about that trip from Boston to North Carolina is learning how to seize the moment. I had never been to Washington D.C. before and suddenly here I was, driving down Pennsylvania Ave. I felt so excited; I wanted to stop and sightsee but Paul was anxious to get to our destination. "We'll come back some other time," he said. As it turned out, I didn't get back to see our nation's capital until I was forty-five years old. You see, it took me a long time to find a man who would "brake for scenery." On that trip I also learned that I no longer had control over my own body because I began waking up each day throwing up with morning sickness; not so romantic for a honeymoon. This was small potatoes compared to what the U.S. Army was about to show me as to who was in charge of my life.

Fort Bragg was a shock for me. When we arrived we had to live in a dormitory style barracks for married couples. Paul would take off every morning at 4:00 am to do God-only-knows-what, and I was left alone in a room with no pictures and dealing with my morning sickness. I felt so lost. I had no sisters; I was out of my litter. I had no school to go to, no apple tree to hide in, just me. I called home crying one day and my mother more or less said to me, "You made your bed, Renie, now you've got to lie in it," her firm Scottish attitude striking at my heart. When I hung up the phone, I hugged myself trying to feel my father's Irish arms around me again. Within a few days, my mother's firmness brought out my determination to make a good bed for myself to lie in. I went to the army information office that day and asked where else married GI's could live besides the dormitory. They told me where to find housing, and by that evening I had rented us a furnished house in a neighborhood full of GI's and we could move in that weekend. This was a military

Irene Isobel Carver

town; they were ready for me. I called my mother first thing.

By the time Halloween came, Paul and I were all settled into a white two-bedroom track house with a carport. I had carved out two pumpkins and had a bowl of candy ready for the neighborhood children. I was hoping to meet our neighbors that night since I was playing house for real for the first time, and I was having fun; I wanted to find a friend. Everything changed that night. As soon as Paul got home from his duty, he went in the bathroom and smoked a joint. He immediately became reclusive and went into our bedroom, shutting the door and telling me he didn't want to meet any of our neighbors. I felt abandoned and scared as I watched Paul close the door on me. I had only smoked pot a few times with Paul the previous summer before I became pregnant. We had fun, but everything was different now. I was pregnant and smoking was not an option for me. I hadn't seen Paul smoking by himself, so I was unprepared for this moment. Paul stayed in our bedroom all evening, and I introduced myself to the families who came to our door like the good Bostonian I was; but the wind was gone from my sails and I still had to lie in this bed that I made.

When the trick-or-treaters stopped ringing our door-bell, I blew out the candles in the pumpkins and Paul came out to the living room and turned on the television. We sat together on the couch and watched the Beverly Hill-billies, holding hands. I didn't say anything about feeling abandoned. I was really confused and insecure about how I should feel or be in this new role of wife and homemaker. Paul and I were both silent as we watched television. Eventually our laughter at the show turned into kissing and then we went off to bed, as the alarm would ring at 3:30 a.m. for Paul's morning duty.

When I awoke it was November, a new month, and I could change the calendar. I loved doing that—getting a new start, having new energy and a clean slate. My mother and I would ritually change the kitchen calendar together. I resisted the temptation to call home because I needed to be a little careful of the phone bill. Instead, I went to a local second-hand store to look for an end table to put by the kitchen door to place our keys and pocket stuff on when we walked in. As I drove along the sparsely treed streets, the car radio DJ said there was to be an important football game on Saturday at the college in Durham, North Carolina by rival teams. It felt like a great gift hearing that because I was wondering what I would do all day Saturday when Paul had to be on duty. I hadn't made any friends yet. While I listened, I felt myself take a deep breath, feeling a little taste of home filtering into the warm November air. I missed the crisp fall air of New England but did not want to admit it to myself as I struggled to shift into my new world. Breathing in the thought of college football resurrected my homesickness and I allowed myself some tears as I drove.

I didn't say anything to Paul of my plans to drive to Durham because I didn't want him to think of a reason to discourage me. I needed an adventure. I called my dad and told him I was going to the game because I wanted him to be proud of me; yet I found myself fibbing and telling him Paul was going with me, not knowing why. It was only about a two-hour drive from Fayetteville, North Carolina to Durham. I was a bit nervous driving alone in this unfamiliar territory. Once I found the stadium I felt right at home with the college football scene. My New England sports roots ran deep and it was easy for me to people-watch and pretend I was close to Harvard Square.

Irene Isobel Carver

I left at half time because I didn't really care who won the game and I wanted to get home before dark and before Paul got home from his shift. As I drove home I felt proud of myself for having had the courage to take off on my own. I was able to see myself without the backdrop of my family and it was exciting. *Yup, a new slate*, I thought to myself as I pulled into my carport.

I discovered even more about myself a few weeks later when Paul's platoon was sent on a weekend assignment. Paul didn't want me to be alone so he arranged for a friend's wife, who was also pregnant, to come stay with me. On that Friday night, Maria Hernandez from San Antonio, Texas arrived at my door. We were both due to have our first babies in May, so it was easy for us to curl up on the couch and talk all evening. At bedtime Maria seemed both amazed and afraid that I did not have at least two bolts on each door. "Well never mind," she said, "I have my gun with me," and she pulled a small pistol from her overnight bag. Now it was my turn to be amazed and afraid. I had never even seen a gun let alone have one in my house. The surprise must have shown on my face as she said, "Oh don't worry, I always sleep with it under my pillow when Emilio is away, and I'm a good shot." I don't think either of us slept that night because she was very nervous without bolted doors and I was waiting for a gunshot all night. The next morning she made polite excuses and went back to her own house. After she left, I thought a lot about how I was raised and how we never even locked our doors at night or during the day. I couldn't remember ever having a key to our house, and I had never heard of a robbery in our neighborhood. I never imagined that guns were an everyday part of some people's lives.

Homesickness overtook morning sickness as I stared at myself in the mirror, wondering how I would ever find a friend. Life itself was soon to become more intense than my loneliness.

Irene Isobel Carver

Chapter Seven

Death

THE PHONE RANG ONE EVENING JUST BEFORE THANKS-giving as Paul and I sat curled up on the couch watching TV. It was my sister Clare calling, but it wasn't a cheery holiday hello; it was the sharpest words I had ever heard. "Donny has been killed in action in Vietnam," she said rapidly as soon as I said hello. I screamed when Clare said those words and dropped the phone. Paul jumped up and grabbed the phone, putting it to his ear. Poor Clare had to repeat the whole story to Paul about how Jimmy Bartlette had called her and told her just an hour earlier that our pal, Donny Beam, was killed in action. I sat on the kitchen chair next to Paul, holding the baby forming in my womb, trying not to scare him with my deep sobs. Paul hung up the phone and without saying anything he touched my shoulder and went to our spare bedroom shutting the door. I looked at the closed door and decided to leave Paul alone and call Clare back for more details. She answered the phone on a half ring, hoping I was calling.

We relived the senior prom together, remembering Donny looking so handsome in his army uniform with Eileen next to him in her burgundy dress that Clare and I had helped pick out.

"Who told Eileen?" I wanted to know. "Was she okay?"

Tears filled my eyes as I lovingly remembered Eileen, my high school buddy, who had loved Donny all through high school, even when he ran around with other girls. She just adored him no matter what. It was too soon, Clare didn't know the answer to any of my questions. She called me first because she knew Paul would want to know, since he and Donny had been close high school pals.

Paul finally emerged from the bedroom, eyes swollen from crying and fists still clenched in rage. I silently made us tuna fish sandwiches and Paul sat out on our back steps smoking a joint. At this point he just didn't care if the neighbors saw him and neither did I. After eating, I lay down on the living room couch and floated into a painful daze, remembering Donny as I hummed the song "Moon River," which was the theme song at our prom. I remembered seeing Donny take a small flask from the top pocket of his uniform and raise a salute to Paul and me who were dancing nearby. He had become a man of the world now and could do such things. Then I flashed back a few years and saw us all crammed on a toboggan, legs wrapped around each other, screaming wildly as we flew over snow banks, all of us tumbling like a pig pile at the end. Donny would stand and say, "Let's do that again," as he headed up the steep hill, pulling the toboggan behind him. There he was, ready for more life, more wildness, and now it all came to a sudden stop.

When I woke up the next morning, Paul was heading out the door to report for duty. He saw me open my eyes as he walked by the couch, and he squatted next to me and squeezed my hand. He looked down at the floor, his bright blue eyes puffy and raw. We could not look at each other directly; we had to squint to bear life that day. Paul and I didn't get to go to Donny's wake because Paul could not get a leave and we didn't have money enough for me to travel home. So we relied on friends to tell us all about it. Death became very real to me that week. Paul and I mourned in silence, far from our hometown, where our first casualty of the Vietnam War was buried. Even though we were not there, we could imagine the bugles blowing taps, shattering the frozen silence of that November day.

I finally talked to Eileen a week after the wake. I was dreading this and needing it at the same time. But I was surprised; Eileen seemed more at peace than I would have thought. She told me her story: how she knelt next to the open casket by herself just before it was closed, and how a red rose in a bouquet next to Donny's shoulder moved. She kept repeating, "The rose just moved. The rose really moved. I kept looking at it and then I'd look away, and then look back, and it would move again." She said she finally stood up when someone else came up to the casket; she leaned over and took the rose. I'll never forget the sound of Eileen's voice; it was melodious, like an angel, and she said, "It was Donny; he gave me the rose.

THREE MONTHS LATER—FEBRUARY 22, 1968

I was six months pregnant. The baby was growing fast, kicking a lot, and all seemed to be well. Paul woke up that morning at 4:00 a.m. like he always did, to report to the base. I puttered about that day, going to the grocery and deciding for the third time that week to make macaroni and cheese for dinner, one of my pregnancy cravings. Paul's schedule was like clockwork, so I was straining the noodles in preparation for his arrival home when I looked up to greet him, and saw the whitest face I had ever seen looking back at me;

every freckle seemed to be leaping off of his face. I placed the colander in the sink and steadied myself on the chair as I asked him what happened. "President Johnson came to speak to us today," Paul said as he flopped into a kitchen chair and continued robotically. "He said he is sorry, but that he has to send the 82nd Airborne back to Vietnam because of the Tet Offensive." The heaviness of these words stunned me. I reached over and put my hand on his, "Can they do this?" I asked, "Isn't everyone supposed to do just a one-year tour of duty in Nam, and you already did yours?" "Yes, that is why the President himself came, because they are going to break this rule," Paul said, as he began to shake off the shock.

"Maybe we should just leave and drive to Canada," Paul mumbled.

"You mean go AWOL, desert the army?" I asked softly. Paul stood now, staring out the front window, so I went to him and took his hand.

"Paul, if we did that, then I would have to have the baby in Canada, and we wouldn't be able to come home and see our families."

"Never mind, that was a stupid idea," Paul said, as he sucked in a deep breath and turned abruptly to look at me. "We're going in four days, so I guess I better call my parents," he added, now suddenly standing, looking stiff as a board. A wildness erupted in me and I grabbed hold of Paul, pulling him fiercely to me.

"You go Paul, you go to Canada, and I'll go home to my parents' and have the baby there."

Suddenly, after those words blurted out of me, we both seemed to emotionally collapse with the tension. We sat on the couch, and without understanding what was happening, the fright and rebellion all floated far away from our consciousness and we surrendered our lives to the huge government war machine. We were just too young and overwhelmed with a baby coming to make any radical moves. We didn't move or talk for quite awhile. In the silence something shifted, and standing, Paul said, "No, the President said we will only have to stay in Nam for three months; I can do that," and he walked over to the phone and called his parents.

"War, What Is It Good For, Absolutely Nothing" —*Edwin Starr*

As fate would have it, Dora and Ed had good friends who were driving to Florida from Massachusetts that week to spend the remainder of the winter there. They said they would be glad to drop Paul's parents off in North Carolina to be with us, and when Paul left for Vietnam, they would drive back to Boston with me in my little Dodge Dart. Paul and I were so grateful for this much needed help. We were both just going through the motions of life on those last few days together; we had to hold back our emotions. I was like a shell of myself, going about the house and packing the few little items that I had recently collected in an effort to make my house a home. One night the four of us went to the movies to see *Cool Hand Luke*. Paul Newman would go on to get an Academy Award for best actor in this film. We thought we would distract ourselves from our painful reality. All I remember is sitting there staring straight ahead at the screen while Paul fiercely held my hand. On the way out Dora said, "Well, that was depressing," which made me realize I was beyond depression; I had become numb.

February 26th arrived, and before Paul left for the barracks at 5:00 a.m., the four of us stood in the living room acting as bravely as we could as we hugged our goodbyes. Paul put his hands around my belly and said, "See ya in three months, wait for me." "Okay Spec. 4, we'll do our best," I saluted, kidding, trying to hold every cell of my body in place as Paul turned and walked to the car with his father who was driving him to the base. Dora went to the kitchen to make tea for the trip home as I stood and watched Paul disappear into the distance, thinking we each deserved our own Academy Award that morning. While the three of us made our way north, the 82nd Airborne was being flown to Vietnam, and parachuting into the surrounding area of Hue, into the heart of the battle known as the Tet Offensive. All I knew was that the word Tet had something to do with the Lunar New Year and that Paul was there against his will.

Only four months had passed since I had left my childhood home and here I was at the door again, and oh how I loved the sight of that red door. It sparked in me a poem I so loved, and as I walked up the stairs to my bedroom, I recited the words. "I will go back a little while and be with old untroubled things, there is the tree no wind could harm that embraces the far returning heart."

I felt as if a lifetime had passed and as I wrote in my journal that night, I realized how much I'd changed. I was no longer the girl who was raised in that house. I was now married, six months pregnant, had lost a friend to death, and more war loomed before me. *Buck up, Renie,* I wrote in my journal.

On the drive home, I wondered what I would do while I was at my parents' house, but I found it was easy to stay busy once I was home. Dora, who was quite a seamstress,

Irene Isobel Carver

decided to teach me how to sew in order to keep us both busy and our minds off the war. I would walk the mile to her house each day for exercise, sew for hours, and then walk home for dinner at my parents' house. Before I knew it, I had more maternity dresses than places to wear them, so I picked out some spring fabrics to make skirts for after the pregnancy. Mini-skirts were the style and they didn't require much yardage. I could afford to experiment with new and wild fabrics. I even made a white mini-skirt that was held to the top by gold chains. When Clare saw it she said it was very "go-go" dancer for a pregnant woman.

"Well, pregnancy does end," I said back to her.

"Yeah, but …" and she stopped there, realizing she was opening her big mouth when she knew she shouldn't. I didn't care; it felt so good to be home with my sisters, I even found those old annoying comments loveable.

My parents were sixty-two and sixty-four years old in 1968, and their faith was being tested. Besides having me home and pregnant, and with all the fear of war, their baby, Brigette, who was thirteen, had been diagnosed with a curvature of the spine. She had a forty-eight degree curve, which was quite serious. She was given two choices by her doctor: One, she could wear a brace from her hips to her chin all through high school, only taking it off to sleep; or two, she could have an operation where they took a piece of her hip bone out and fused it into the place in her spine where the curve began. With this choice, she would have to lie in a hospital bed for six months and do school on television. Brigette chose the second option. When I came home that February, Brigette was in the hospital school; the operation had been successful. Between maternity dresses and mini-skirts, I also began to make pretty frocks for Brigette to wear in her hospital bed. When I showed her one of my mini-skirts, she asked that I make her some too. She, like me, held the attitude, *this experience will end you know!* Now if only this damn war would end, was the cry from the deepest part of our national psyche. The more televised the war became, the louder and more intense the anti-war demonstrations became.

WHERE WERE YOU IN '68?

I waited anxiously each day for the mailman to come, hoping for a letter from Paul. Finally, on March 11th a letter came. "Oh thank God, he's alive," said Dora when I called immediately and told her. Then I went to my room to read and savor every word:

My Rene, I thought of you right away when I was literally dropped into this war again. After I folded my parachute, I leaned against a wooden beam and looked around me. I could tell right away that I was in a bombed-out church of some kind. I thought of Our Lady of Mercy and how horrible it would be to find our church bombed to bits as this one was. After gulping some water from my canteen, I looked up and saw a steeple of red and orange, leaning and ready to fall. There were beautiful carved dragons leaning over, as well. How sad; what a waste. I really have no clue what we are doing here. But here I am and I know you are praying for me so I plan to be okay and to be home before you know it. How are you? I can picture you at your mom's house having tea and chocolate chip cookies. Have one for me. I'll write as often as I can. Don't worry I will be okay; just take care of yourself and the baby. I love you. Write back to me. Paul

I read the letter about five times and then immediately wrote a long letter back telling him all about my sewing with his mother and about Brigette. I put his letter in my purse to show to Dora, and took my letter directly to the post office to mail. What a relief; my heart could rest a bit. I had an address and we were connected again. I wrote and mailed a letter to him every single day:

Paul O'Connell Ra11468011
Paul O'Connell Ra11468011
Paul O'Connell Ra11468011

It was the same, day after day for three months—sending and waiting, sending and hoping, sending and praying, sending and crying, receiving and weeping. That was how my personal world was spinning in the spring of 1968, which insulated me a bit from the larger picture of what was happening in our world. I have heard it said that history repeats itself, but I pray with all my heart that the spring of 1968 never comes around again; it was straight up HELL ON EARTH for me!

In America, the Civil Rights Movement was in high gear with the beloved Martin Luther King Jr. as its leader. He was a pacifist reverend, planning peaceful demonstrations around the south. With his eloquent leadership a change of consciousness was taking place, an identity shift from Negro to African American. "I'm Black and I'm Proud" became a chant that was deeply moving people, awakening the black culture to a new way of being and thus, awakening us all.

On March 28, 1968 Dr. King was in Memphis to lead a peaceful demonstration, when all hell broke loose. The black city workers—the trash collectors—were protesting against the way they were unfairly treated. A documentary I watched afterwards pointed out how the FBI planted troublemakers to stir up violence. They grabbed sticks off the picket signs and began to smash windows, and the police were right there to begin beating the blacks. It turned into a riot, thus sabotaging Dr. King's plan for a peaceful demonstration. Just after this incident, on April 3, 1968, Dr. King gave his famous *I Have a Dream* speech; it was to be his last.

Even now, when I watch Dr. King give that speech, it feels more and more like he was Jesus in the Garden of Gethsemane, taking on his crushing Cross and surrendering to God's will. It seems to me that he somehow knew he was about to give his life for a great cause. That speech of love and hope was his response to the evil power of ignorance demonstrated that day in Memphis in 1968. Thank you, Dr. King, for being a role model for such a magnificent soul course for us all.

On April 4, 1968, the power of evil once again stepped in and took the life of this beloved man. Cities all across America broke out in riots. I remember sitting on a bench along the Charles River saying my daily rosary for Paul's safe return; my novena. I thought surely some very evil energy has come to earth, and Jesus' words reflected back to me, "What man has meant for evil, God will turn to good." That phrase, that biblical quote, saved me from depression throughout the continued evil that was to come. In the meantime, President Johnson must have been graced with some of that goodness as he began the Paris Peace Talks. He said he would not run for another term as President. At first I was hopeful that with the Paris Peace talks Paul might be sent home early, but those thoughts were quickly dashed as we watched the slow progress of these talks.

The murder of Martin Luther King Jr. sucked the hope out of us, but not all of it. The presidential elections were coming up in November and most of the peace activists were working hard for Senator Eugene McCarthy, whose platform was all about ending the Vietnam War. Hope lived; evil had not taken us down. McCarthy had his own army of college students whose motto was "Be clean for Gene." They were keeping the light of hope alive in young hearts. A curve ball to McCarthy's campaign was thrown when Bobby Kennedy decided to run for President instead of waiting for the 1972 election like he had planned. As we know, Bobby Kennedy was very charismatic and he ended up winning the Democratic nomination over McCarthy, on June 5, 1968. He was also running on a platform of peace. In his acceptance speech, he said, "The divisions between blacks and whites, and the divisions over the War in Vietnam can be overcome. We can start to work together." It felt like the path to peace was still possible and that is what we needed to believe. This is the world that my son was born into, on May 20, 1968.

I think pregnancy kept me anesthetized because I just did not have the energy to create new life and respond to the current tragic environment that surrounded all of us. As I look back, I think saying the rosary every day was weaving an etheric bubble of light protection around me. I kept breathing, hoping, and trusting God. I never watched the news and I ate a lot of ice cream, which was beginning to show on my face, but it soothed my soul each evening; I was addicted to mocha almond fudge.

On May 19th, just days before Paul was due home, I awoke in the night to go to the bathroom and there was a spot of blood. I woke my parents and my mother called the doctor. The doctor told me to go right to the hospital where he would meet me. My dad drove me to the hospital; we were mostly silent but I asked him if he had been afraid with each of us that something would be wrong with the baby. He said that most babies were born perfectly healthy and he just trusted that. My dad parked the car, walked me into the hospital, and admitted me at the front desk. He gave me a big hug, a reassuring smile, and then left. As an orderly pushed me down the hall in a wheelchair, I became fearful. What was I doing here alone? Everything suddenly felt very unnatural, as if a hole had been punctured in my protective bubble. I guess it was the reality of impending childbirth that dawned on me. OUCH! The doctor took one look at my fear-drenched face and easily convinced me that I should have anesthesia to knock me out so I could avoid all the discomfort of labor. The nurse on duty assured me all would be fine, she would be there with me. That is how it went and all I remember is that nurse at some point yelling PUSH! I told her I was afraid to push because I might have to go to the bathroom. She gave me a stern look and said, "Don't worry about that, just push." I pushed, and at 11:20 a.m. my son was slapped on the bottom, cried out, and took his first breath.

I didn't know what we were going to name the baby. Paul and I wrote about it a little in our letters, and Paul always said, "Let's just wait till we see him." I thought Paul would be home from Nam by the time of the birth, and we would discuss it, so I didn't really have any ideas for a name and I didn't know if it would be a boy or a girl. But when I looked at my son for the very first time, with strawberry blonde hair like his dad's, I said "Hi, Paulie" and that was that. Prince Paulie had been born! We had the nursery set up at Dora and Ed's house since we planned to live with Paul's parents until Paul was discharged from his three-year tour of duty that coming October. That would give us time to save some money and to adjust to life with a baby.

Irene Isobel Carver

On May 22nd I came home from the hospital with Paulie. We got a call from Paul that he was in Alaska going through medical clearance and we could expect him home on the 24th. He was out of Vietnam and that was all that mattered! It would have been a time of great celebration for us except for the sad news that Dora and Ed had been withholding from me until I got home from the hospital. Our friend, Teddy Reid, had been killed in action in Nam on May 13th. Teddy was one of the three high school friends that Paul had joined the army with on the buddy system. I screamed out loud when Dora told me, and the baby jumped a bit in his sleep. I sank back into the familiar and well-worn couch, searching for an anchor. The wooden harp-shaped chimes that hung on the front door anchored me in. Dora's mother had brought them from Sweden and knowing the history of them steadied me. "Oh my God, how will we tell Paul?" I asked. Ed quickly answered, "Let's let him get settled and see you and the baby for a bit first. But we have to tell him fairly soon before someone calls here; the news is all over town as Teddy's body is being flown home right now." Dora sat down next to me and squeezed my hand. "Maybe you should go upstairs and rest while the baby is sleeping and I am going to go make a meatloaf, as Paul always loved that."

I made myself a cup of tea and took it to my room. I knew I wouldn't sleep, but I did need to be alone. I sat at the bedroom window looking at the tiny maple leaves starting to bud. As I stared into the cloudless blue sky, I remembered the last time I saw Teddy. He threw a big going away party for himself at the Commander Hotel in Harvard Square, and he came to my parents' house to invite me. He sat on our living room couch in his uniform, telling us how he had decided to "re-up," since his one-year tour of duty in Nam was over and he wanted to go back. I watched him as he proudly told my parents how he had become a Green Beret and that just a few men are chosen for this elite force. None of us really knew how to respond; most everyone was trying to avoid the war, and there was Teddy asking to go back. We all stood and my dad patted Teddy on the shoulder wishing him luck; I assured him I would be at the party, and I was.

Teddy rented two rooms at the hotel. It was old home week for our high school crowd with kegs of beer flowing and music blasting. I could not enjoy myself as I sat there, pregnant and wondering why Teddy would want to go back to war. I sat next to him on the bed, telling him I needed to go home—pregnant you know—and he showed me his key chain. On it was the ear of a Viet Cong, or a "gook" as Teddy called him. It was a real human ear, all dried up and pierced onto Teddy's key chain. I remembered Paul telling me that in training they had to chant "kill-o, kill-o, kill, kill." At that moment I realized that the army brainwashed people into a hypnotic killing frame of mind. Teddy had been trained to kill and he could not just take off his uniform and join the civilian world. He was a Green Beret, a trained and proud soldier; he fit in in Vietnam and he no longer fit in at home. I got up, moving away from the petrified ear and Teddy. I joined the mingling crowd, gradually moving toward the exit door. As I was leaving, I turned and caught Teddy's eye. We flashed each other a big goodbye grin and he lifted his glass of beer in a final toast, "see ya," we both mouthed as I lifted an invisible glass. I knew then, standing in the doorway of a hotel room in Harvard Square, that I would never see Teddy alive again; he was making his choice. I just had to turn and leave.

Irene Isobel Carver

The baby's cries brought me back to the present. I picked him up from his bassinet and put him to my breast. *What a time to be born*, I thought, *in the midst of war, tension and assassination.* I wondered if the baby could feel any of this in the milk from my breast. Was my memory of Teddy flooding into him? I decided I should just put thoughts of Teddy out of my mind for now and think about what I should wear for Paul's arrival home in two days. I decided on a silky yellow pantsuit that hid a lot of my baby fat. Then I snuggled up with the baby and we had a long, calm sleep together.

The next day Dora and I stayed busy cooking. She said I could spoil the baby's milk if I kept dwelling on death and we should just think of recipes that were healthy for all of us and ones that Paul liked. So we started with Swedish meatballs and moved quickly into Swedish butter cookies. All the while Dora was sipping on a glass of whiskey. I was feeling very happy not to be pregnant and the thought of being kissed really soon made me flutter. Dora protected me the whole day and told everyone who called that I was sleeping. Her female instincts were keen and she knew a new mother had to put sleep and calmness before anything and everyone. This would be my one and only day of complete quiet. I allowed myself to be suspended in time. I curled up in my bedroom with the baby and only came out to eat her homemade chicken soup. At the end of the day I called my mother to say hi and good night.

May 24th arrived and I woke up nervous, knowing my psychic rest was over. As Dora and I waited for Ed to return from the airport with Paul, we thought we would escape into television. I quickly bypassed the news but not before I saw students at Columbia University being dragged out of buildings and being beaten. Was there a sane corner on earth? I wondered, as I switched channels as fast as I could. I finally found Dick Cavett talking to Ann Margaret and settled back to wait for Paul and Ed to get home. I felt really cute in my yellow silk lounging outfit and gold humming-bird earrings. I took a deep breath and thought, "*I can do this; we are going to be okay.*"

It was 3:00 in the afternoon when I heard the car doors open and close and both Dora and I sprung to the window. There was Paul in his uniform, looking just like he did the morning he left, three months ago. We watched him drag his huge duffle bag out of the back seat, sling it over his shoulder, and head up the front steps. Dora rushed outside to greet them and I knelt on the couch, peering through the Venetian blinds. I was suddenly petrified. I backed across the room and stood next to the baby's bassinette. I was afraid I was just going to blurt out, "Teddy was killed." I needed the baby to hold me back. Paul saw me, dropped his duffle bag, and held out his open arms. A frozen wall of fear around me cracked and I ran into his arms. Time collapsed and it was as if nothing at all had transpired between our Fort Bragg house and this moment. And yet everything had happened. The baby began to cry and Paul walked to his bassinette and looked in.

"I better not touch him until I get cleaned up," he said.

"Okay, you go take a shower and I'll bring the baby up to our room and you can change him with me and get the full baby viewing."

"No," Dora chimed in, "give me the baby and you two go up stairs, take a little time alone." Of course she was right, so we followed her wise advice and hopped right into bed.

"The doctor said I should wait six weeks to have sex," I

Irene Isobel Carver

said, in between kisses that were covering my face and neck.

"Why?" Paul breathed.

"Infection, I think," I said as I flung the top of my pant-suit to the floor.

"I just passed a medical inspection; I'm healthy," Paul whispered, "any other reasons?"

"I don't think so," I surrendered, "I guess six minutes will have to do."

We laughed and rolled around the bed in joy. *We had survived war again*, I thought, *and the whole damn world is spinning out of control, we may as well enjoy the ride*, and we did.

When I opened the door of the bedroom I felt the flood of reality immediately. The heaviness that had been weighing on Ed's shoulders was reaching overload and had to be dispersed. He was leaning against the kitchen sink looking weary when I walked in. I checked the baby. He was still asleep, so I went and took a shower, hoping that would give Ed the opportunity to tell Paul about Teddy before dinner, as we had planned. As I showered, I actually felt moments of anger at Teddy for putting himself in harm's way and causing the rest of us more shock. God, I just wanted to go dancing or go to the drive-in and be happy. Happy—that suddenly felt like a far-off reality.

I decided I didn't want to go to Teddy's wake. I had said my goodbyes to him that night in Harvard Square and I wanted to remember him flashing that last grin at me, holding up his glass to life, not lying in a casket looking all stiff. Of course everyone understood; a new mother receives a lot of grace, thank God. I was turning inward in a deeply protective way and no one questioned me. In fact, I think

Paul was relieved. He wouldn't have to be responsible for me; he could just spend time with friends that he hadn't seen in awhile.

That night, when Dora and Ed went to the wake with Paul, I got to be alone in my in-laws' house for the very first time. As the baby slept, I began to peek around a bit, just enjoying the quiet space. In the dining room, I was drawn to the beautiful hand carved mahogany hutch. Who had actually hand carved roses in the wood? I wondered, as I ran my hand over the opening petals in awe of the beauty. I opened the drawer and saw neatly stacked embroidered doilies and linens of every size. The next drawer was filled with old family photos with mostly Swedish names on the backs. I shut the drawer, bored now. I guess I hoped there was something hidden or secret to discover. *The attic*, I thought—that tiny door in our bedroom that I had yet to open; *I'll go check that.*

The door was a bit stuck, but it opened, and I headed up the stairs. I spotted a hand-painted picture of Olga, Dora's mother, hanging on the wall. Her stern eyes seemed to chastise me, "And just what are you looking for young lady?" I stopped in my tracks, rather spooked, and went back to the living room. I turned on the television but couldn't concentrate on anything. I went to the kitchen and pulled back the delicately flowered curtains so I could look out at the night sky and I began to talk aloud to myself, or maybe to Teddy. "Where are you really, Teddy? Is it only your body in the casket that everyone is looking at tonight? Did your soul get to go right to heaven just for being a soldier, or did you have to go to purgatory for taking that man's ear and putting it on a key chain? That must have been a sin, I chastised, as I waited for a twinkling star to answer me. Then I heard

Sister Amadeus, my high school teacher, saying, 'Pray for the souls in purgatory.' " I thought that must be the answer and for the first time in my life I actually cared if any of these ponderings were true.

The front door opened, startling me, as Dora and Ed walked in. They said that Paul was going to stay at the wake with friends and he would be home later. "He'd call," they said. Well, later turned out to be the next afternoon at two o'clock. Thank God I had stayed at home. The wake turned into a major send-off party and it was still going on. In fact, everyone planned to keep it going on until the burial. So Paul would come home and sleep for a few hours and then get up and go to the next designated party house. I didn't care, I was just glad no one expected me to be there. But I did plan to make it to the cemetery for the funeral the next day. Both of Teddy's parents were already deceased. His father was a local policeman who died in the line of duty and his mother passed away soon after. This meant that Teddy's two sisters, who were my age, now had to bury their brother; it was a cruel time. I wanted to bring them a card with pretty words and some daisies. If they could bear this, I could also. *Courage, Renie*, I told myself—chin up, and all that.

I went through my closet looking for something black to wear but I had nothing except the cheery spring dresses I had sewn with Dora. I asked Dora what I should do. She looked in my closet and pulled out a royal blue dress with a white collar. "Here, wear this one," Dora said, "You look really beautiful in it and I think we could all use something to brighten us right now."

I was relieved at her attitude, and asked her if that was what she was reading about in her book, *The Power of Posi-*

tive Thinking. "Yes, that is the idea, how our minds create our reality; you can read it too if you want," she said, and walked to her room to get ready. I noticed she wore a black dress but put on a bright red pendant with it. *I guess Lutherans think differently than Catholics*, I thought. *My mother is going to think it very strange when I show up at the funeral in bright blue*, but I was starting to let go of that old way of thinking. War was changing me.

There was a huge crowd surrounding the burial plot that fanned out way past hearing range of the priest, when the casket was lowered into the ground. My heart ached as I looked across the rows of tombstones at Teddy's sisters. *At least they have each other*, I thought; my only comfort as I watched them receive the American flag that had been draped over the casket. The sharp sound of Taps being played behind us rang through the surrounding maple trees, which were beginning their spring bloom. I could feel Donny's slate gravestone only rows away, and I hoped that Donny and Teddy were watching us from a world that didn't hold the pain we were all feeling. We were all invited to go back to one of the sister's house following the burial. By now, I was ready to talk to people and socialize a little bit, so I asked Dora if she could take care of the baby for a couple of hours. I was not ready to take him out of the house yet; he was only a week old. Of course they said yes, and thus began a lifetime of my precious in-laws helping me every step of the way.

AND MORE DEATH

Paul had a month's leave and did not have to report for duty until June 25th. He made one very close friend in Vietnam, Don Phillips, who lived in Foxboro, about forty-five minutes south of Boston. They were like brothers, Paul told me, as he headed out the door to visit him with a plan to spend the night. Paul said they needed to drink beer and decompress. This became a weekly pattern. I didn't really care, since I was resting a lot and taking the baby on long walks in the carriage, trying to get my tummy flat again. June was just around the corner, and I wanted to fit into the cute summer clothes I had made with Dora.

I was beginning to come out of my protective cocoon a bit and join the world, just as the next big slam hit. It was June 6th. Paul was in bed sleeping after a late party with friends and I got up early as usual. I walked downstairs carrying the baby, expecting to see Dora making coffee and Ed shaving in the bathroom like they did every morning. Instead, they were sitting side by side on the couch holding each other and weeping as they watched a special newscast on television. I headed to the kitchen, not wanting to join any drama and calmly lay the baby on the changing table. I thought it must be a special broadcast honoring Martin Luther King. Then the words from the TV filtered into the kitchen; I could not escape them:

> Senator Robert Kennedy was shot and killed in a Los Angeles hotel last night at the California State Primary. He was giving an acceptance speech when he was shot by Sirhan Sirhan.

I wrapped the baby in a blanket and quietly walked out the side door that led to the backyard. I sat in a chair under the cherry tree and began to nurse the baby. "We are not going anywhere near that horrible television," I assured the baby and myself. I stroked the baby's head and looked up into the cherry blossoms, which were just beginning their bloom. I realized that Bobby Kennedy's mother had just lost another son. I felt my son's mouth on my breast and the name Sirhan Sirhan echoed in my brain. Bobby stood for peace, Martin stood for peace, I said to myself. There is some force so evil that it will kill mothers' sons rather than allow the hope of Peace on Earth. How do we live in a world that allows such horror?

I burped the baby and switched him to the other breast and saw Ed at the kitchen window looking at me. Dora walked out with an afghan and wrapped it around us and asked, "Did you hear?" "Yes," I answered. "I'm saying the rosary for Rose Kennedy. My God, Dora, how does a mother's heart bear the senseless death of yet another son?" Dora squeezed my hand, kissed the top of my head, and walked back into the house. She had no answer to my question, but Mother Mary did—*Grace*. I held my baby tight and hummed Amazing Grace.

Boston was at half-mast. When Paul woke up and heard the news, he summed it up pretty accurately when he said, "This fucking world sucks," and he lit a joint right in the middle of his parents' kitchen. Ed calmly said, "Would you take that outside, Paul?" and he did. People all over the country watched as Bobby's body was taken from Los Angeles to New York by train. America's heart was broken again and hope was buried alive.

SINGING IS PRAYING TWICE

When I look back and wonder, how do we live in the midst of such horror? My response is to quote the American protest singer, Phil Ochs who said, "In such ugly times the true protest is beauty." And it seems the Divine spirit of love agreed with him and sent us music. We were the "children of god" and we needed help. Our tender young souls were being crucified. God knew how to talk to us, and our world exploded with musicians. Grace and inspiration came through music and I think it saved our lives and our psyches.

The war in Vietnam seemed to be created by evil itself, but if man created this evil, then God could turn it to good. This is what I was taught growing up. I believed that music, dance, and brotherly/sisterly love was helping us to heal. This was a time of grace that gave birth to many bands such as the Youngbloods, Crosby, Stills, Nash & Young, Buffalo Springfield, James Taylor, Carol King, Cat Stevens . . . the list could go on, but those are the groups that really spoke to my soul, and whose lyrics gave me comfort.

And there was marijuana; a beautiful, mind-expanding herb that was such a gift. Straight society liked to call it the "gateway drug," negatively implying that it opened the door to all other destructive drugs. Well there may be some truth to that, but before it leads to other drugs, it is truly the *gateway* to a higher consciousness where we know we are One Human Family and, therefore, would be incapable of dropping napalm on human beings.

Let Freedom Ring

One Saturday, as Paul prepared to take off for Foxboro again to party, I asked if Paulie and I could come with him this time and not stay overnight. I said I wanted to meet his friend. Paul looked very reluctant and began to tell me that having the baby there was not a good idea because everyone would be smoking pot. Once again, I stayed behind. When Dora saw my sad face, she asked me about it and I fibbed, and said that I was nervous to take the baby out to a strange place and left it at that.

Paul didn't come home that night. In the morning, Dora, looking a little worried, sat me down and said that keeping a marriage together is mostly the woman's job. Men can stray if we are not careful, she cautioned, and I got her meaning. I decided that night to stop breastfeeding the baby; I wanted my freedom back. I asked Dora if she knew how to wean the baby from the breast to a bottle, and luckily she did. She supported the idea; I think she could see more than I could about her son. The baby took to the bottle easily and my milk dried up pretty fast. I felt a new sense of life opening within me; having my body back to myself was exciting. I was going to turn twenty in a couple of weeks and it was great not to have milk leaking on my shirts. When I told Paul I was going to wean the baby he said, "Good idea; now you can try smoking pot if you want to."

Paul had to report back to duty in late June, so his Foxboro friends were throwing him a send-off party. This time I was prepared. The baby was weaned and Dora said they would babysit overnight so we wouldn't have to drive home. This was going to be my coming out party; I was ready to give pot a try—open the damn gate, here I come! When we got to the spacious country house in Foxboro, the stereo was set up in the private backyard and the Rolling Stones were blasting "Jumping Jack Flash." I felt out of place looking around at all the hip chicks in bellbottoms, paisley tops, and dangling earrings.

Oh God, I look like my sister, Clare, I thought, as I looked down at my pink seersucker mini-dress with puffy shoulders caps. I suddenly felt like miss goody two-shoes and I wanted to walk away. Paul held tight to my hand and walked me over to meet Don and his girlfriend. They handed Paul a joint as they greeted me, and I watched as Paul took a couple of puffs and then handed it to me. I copied how he had sucked in a couple of times, held the smoke in, and then blew it out. "Hey, good lungs, Rene," Paul said, "most people cough a lot the first time they smoke," and he put his arm around me.

I stood staring at Liz, Don's girl. She wore small peacock feather earrings. I thought, *I don't feel any different; I wonder what the big deal is with pot?* Then I looked across the yard and saw three picnic tables set up next to each other full of dishes of food. I realized I was hungry, so as Paul and Don talked, I walked over to the food table. Everything looked so beautiful that I didn't notice people around me for a long time. I grabbed a fork and began to sample each dish. I hardly recognized anything. Finally, I said to the person standing next to me, "What the heck is that?" as I pointed my fork at a grainy green something. The girl burst out laughing and said, "Tabouli, I think." "What the heck is Tabouli?" I laughed and looked up at her. She had on platform heels and towered above me with her long, pin straight black hair hanging over her shoulder; she put spoonfuls of food on her plate. "The plates are down there," she said, and I suddenly realized I didn't have a plate; I had been using just my fork to sample the food, and then I realized I was very HIGH! Luckily, with my focus on food, I forgot how very un-cool my outfit was, and I was just having fun laughing with myself. Paul walked over and I said to him, pointing my fork, "What is that? I've never seen most of these foods before." "It looks like tofu with tahini sauce," he said so nonchalantly. It sounded like a different language and I burst out laughing. I had to put my plate down so I wouldn't drop it, as I doubled over laughing, repeating, "Tofu with tahini!" Thinking I would wet my pants, I asked,

Paul, "Where's the bathroom?" "Good weed," Paul said, and smiling added, "The bathroom is in the kitchen, the door to the left."

The rest of the day seemed to pass in a haze of Jefferson Airplane and food. Eventually, I ended up in a chair under a shade tree with iced tea in my cup. I became very aware of my eyelids in the sense that I couldn't keep them open. I remembered a cartoon where goofy held his eyelids open with toothpicks and I could relate. They were closing; they had a mind of their own. I went to our car and got our sleeping bags. I found a corner in the back of the yard where I didn't think I'd get stepped on and made a cozy overnight spot for us. I found Paul and told him where I'd be and then lay down and let Joe Cocker sing me to sleep, "I get high with a little help from my friends, I get by with a little help from my friends." Sometime in the night I felt Paul snuggle up next to me. In the morning, when I was actually in charge of my eyelids again, I sat up and looked around. I saw people still passing joints and laughing. I heard Joan Baez's voice in the background and it sounded like a lullaby, which made me sad. I missed the baby; I wanted to go home. I was only forty-five minutes away, but I was homesick. Luckily, Paul agreed with me when I shook him awake, and suggested that we head out. We walked over to the food table to see if there was anything that resembled breakfast. Paul accepted a joint from someone standing next to us but I quickly walked away. Paul followed with a tortilla shell in one hand. As we walked to the car I remembered how much the pot had altered my mind, so I took the keys from Paul and said I wanted to drive.

Soon It was the Fourth of July, 1968, and time for my

Irene Isobel Carver

family to celebrate. Brigette was home from six months in the hospital school after her scary operation. She had just turned fourteen in May, and was beaming with joy because her newly budding breasts were finally free of the full body cast! Our family baby was home. Paul had made it home from war and was stationed at Fort Devens, Massachusetts for the remaining three months of his tour of duty, which was only forty minutes from us. I was turning twenty years old. Finally, we could all take a sigh of relief.

I learned an important life lesson on my twentieth birthday. We were having a cookout in our backyard and I had just fed Paulie, who was now six weeks old. I put him upstairs in one of the bedrooms for a nap. He didn't go to sleep and we could all hear him crying through the open window. I wanted to go up and get him but my mother and aunt both told me not to. They said I would spoil him and that I should just let him cry himself to sleep; otherwise, he would be the boss and I'd be jumping to his command. I tried. They could see the tension on my face and tried to reassure me all was well. But I could not stand to hear him cry, so I sneaked around the front of the house and up the stairs to pick him up. As soon as I did, he let out a big burp and then went right to sleep. I never again listened to anyone's advice when it came to my child.

Paul was discharged from the army in October and went right to work for the post office. He hated it. It was a government job and he'd had quite enough of the government. Paul was beginning to let his hair grow long; his marijuana use was beginning to show. He definitely did not fit in at the post office but he wanted to stay through the Christmas rush because we needed the money to move out of his parents' house, which we wanted to do by spring.

We had saved all his military pay for a new car.

As New Year's rolled around and the tragic year of 1968 was coming to an end, the stark differences between Paul and I was finally apparent as we tried to decide what to do to celebrate New Year's Eve. I wanted to go to the supper club, Blinstrubs, with some other couples, friends from high school, and have dinner and be entertained by a comedian. I wanted to get a new dress and socialize. Basically, I was pretty straight. Paul just wanted to go to a party at his friend's house in Cambridge, smoke pot, and listen to music. We tried to fight this out a bit, but we were living at Dora and Ed's house and had no privacy. I swallowed my disappointment and let Paul win. After all, he had just been to war, I rationalized, as I called my friends to tell them we would not be joining them on New Year's Eve.

I had only smoked pot twice since the Foxboro party and the only change I saw in myself was that I began to dress a lot more hip. I put away all the dresses that I had sewn with Dora and replaced them with bellbottoms and vests. One day I smoked pot and went with Paul to one of his friend's house where I learned to make macramé plant holders out of twine. But that does not a hippie make! My consciousness had not shifted, until of course, it did.

What I mostly remember about New Year's Eve, 1968, was all the silence surrounded by music. We all sat around the living room passing joint after joint. The music was blasting from large speakers set on shelves in diagonal corners of the walls. No one talked much. I don't think I actually could talk; the music said it all. We were partying with Jimi Hendrix, The Doors, Cream, and Jethro Tull. I heard The Velvet Underground for the first time. We were all hypnotized, entranced, rocked, and lulled into a world that took us inward. I had done my best to dress up to feel like it was New Year's Eve but in this world, that just meant a sash of silk on my bell bottom jeans and a beaded choker at my neck. I took a puff of the joint each time one passed by me, and I began to have my own private party in my head. I began going through stages of reality. I saw my friends sitting at the nightclub, white linen tablecloths decorated with party favors. I watched them stare, laughing at the comedian on stage that looked like a marionette puppet in my vision. I walked into their gin and tonic reality and I literally slid off the couch and lay on the floor laughing with them at the puppet. A few people looked over at me from the movie show in their heads but everyone was too engrossed in the awesomeness of the music; there was no need to communicate with me about my "trip."

When I looked up from my new perspective of lying on the floor with my feet on the sofa next to Paul where I had been sitting, I really saw Paul's face. Jim Morrison was taking everyone deeply into their subconscious; everyone was "breaking on through to the other side," but I didn't join them. I had laughed myself conscious. I could see the suffering on Paul's face; it was the twitching of the muscles in his jaw that alerted me. I closed my eyes. I didn't want to see the pain of the movie picture running through his mind, I didn't want to witness it. I got up and sat next to Paul on the couch. I put my head on his shoulder and I squeezed his hand, wishing that we were at a club letting a comedian take us out of ourselves, helping Paul forget.

Paul chose a path for himself and I let him lead me into this new awareness; it was surreal. Smoking pot was like lifting a veil from my mind, enabling me to see the world from a whole new dimension. It was the "Magical Mystery Tour" that the Beatles sang about. You could either get on the bus or not; there didn't seem to be a middle ground. There was definitely a cultural revolution going on, and Paul and I were among the millions of young people who were making the choice to leave the known straight reality, taking a new path of self-exploration. We had a term for this: you were either "straight" or you were a "head." In the Jefferson Airplane song "White Rabbit" are the words "feed your head," meaning feed your consciousness. You were either "turning on" or not, and the two worlds did not seem to understand each other.

People who were not turning on were still playing charades at parties, drinking alcohol, planning their honeymoons in the Pocono Mountains, and they still bought stereo sets in cabinets as furniture for their soon-to-be suburban homes. To the people turning on, music was everything. We were buying speakers and amplifiers that could magnify the incredible music that was bursting onto the world stage. Janis Joplin would rock us at night and Judy Collins would serenade us in the morning. By the weekend there would be the release of yet another new album by the Grateful Dead, the Stones, The Who; take your pick. It was a smorgasbord of sensual immersion. It was as if the heavens sent us music and lyrics as a survival technique that assuaged the ugliness of war. Music defined us. It could pull us together on a bad day and blow our minds open with truth and reality the next.

I suppose marijuana was the gateway to mind expansion because we wouldn't consider drinking alcohol, as that was the drug of the establishment. Like Dr. Timothy Leary, we were discovering a "brave new world." Dr. Leary was a

Professor at Harvard University and was working with an experimental drug called LSD. It was being tested to see if it could help schizophrenics. As the story goes, Dr. Leary decided to try this wonder drug himself. Once he saw the world from this lofty new dimension, he chose to leave the straight academic world of Harvard University and pave a path to enlightenment; he dropped out of conventional society.

I was twenty years old and enjoying my new reality, but I was being very careful as I approached the gateway to more mind-expanding drugs. I was, after all, a mother, and I had always been a very prayerful person, so I was taking baby steps on this path of self-discovery. I watched Paul and his friends when they took acid, and after it was proven pure, I would take half the amount Paul had taken. Of course, the baby was always with Dora and Ed. Being a mother provided a very healthy boundary for me.

Now as I sit with more than forty years of twenty-twenty hindsight, do I wish like hell that I had won that New Year's battle of wills and dragged Paul off to the nightclub world? The answer is: I don't know, but I wish I had known I was choosing a major fork in the road of life. I guess that is the trick of life on earth; we don't get an overview until things are behind us. It was becoming more and more obvious that Paul and I needed to move out of Dora and Ed's house. We needed our own "pad," so we put our names on a waiting list for the new high-rise apartments in Cambridge. On April 1, 1969, we were accepted and were given an apartment on the 9th floor—apartment 9N. It turned out to be quite a fateful placement as the people in 8N were to become important friends in our lives.

We had a two-bedroom apartment with a balcony porch

that was six feet long and four feet wide. There was just enough room for a barbeque, a small wading pool for Paulie, and a glimpse of the sunset each evening. We were happy! We easily collected furniture from our families; they would give us their couch and get the new one they had been wanting. An end table here and a lamp there, and we were all set. We bought a bedroom set with our savings and, of course, the much anticipated stereo. What fun we had painting the living room a soft yellow and putting up the shelves for the stereo. We hung a Mexican rug on the wall and began our new life on our own—no parents, no military, pure freedom.

Just before Paulie's first birthday in May, a friend of Paul's offered him a job on a construction crew in Boston. Paul said yes in a heartbeat and was finally able to quit his job at the post office. Paul started at $300 a week. After three months he would be able to join the union and we would have medical benefits. Life was good. I loved playing house and now I could begin to think about how I wanted to spend my twenty-first birthday. Well, that was easy. The Newport Jazz Festival was held every Fourth of July weekend in Newport, Rhode Island, and that sounded perfect to me. Did I dare to ask Dora to babysit overnight? She and Ed had already agreed to take the baby for three days in August when we went to the Woodstock festival, for which we already had our tickets. I didn't feel I could ask my parents because they were still adjusting to Brigette's operation year and now her return home. I mustered up the courage to ask Dora and, of course, she said yes; they loved having Paulie and would take him anytime I wanted. God, how I lucked out in the in-law department; I love them dearly. Don't tell me any bad mother in law jokes, man.

Irene Isobel Carver

Chapter Eight

Turning 21

ON THE MORNING OF JULY FOURTH, WE DROPPED
Paulie off bright and early at his grandparents' and I asked
Paul to stop at a pay phone so I could call my mother. At the
last minute I realized I could not leave town without calling
her. This was our only totally private day together that I did
not have to share with any of my sisters or brothers. There
I stood, turning twenty-one years old in a phone booth in
Cushing Square, listening to my mother tell me, like she did
every year, how beautiful it had been in Maine on the morning I was born and how completely adorable I was. Best of
all, she had gotten her wish—I was a girl! As I hung up, I
looked down at my white skirt that was attached to the top
bolero with gold chains, my midriff showing, and I still felt
completely adorable, especially with all my pregnancy fat
gone now—until I made the mistake of asking Paul how he
liked my birthday outfit. "Well, it looks a little like a go-go
dancer, a little straight," he said. Realizing quickly that blurting out the truth was a bit harsh, he added, "But you look
beautiful, anyway." To hide my hurt feelings I slid closer to
him on my seat and said, "Well, I guess we're gonna have
to go-go dancing," and we laughed the tension off.

As we drove along Route 2, I remembered a time the
previous month when Paul had picked up a woman hitch-

hiker and she asked if we had any "bread." Well, this was just before I knew that "bread" was hippie slang for money and Paul had to apologize for my dense response. Poor Paul, he was always just one step ahead of me in hipness and I always felt just a tad un-cool in his eyes.

The Jazz Festival was set on a hill overlooking the ocean. We found a shady spot for our blanket and lay back to enjoy the music. The only performer I remember at the Festival that weekend was Alice Cooper. I think it was because during his performance it dawned on me that it was my twenty-first birthday and I had no alcohol with me. We were "heads," we didn't drink alcohol; that was for the straight people, but at that moment my old programmed thinking said, *I should find some wine just for a toast.* After we smoked a joint, I looked around spotted a couple with an open bottle of wine. I walked over to them and asked if they would mind giving me a small sip to toast my twenty-first birthday. They handed me their bottle and as I raised it to my mouth for a gulp, I caught a glimpse of Alice Cooper on stage. He seemed as crazy as his female name, with black tears painted on his face like a jester, and his hysterical guitar playing. He was awesomely crazy. Life was exploding in our faces, new meaning was everywhere, I was alive, and soon we would go to Woodstock!

ALL THE WORLD'S A STAGE

After Woodstock, our lives went back to a routine but I had a new awareness. I began to look for opportunities to get Paul to talk to me about how he was feeling. I knew something was wrong with his nerves but I didn't know how bad it was; nobody did. It would take another ten years before the diagnosis "post-traumatic stress disorder" existed.

One night after I had put Paulie to bed, I curled up next to Paul on the couch and said, "I felt pretty bad at Woodstock when Country Joe sang about Vietnam; that must really have hurt you." I was hoping he would open up and we could talk, but instead, he abruptly stood up and said, "I'm going out, be back in an hour," and he quickly left. I felt like I had been slapped and I was worried about him. As I wiped away my tears, I wondered, "What the hell should I do now?" I turned on the TV. Richard Pryor's show was on and he was mocking the trial of the Chicago 8, joking about how now it's the Chicago Seven and Judge Julius had Bobby Seale bound and gagged. "It's the battle of the Hoffmans—Abbie and Julius—round three tomorrow folks, get your popcorn now." I found myself laughing, too, and before I knew it, Paul walked in the door. He walked directly to our bedroom and I followed, wanting to know what the heck was going on. I watched as he opened our nightstand drawer and then closed it. When he turned and saw me I asked what he had. He didn't say anything, so I opened the drawer and saw a small baggie of white powder. I held it up, "What is this?" I asked, my cheeks burning.

"Don't worry, I'm saving it for Friday night. It's heroin, it helps me relax after the work week." I put it back in the drawer quickly, afraid of it. I knew Paul had one friend that was using heroin; I had seen tracks in his arms and asked Paul what they were. He had said that Rich had snorted heroin in Nam and now he was shooting it with a needle, thus the tracks. I had been frightened then for his friend, but now I was frightened for myself. In my panic I blurted out, "Paul we can't be spending money on something like this, please don't buy this shit." He turned and walked away and said over his shoulder, "I'm the one working all week for the money, I'll spend it how I want." I burst out crying and Paul turned and said, "It's only ten fucking dollars, give me a break."

That night as I tossed and turned myself to sleep, I found myself rationalizing that it couldn't be too harmful if he only did it on the weekend. But deep down I felt myself spiraling into an abyss as more and more drugs were being introduced into my life. A few days later I found a way to ask Gwen, my downstairs neighbor, what she knew about heroin from her nursing perspective. I think she evaded my question by telling me how Leslie, our neighbor in 8H, had just left her husband because he was smoking pot and using LSD. "She just packed her bags and left," Gwen told me. I knew in that moment that I wouldn't leave Paul; we were married, for better or worse.

Soon after the heroin experience, a friend told me that she had taken a hit of some blotter acid and her trip was the "most superior" experience she ever had. She said she had gotten clarity on many of her own life questions and she was going to do it again that weekend; she would sell me some if I wanted. Well, I was feeling like I could use a few answers myself, so I made my plan. Dora said she would take Paulie Friday night and all day Saturday and Paul and I organized a party at our apartment for the occasion. Gwen and Randy decided to join us for their first "trip" also. I was inching cautiously into this world of mind expansion, so Paul cut one tiny blotter in half with a razor blade for Gwen and me to split. I quickly put my half under my tongue, and playing hostess, went right to the stereo and put on our new Traffic album. Within fifteen minutes I knew I was "getting off." I could feel the chemical rushing through my body, sending chills up my spine, and then the tapestry on my living room

Irene Isobel Carver

wall left it's two-by- three-foot boundary and took over the entire wall. It was glorious! Then it floated across the room and out to the porch with me right behind it. My friend, Tim LaPasse, who had taken a full hit of the blotter acid, slid open the porch door and joined me.

As Tim began to ramble on and on about his theory of God, I looked at him and said, "I cannot hear about God unless I am on a swing." So we walked out of the apartment and down the hall. We stood looking at the elevator door for a few minutes in silence and when it opened we looked at each other, turned away, and walked the nine flights of stairs to ground level. LSD and elevators were definitely not a match. At the park, Tim began pushing me on the swing and telling me his God theory. I felt he meant that God was the wind, and then I saw his words floating by me in the air. I reached out and caught the word "domain" and tucked in my shirt. I hopped off the swing in mid-flight and said, "Holy shit, *Alice in Wonderland* is true." We began to discuss the children's stories that we liked and we both agreed that the *Three Little Pigs* was our favorite. We might have walked off together to build our house of straw except we suddenly recalled we were connected to a party on the ninth floor. Walking into the lobby, we closed our eyes and took the elevator up. When I walked into the apartment the first thing I saw was Gwen doing the dishes. I asked her what she was doing and she said, "I'm trying to feel normal, and whatever you do, don't look in the mirror." I think Gwen was up all night washing something or other and, needless to say, she never took acid again.

As the sun rose in the morning and we were all coming down from our trips, Tim and I tried to remember who the God was that we had figured out in the playground.

Tim was really pissed off because he could not remember; he had completely forgotten all that he had figured out about God. I tried to assuage his frustration by telling him I remembered the domain of God is within us, and I put my hand on my heart where I had placed the word. But it was impossible to give him what was inside me; hopefully he'll have a flashback someday. I watched Paul roll a joint at daybreak and I realized that I had no idea what his trip had been like. As I was growing, we were growing apart. If we were music, I was the Moody Blues and Paul was Lou Reed.

We were really enjoying the mind-expanding benefits of marijuana, so our group of friends began to buy pounds of it. This would cost about $200 and we would all chip in. It would come in a "brick" about a foot long and six inches wide. Every couple of months we would buy one; what a cool experience it was to have this earthy, vibrant, and alive herb right into our living room, opening our minds to new ways of thinking and new ways of seeing the world. We would spread out newspaper and place the pound of marijuana in the center, admiring its beauty before breaking it open; it was our holy ritual. Marijuana was our teacher; we treated it with respect. We would proceed to gently pull it apart, slowly exposing the flowerets with branches and seeds, marveling at the clusters with curly, fuzzy buds at the ends. The pungent, earthy smell would fill the whole room and we would begin to expand with just its essence. Gradually we would create sixteen even ounces and begin to sift the seeds with matchbook covers, letting the seeds roll out and into a pile.

On one of these Friday evenings, after everyone had gone home, I took our largest bud of pot, put the stem behind my ear and let the bud rest on my temple. I felt

Irene Isobel Carver

beautiful. I put on the *Surrealistic Pillow* album and as Grace Slick sang, "Feed your head," I danced around the room, floating like the smoke that was rising from the joint Paul had lit. It was a nirvana moment that I will always remember as I danced up to Paul and stopped to take the smoke from his mouth; life was in slow motion, to be captured forever. I looked into Paul's bright blue eyes and for a moment it seemed as if the pain had been lifted, a brief reprieve, and I think he felt beautiful too.

Crisp and gorgeous fall days were upon us in New England. Paul and I decided to go camping in Franconia Notch, New Hampshire for the weekend, hoping to get pictures of Paulie with the pumpkins and red and orange maple trees all around us. This would be Paulie's first camping trip; we were excited. Paul was late getting home from work that Friday evening so I put on the evening news to distract me. Abbie Hoffman had somersaulted into the courtroom for the trial of the Chicago Seven that was now in its second month. What theater Abbie was creating for us all as he mocked the judicial system every chance he could. One day he and the other defendants showed up for court dressed in long black judge's robes. When the judge ordered them to remove the robes, they all were wearing police uniforms under them. God, how I loved Abbie Hoffman! He and the Yippies—the political hippies—were courageously staging all these stunts to try to get the attention of the world. They were trying to show the absurdity of the greed of the capitalistic world that was paying for the Vietnam War and Abbie was quoted as saying "It seems like the U.S. government has a war policy created by Lucifer himself." Abbie was a revolutionary to the core and using humor to express his rage was only one of the amazing happenings of the Sixties.

When Paul finally got home over an hour late that night, I could tell by his dilated pupils that he had gone to Central Square to buy the heroin that he now needed to get through the weekend. For awhile he did a good job hiding the fact that he now had to go "cop smack," as he called it, on Wednesday nights. He wasn't able to make it till the weekend without some withdrawal symptoms happening, like stomach cramps. He was able to show up for work every day, but the emotional weight he had been carrying ever since coming home from the Tet Offensive in Nam was becoming heavier and heavier. The problem now was that he was trying to let smack help him carry that burden; instead he was carrying the monkey of addiction on his back. It was a sad and scary cycle to watch develop. In hindsight, I wish I had yelled and fought with Paul over this, or maybe I should have been like Leslie in 8H and just walked out, but I didn't do either. I guess I was having my own emotional trouble, watching Paul's psychic pain and taking care of an eighteen-month-old. So I chose to stay in some form of illusion myself, smoking a joint each night after I put Paulie to bed, and reading a Harold Robbins novel or just zoning out to music.

Three things saved me that Christmas of 1969. First, my friend brought me an incredible leather purse when he came home from Morocco. The purse had three small mirrors inlaid in the leather and fringe all along the bottom. I felt like I finally made it to the "hip" part of hippie. Secondly, there was a new Buffalo Springfield album with the song, "Expecting to Fly" on it. The lyrics gave words to how I felt. I was on the "edge of the feather" while Paul was trying not to stumble. The music was a comfort to me. I felt that Neil Young understood life as we were living it. That is what makes musicians and music so incredible; they write the lyrics and music that provide the soundtrack to our lives. The third thing was Paulie, of course. He was just nineteen months old, and he could pull me out of the darkest abyss by just having come so recently from God. It was his second Christmas and he was at such a cute age. It was fun to buy gifts for him and take pictures of him. He gave me the reason to pretend that Paul would eventually snap out of this heroin thing. At least, that was my thinking at that time.

New Year's Eve arrived. The traumatic and enlightening decade of the Sixties was at last coming to an end. Once again, Paul and I had a battle of wills as to how to celebrate. I wanted to go to a party we were invited to near Cape Cod, at the house of one of our high school friends. But Paul absolutely refused to go, calling them "phony hippies." His alternative was to stay home, smoke pot, and listen to music. I told him I needed a plan that included dressing up a bit and getting a babysitter. When seven o'clock arrived and Paul said he'd be back in a while as he walked out the door, I knew he was going to get his fix and that that is all he planned to do for the evening. Fortunately, I had taken Paulie to Dora and Ed's house earlier in the afternoon to spend the night. When Paul left, I decided I was not going to sit around watching him nod out on life while the rest of the world brought in the Seventies.

I put on a Creedence Clearwater album and turned up the volume to drown out my own thoughts, as I picked out my outfit. I put on my orange flowered mini-skirt with a matching bolero, beige tights, and my knee-high brown leather boots. I turned on the TV and watched the early New Year's Eve festivities while I waited for Paul to return with the car. When he walked in the door I stood up, grabbed my knee-length army issue woolen coat, and held out my hand palm up for the keys. He put them in my hand and said, "Where are you going?" I didn't look him in the eyes because I didn't want to take a chance of changing my mind. As I walked past him I said, "I'm going to Lauren's party." And I let the door slam behind me. The radio entertained me for the hour-long drive and the top one hundred songs of the decade kept me from dwelling on the fact that Paul was choosing heroin over me, over life.

Paul

Paul stood, feeling the slam of the door in his face, then turned quickly and walked to the bathroom, holding onto the little package of white powder that he had in his vest pocket. "Don't think about it, don't think about any of it, just get your stuff," he told himself as he opened his suede pouch filled with his syringe, thick rubber medical band, spoon, and matches. He laid everything out neatly on the sink while he sat on the toilet lid and rolled up his sleeve. Just above his elbow he tied himself off with the rubber band. He had to hold one end of the rubber band in his mouth while he wrapped the other end around his arm. He pumped his fingers and palm open and closed a few times to get the blood flow rushing to his vein, his main vein which now rose up in the crease of his elbow waiting, burning, primed for its job of receiving the needle. Then Paul emptied half of the powder into the spoon, added a few drops of water and lit a match.

As soon as he smelled the sulfur from the match, his body began to shudder with anticipation; relief was on the way. He held the match under the spoon and cooked the powder. He took the syringe and sucked the liquid into it. He tapped his vein with two fingers and inserted the needle. He gently transferred the liquid into his vein, unleashing the rubber band, and instantly every muscle in his face dropped. His head followed and his chin hit his chest, which jerked him up. He took the needle out of his arm and laid it on the counter and let himself lean back against the toilet. With the tension gone from his brain he could begin to think. Shit, its New Year's Eve, and Irene just took off. He licked the spoon and put all his stuff neatly back into his pouch for the next time. "Thank God, this will hold me for the night," he said into the mirror as he looked at his eyes and scratched his nose. He loved the itchy feeling he got once heroin was in his blood, he didn't know why but it felt good. Then a knock came at the front door. He hoped it was Irene and that she had forgotten her key but his hopes were dashed as he looked into his friend Kobb's eyes.

"Hey, happy fucking New Year, where's Irene and the baby?"

"The baby is at my parents' overnight and Irene just took off, pissed that I didn't want to go to Lauren's phony piece of shit friend's party." Kobb lit a joint and walked over to the stereo. Seeing that Creedence was already on the turntable he just pushed the play button and passed the joint to Paul.

"No, I'm cool man," Paul said as he waved off the joint. "I just did a bit of smack and I like that rush all by itself, but thanks," and he flopped onto the couch.

"So where's the party?"

"Down the fucking Cape; she must be out of her mind

driving there."

"Well, I'm up for a drive; how far down the Cape?'

"Marshfield," Paul said.

"Hey that's hardly the Cape; it's about an hour. I'll drive if you want to take off and surprise Irene." Paul was feeling like his other self now with the junk in his blood. He was the Paul who could think without wanting to yell, the Paul who thought he could, maybe, bear life.

"Sure, what the hell, it's New Year's Eve; I guess I can bear those bullshit phony hippies for one night to make Irene happy," Paul said as he grabbed his coat.

"Yeah, and maybe I'll meet a chick to ball if I'm lucky," Kobb said as he sucked down one last hit of the joint and opened the door. "Ready, set, rock and fucking roll," Kobb chanted as he, too, flung his coat over his shoulder.

When I arrived at the party, I felt a little uncomfortable entering alone but the house was packed and it was easy to just melt into the crowd. Eventually, I saw Lauren, and I lied and told her that Paul was sick. She gave me a kind of sad look like she knew what kind of sick Paul was, and it hurt her too. We had all been high school friends and I knew by now she had heard through the grapevine that Paul was doing heroin. She kissed my cheek and we both knew we would keep up a pretense, at least for this evening.

After I smoked some pretty powerful weed that was being passed around, I found myself standing back in the corner of the kitchen just watching and observing since I didn't know many of Lauren's new friends. The weed felt like a truth serum and I suddenly knew these people were mostly drug dealers. One guy had on red leather boots that had blue and white stars on them. He looked like a clown to me with his pant legs tucked in. I guess this was the phony hippie image Paul had referred to. They were the opposite of the real hippie spirit of non-commercialism; people who lived in their beloved old bellbottoms with patches on them. I looked across the room at Lauren talking to a guy with a heavy suede leather jacket on, with long fringe hanging from the sleeves. As he laughed and gestured I saw a thick gold watch flash on his wrist.

Just then the kitchen door opened, I saw Paul and his friend Kobb walk in. Paul looked so handsome to me in his blue denim shirt with his black leather vest and Levis. I found myself grinning with joy as I walked across the room to meet him. As we hugged and kissed I could see how dilated his pupils were, the tell tale sign of heroin use. Sadness hit my heart with a sharp pang as I realized how very much I loved him and yet, was helpless to help him. The three of us stood apart in this crowd of "pretty" people and we laughed at some of the pretentious outfits the men were wearing. Right after everyone kissed and rang in the Seventies, Paul, Kobb, and I left. I gave Kobb a big kiss as we stood next to his car watching our breath in the cold air of a new decade. I thanked him for driving Paul down to the party. He said he was happy to do it, that Paul had helped him often, and that he was fine to drive so Paul could drive home with me if we wanted. Paul gave him a big hug, also knowing what a real pal he was.

As we drove into the cold, star-filled early morning air, Paul reached over and squeezed my hand and said, "Now, you probably know why I didn't want to be with that bunch of phonies." Then he adjusted the seat to a lie-back position and closed his eyes. "But then I got loaded, and I realized I could suffer through them to be with you," he said. I turned the heat up a notch as my eyes filled with tears and I realized it was people like Lauren's friends that were selling the heroin that Paul was buying, to bear the glare of a world of gold watches.

It took a bit longer to get home, as I was high and afraid to drive over sixty mph. But we made it amidst the occasional firecrackers that burst color into the black sky, and the radio kept me company as Paul slept. I listened to the sound track to *Easy Rider* with Steppenwolf singing, "I've smoked a lot of grass, I've popped a lot of pills" and then I tried hard to grasp the next words, something about, "the spirit couldn't kill." I looked over at Paul and prayed that this junk, this heroin, would not be able to kill his spirit. And that became my 1970 New Year's wish.

By 3:00 a.m., as we snuggled into our warm bed, I heard Paul mumble into my ear, "I was right—bullshit, ego-tripping, hippie hypocrites—capitalists in disguise," and then we let sleep have us.

Chapter Nine

Cooking 101

I LOVED BEING A MOTHER. IT WAS SIMPLY MY NATURE to be happy to stay at home with Paulie while Paul worked to pay our bills. I was content with my housewife role. I didn't regret leaving college or not earning money of my own, like my sister Clare was doing as a secretary. Paulie felt my contentment and was a happy little boy. I was a creature of routine, like my mother, so my days hummed by rhythmically, despite Paul's inner demons. I would take Paulie to the park across the street in the mornings after Paul went to work, and Gwen and I would talk while our boys played in the sandbox with their tiny trucks. Then we would come home for lunch and Paulie would take a two-hour nap from one to three, while I curled up to read in peace. I loved being transported from my ninth floor apartment to a world that Irving Stone or A.J. Cronin had created. When Paulie woke up he would have a snack and then we would head out for our two- mile walk to the library, where both of us would stock up on reading material. It seemed we always had *The Little Engine That Could* close by. Once we were home I would decide what to make for dinner while Paulie contentedly talked to the pictures in his books.

Gwen's Italian cooking made me realized that my mother was a very bland and routine Scottish cook. The only spices that I knew existed besides salt and pepper were rosemary and thyme, which my mother used in the turkey stuffing a few times a year. The wildest my mother ever got was to toothpick an onion to the top center of a roast beef, and then we knew it was Sunday! I had my work cut out for me and I knew it. I asked Gwen if she would teach me some of her recipes. She happily agreed and said the first class would be about how to shop. So one winter afternoon, instead of going to the library Gwen introduced me to the magical world of tiny, ethnic neighborhood stores.

First she took me to her favorite shop, Quido's, tucked away in a cobbled alley behind a three-story house. We left the strollers in the car and carried our two-year-old boys on our hips. We passed through a narrow wooden door as a bell jingled over our heads, where we stood under a ceiling that had foot-long pepperonis and linguiça hung from strings. "Bonjourno, bonjourno, Mrs. Genoa, and how's our little Joey today?" asked the white- aproned owner. I looked around amazed. Where the heck had I been all my life? This store was right in my hometown and I suddenly felt like I was in Italy. Gwen nudged me to pay attention as she ordered provolone cheese, some sliced thin for baking, and some sliced thick for cheese and crackers. The owner then cut the strings that held two large pepperonis to the ceiling rack and rolled them up in crisp white paper. Joey began to slap the glass display window so the owner quickly handed both the boys a fat, black olive. Joey popped his in his mouth with juice dripping out as he grinned in delight, and Paulie just looked at his, as stunned as his mother at this foreign object. I took his and broke it in half and shared it with him so he would give it a try.

Then we went to the Armenian side of town because

Gwen said they generally had the freshest produce, just in from the Boston marketplace. I watched her pick out bunches of cilantro, parsley, green peppers, and mushrooms and I followed suit, filling my own basket. She then instructed me to select five pounds of tomatoes. She smelled each one before she put it in her bag. Since I didn't know what the tomatoes should smell like, I just kept the color about the same as hers. When we left the market Gwen said she was going to make her spaghetti sauce this Saturday and I could watch her and make my own batch in a pot right next to hers. "For tonight's dinner, we'll go to the butcher down the street who pounds a great veal and who has the hot sausages Randy likes best," Gwen said, as we sped off in her green Volvo to stores I had only driven by before.

I realized I was quite tired; this was not at all like the one-stop shopping I was used to. Before I could suggest maybe this was enough of a class for one day, Gwen said we had to go to her favorite bakery to get the best rolls and that I should know who makes the best cannoli in town. I kept quiet and I was soon looking into a case of chocolate and cream-filled pastries. My mother's voice came whispering into my head, "In your mouth for a minute, on your hips forever." I didn't want to offend Gwen, so I tasted my first ever cannoli, and my eyes rolled up into my head with pleasure and guilt.

Paulie and I were both weary by the time we got home. While I put all our new food away, Paulie decided to lie down on the floor with a bottle of apple juice and fell asleep. I had just enough time and energy to put three fat sausages in a pan, puncture them all with a fork many times as Gwen had instructed me on the way home, put sliced mushrooms and green peppers in the pan and cover them. I let this simmer until Paul got home from work. Then while he watched in amazement, I drained the fat out of the pan and added a cup of marinara sauce. All that was left to do was to put the sausages into soft, freshly baked Italian rolls and life on the ninth floor was temporarily transformed; at least I was transforming. Did I think new food could replace Paul's need to escape from our life? No, but I was hoping my love could. I was only twenty-one, after all. Was I full of illusion and delusion? I wonder now as I look back, but still, I prefer to call it hope.

As spring of 1970 blossomed, I caught tie-dye mania. Color therapy was seeping into my life like manna from heaven. During the week I would drag Paulie around to all the Goodwill stores and collect white cotton tee shirts of all sizes to get ready for the weekend, when I would turn my kitchen into a bubbling bath of dangerously hot colored water. At the Salvation Army I found a few old aluminum pots that were large, worn, and dented, most likely retired after years of faithfully boiling lobsters. Then came the color, which was actually the easy part. Every grocery store sold Rit dye in an array of colors for only thirty-nine cents a box. I would buy every color the store had in stock, move my spices out of the way, and let the dye take over.

Paul would take Paulie to the park to make sure he was out of harm's way while the boiling and submerging began. Tie dying was an awkward process with pieces of a shirt hanging out of one pot, strutting its new royal blue, while another part of the shirt, all twisted up in elastic bands, was dangling into a different pot, bubbling in yellow or green, or whatever my favorite colors of the week happened to be. I began giving my experimental tee shirts away to friends and they started bringing me all types of material to be dyed.

Irene Isobel Carver

As I got the knack of it, I began making wall hangings and tablecloths. I even found some terry cloth and transformed it into rainbow seat covers for my friend's Volkswagen bus. No white material was allowed to stay that way. I saw it only as a canvas for color. One morning, as the sun shone in while I was changing Paulie, I looked at his white diapers and thought they looked terribly plain. I was just going to have to give this little boy his own signature colors! So I set to work that night, dying half his diapers in spirals of green, yellow, blue, and red. Then, in the light of day, when I went to put one on Paulie, I became concerned that his urine could cause the dye to soak into his skin so I decided to put the diapers away until I could figure this out.

Clare called me from work to tell me to turn on the news. She sounded angry with me when I hesitated. She knew I generally refused to watch the news and said, "Just watch the damn news, Irene" and she hung up in my ear. I decided it must be pretty important or she wouldn't have called and ordered me like this. So I put Paulie in his crib with a bottle of apple juice and turned on the TV. All programs were interrupted with the news flash that National Guardsmen had killed four students at Kent State University in Ohio. The demonstration that had been going on there all week-end had gone terribly wrong. The protest was organized because the United States had now begun to bomb and invade Cambodia. The war was spreading, not ending as we were all hoping. Frustration and anger were coming to the surface on college campuses all over America, but no one had expected this—four students shot and killed and ten more wounded.

When Paul came home from work a few hours later, he

sat with me on the couch and we watched the six o'clock news; it looked like war in America. The students were trying to physically push back the guardsmen and soon there were bodies bleeding and people screaming in disbelief. I was scared. I thought of my friend Patty who was at the University of Illinois.

Paul stood up and I heard him punch the wall as he walked down the hall to our bedroom yelling "The military sucks!" The baby began to cry from his crib, but Paul didn't stop and I knew he was in a hurry to get to his pot stash so he could alter his painful view of the world. I went into Paulie's room and picked him up. My eyes flashed towards the stack of newly dyed diapers folded on the top shelf of the closet. I scooped Paulie out of the crib with one arm and pulled the diapers down from the shelf with the other. As they landed in a pile on the floor, Paulie began to stomp on them one by one as he called out the colors. He was so cute that I just lay down in the middle of the pile and let him flop on my chest. His happy spirit sparked an idea. I hurried to the kitchen with Paulie at my heels to get red and black magic markers from the drawer. Together we sat in the middle of the diaper pile as I drew peace symbols in the center of each diaper with the black marker and Paulie took the red one and began making dots all over his feet. I sensed someone watching and looked up to see Paul standing in the doorway. "Sew them all together and make a flag," he said. "That's a great idea," I said as I leapt to my feet, excited to have Paul with us. "Keep an eye on Paulie while I get my sewing stuff, and I'll get us a snack, too" I said, feeling a twinge of hope that we wouldn't all collapse in pain.

The three of us sat on the floor nibbling on pepperoni and cheese with crackers while I sewed each diaper together

Irene Isobel Carver

at their corners and then added yellow ribbon at each end. When our beautiful tie dyed flag was done, Paul and I tied it across our balcony. We stood back and watched as the spring breeze blew our tribute, through our diaper flag, in soft waves across the evening sky. We took our dinner out on the porch that evening. Paul put on a Joan Baez album and we listened as Joan sang in her trilling and prophetic voice, "winds of the old days will blow through your hair."

Friends called to say they were taking off for D.C. to protest, but Paul and I remained quiet. We sat on the porch and watched as the sky turned from a brilliant red into a soft purple pink. Paulie fell asleep in my arms, and I made a wish upon the first evening star. It was a wish that could never come true, a wish that I had never said out loud until that moment. I wished that Paul and I had been courageous enough to run away to Canada and to protest the war as those students had that day. I squeezed my son close to my heart and I knew he was the reason why we hadn't run to Canada, and I hoped that God could forgive me. I hoped I could forgive myself.

Boston—My Home Town

Two months later the city of Boston did an amazing thing. They hosted concerts every Friday evening all summer at the Harvard Stadium for only two dollars. If this was a ploy to take the attention of young people off the war, it worked—at least in part—as we lined up every week to get tickets to this Romanesque, circular stadium; this gorgeous stone amphitheater, with ivy growing up the sides. In the Harvard Stadium I could easily imagine a gladiator fight being held rather than a Sly and the Family Stone concert. Sly performed one Friday in his multi-colored outfit and his *I'm black and*

I'm proud afro, singing, "I'm gonna take you higher," and that was just what he did. These "Summer Thing" concerts of 1970 brought us many of the most popular bands of the time, but the most memorable concert was Janis Joplin, because she broke my heart wide open along with hers.

It was a hot and humid night in Boston and Janis was singing the blues like only Janis could, rocking all our souls in her longing for Bobbie McGee. "I'll trade all of my tomorrows for one single yesterday," and then she stopped singing and started talking to us. She began begging actually. "So look at all of you out there, isn't there one of you who will come up here, who will hold me, who will be with me?" She held out her hand to one of her stage people and he brought her what we all knew was a bottle of Southern Comfort. She took a swig and then held it out to the audience. "Here, come drink with me." She swaggered; no one moved. This gigantic stadium became silent as the immensity of her loneliness loomed above us all. We were paralyzed in sorrow and love for this amazing and blazing star that, before our eyes, was fizzling out. The existential pain was too great and someone shouted out "Summertime, Janis" and this queen, this goddess of rock and roll, continued pleading for her life as she yelled, "Come on, I really need someone, I need a man." I remember holding my breath when she said this and I chanted in my mind, *come on someone run up there, come on.* But there wasn't a man at the concert that night capable of taking on the challenge of Janis Joplin. So finally Janis saved herself, as she broke into the song "Cry, Cry Baby," . . . "There is only one thing you ever need to do right in this world, it is to just really love one person." There she stood, writhing, singing, giving us her all, giving us a little piece of her heart as her words and her body dripped with passion under a canopy of August stars.

On the drive home that night, I couldn't help but think that every woman at the concert had been hoping for that happy-ever-after ending for Janis; that someone would eventually come to her backstage out of the limelight, but sad to say, we were too soon to get the opposite news. On October 4, 1970, Janis died of a heroin overdose, alone in a hotel room in Los Angeles. The day after hearing the news of Janis's death, I put Paulie in his stroller and walked to the cemetery near our apartment, wanting to honor the sadness weighing on my heart. Thankfully, it was a crisp and sunny fall day so I spread out a blanket, and Paulie and I lay down under a maple tree, letting the brilliant red leaves fall on us, which made us both giggle when they hit our faces. I looked up into the clear blue sky and wondered what in the world was going on. Two weeks before Janis's death, Jimi Hendrix had also died of a heroin overdose. They were both twenty-seven years old. A news headline said they had "lived themselves to death."

Paulie got up and began running around, squishing leaves between his tiny hands and throwing them at me. I would scoop up a pile of leaves and chase him, throwing them back at him. Soon we would tumble back onto our blanket laughing and exhausted. I gave Paulie a bottle of juice to drink so I could lie down in silence and think. I was very glad I believed in another world after death. It comforted me to picture Jimi greeting Janis in the heavenly realms. With his unique guitar style and her passionate voice, I could see them in an eternal purple haze, a celestial duo, free from all the suffering down here on the earth. My sadness began to lift as I breathed in the beauty of the falling leaves blowing around us.

While the bottle comforted Paulie into an early nap, I pulled the edge of the blanket over him. Now I could really let my vision expand on what might be going on for Jimi's and Janis's souls. I saw Jimi with his ancestors from his Black, Mexican, and Cherokee bloodlines. I envisioned them dancing, rattling, and chanting him home. I saw angels rocking Janis' lonely heart in rainbow colors of light as they sang to her. I leaned back against a tree and had a depressing thought: Janis and Jimi had both died of heroin overdoses. Paul was using heroin. As fear shot through me and the sun set behind the trees, I scooped Paulie up and put him into his stroller with the blanket tucked all about him. I walked home briskly and wondered if Janis had overdosed on purpose or by accident. The news reported that Jimi's overdose was accidental but nothing had been said yet about Janis. I hoped there would be more information in the evening paper. I knew that no one was ever going to really know the truth because Janis was alone when she died. Those of us at the Boston concert just six weeks before, knew in our hearts that loneliness was her real killer.

When I got to the house, I sat Paulie on the couch with a couple of his books as I began to prepare spaghetti and salad for dinner. My sense of peace was gone and a nervous energy took its place. I decided to put Paulie in his crib, so I could explore what this new fear was about. Once Paulie was safely settled, I put on the Lou Reed album. I wanted to really listen to his songs about heroin and see if I could figure anything out. What could be going on in Paul's mind that kept him using this stuff? I was afraid. What if Janis's death was an accident? I remembered hearing Paul say things like, "That was some very powerful smack," or "That shit wasn't cut with anything, it was pure."

Irene Isobel Carver

I lay down on the floor near a speaker straining to hear every word. I soon found myself kneeling and rocking back and forth to the soft drum in the background. It was like a heart beat that started slowly and then sped up. I heard the words, "I don't know where I am going, I feel like Jesus' son, I guess, but I just don't know." I rocked back and forth to the slow heart-beating rhythm. "Heroin will be the death of me; it's my wife, it's my life." The music became a fast grating electric sound. "It leads to a center in my head. Thank God that I'm not aware, that I just don't care." When the music stopped, I peeked at Paulie. He was fast asleep. I stared at him, letting his innocence bring me back into my world and out of a junkie's world.

I lay back down on the floor and stared at the mandala hanging on the wall. Once again I was filled with dread thinking that Janis died from an accidental overdose. The song lyrics ran through my mind again—*Shit, Lou Reed loves heroin like a wife, when you're high on it you just don't care. Wait a minute,* I told myself, *Lou Reed was just one person, who else would know about heroin?* I thought of Gwen, who was a nurse, would she know anything?

I called her and bluntly said, "Gwen, I'm worried about Paul and his heroin use, how bad is this shit? What do you know?" "I think it is much worse than people know," she said after a long pause. "My brother has a problem with heroin and his need for it seems to keep growing a little at a time." I asked, "Is there anything I can do to help Paul?" Tears filled the little holes in the telephone receiver. "Do anything you can to get him to stop before it gets worse. Shut him off from sex, anything. Hey, I got to go Joey is crying, good luck," and the phone went silent.

I went back to pacing the living room and my first

thought was that I really believed Paul would choose heroin over sex. I collapsed on the couch and bit off all my fingernails. I needed a plan.

When Paul got home from work that evening, he went right to our room and lit up a joint. Without even saying hi, he got in the shower. When he finally joined me in the living room he didn't say a word, he just went right to our record collection and pulled out Janis's *Cheap Thrills* album and put it on the turntable. I served us all spaghetti as Janis belted out "Summertime," filling our living room with a raw and shocking reality. It took every ounce of control I had not to blurt out all the fear I was feeling. I didn't want to upset the baby or our stomachs as we ate so I just listened, picturing Janis in her orange bellbottoms with a pink boa in her hair.

Paul eventually went to bed, exhausted from the day's construction work. He set the alarm for seven o'clock in the morning to get up and do it again. I stayed up and watched Johnny Carson, still wondering if there was anything I could do or give to Paul that would replace what heroin was doing for him. My chest felt as if there was a hand pressing on it. It felt like I couldn't really take a deep breath and then I had an idea, I could get pregnant! I started breathing and let go of the tension in my shoulders. *Surely if another baby was on the way, Paul would change*, I thought. *He would see that he would have to stop spending money on smack and think about our future.*

I was elated. Maybe we could move to New Hampshire and plant a garden. I could grow tomatoes and make my own spaghetti sauce. *Yes, this could work*, I told myself as I collapsed on the couch exhausted. I kept fantasizing. We could get far from Central Square, far from the heroin. Paulie would be three-years-old when the baby was born;

he would be out of diapers. *This is good; I can handle this.* I walked out on the balcony and smiled up at the sky. I wasn't afraid anymore; I had an escape route.

This is What Illusion Looks Like

When you are the one in the illusion, you can't see it. That is actually what illusion is, right? I immediately stopped taking the birth control pills I had been on for two years, but I did not tell Paul. I thought that part of being a good wife was to trick Paul into what he was unable to see. Lou Reed sang, "He just didn't know, that heroin was his wife." Well, I wanted my wifely role back and I thought this would do it. I needed to take charge.

There is a verse in the Bible somewhere that says, "Rely not on your own understanding." This would have been a good time to heed this reasoning, but it was the energy of free love, free spirit, and for me it was apparently time to throw the baby out with the bath water. Maybe it was Janis's message "freedom's just another word for nothing left to lose" resounding through our lives; I don't really know. It could have been Richie Havens, transforming us all at Woodstock, with "FREEDOM," filling all the places in my cells where dogma had once lived. Whatever it was, I was deep into it, and it just all had to play out. How else do illusions actually get busted?

In mid November, when my period was due, it did not arrive. I was pregnant. I was happy and scared at the same time. I was scared because I would now have to tell Paul, and my plan would not be mine alone or be a secret anymore. I decided to tell him on Thanksgiving night after we came home from my parents' house. Maybe I could drop hints over dinner and pave the path a bit. As we were getting ready to leave for my parents' house, I was dressing Paulie in a new outfit that included suspenders over a turtleneck shirt. I said, "Paulie is doing really good at potty training, by spring he'll be completely out of diapers, no more baby." Paul's response was, "I wish we could cook our own turkey here and not go to our parents' for every holiday."

I watched as Paul combed his shoulder-length hair back and then just let the part fall in the middle; how beautiful the strawberry blonde color of his hair was. I picked up a hair tie and attempted to pull Paul's hair back into a ponytail. He let me do it while he looked in the mirror, combing his beard. "I'm glad Paulie has your hair color," I said as I gave his shoulders a hug. Off we went. I carried Paulie down the hall to the elevator and Paul slung the bright yellow baby bag over his shoulder; the holiday season once again began.

My mother agreed to watch Paulie while Paul and I joined my sisters for the annual Thanksgiving Day Larchmont/Bridgetown football game. I think the high point of the day for me was not who won the football game, but the moment when—after the bone chilling experience of watching a football game in the late November air—I would open the bright red front door of my childhood home and every fiber of my being would be engulfed in the smell of a turkey roasting in a cozy, warm house. I would get closer and closer to perfection as I walked to the kitchen, where a large pot of giblet gravy was simmering. I would take a piece of "crimp bread" from Henry's Bakery and begin dunking it in the gravy. Soon my sisters and brothers would be elbowing each other for the holy space over the gravy pot. Mummy would eventually say "Don't ruin your dinner, kids," but we all knew that would never happen. This year was special. I held Paulie in my arms and taught him the art of dunking those small, white rounds of bread into the gravy. I had a little flash of the following year when I would have a little baby at the kitchen table as we dunked. As I smiled at this vision, I watched Paul walk out to the backyard and saw him slip behind the garage. I figured he was finding a safe place to smoke a joint.

Soon after dinner was over, Paul said he wanted us to go home. He said he didn't want to hang out and watch football, a gladiator sport, and I knew that was what it looked like to him through his marijuana lens. So I made our excuses for an early departure. I figured this would give us a quiet evening to get Paulie into bed, and for me to tell Paul about the pregnancy. My heart raced a bit at the thought. When Paulie was in his crib for the night, I put on my two-piece silk pajamas, made us a pot of hot tea, and lit the candle that was dripping wax in many layers over the sides of a Mateus wine bottle. I put on the Traffic album because it was one of Paul's favorites. I kept the volume low, just for background music, and lifted Paul's legs so I could sit at the end of the couch with his feet on my lap. Paul looked like he was about to doze off after a day of turkey and pot, so I knew I should hurry and get to the point.

"Paul, I have some good news I've been saving to tell you tonight," I said as I rubbed the arc of his foot. "I just found out that I'm pregnant," I blurted out. Paul's reaction came very slowly, like someone being drawn in from very far away by a distant sound.

"What did you say?" The words felt like a wave that was gaining height in anticipation of rounding over into a mighty force.

"I'm pregnant. I just found out this week; I'm due the end of July."

"How can you be pregnant when you are on the pill?" Paul was almost yelling as he pulled his feet from my lap and sat on the edge of the couch.

"I stopped taking the pill after Janis Joplin died. I was afraid you were going to die, too." I could feel my whole body shift into a defense pose.

Paul stood up and began to rant at me. "You *thought* I could die from heroin and you *thought* being pregnant would help the situation?" He looked at me in disbelief. "You must be out of your fucking mind, Irene."

He began to pace, and not leaving a second for me to comment, he said, "Who are you? I don't even know you. There is not a person I know who could even think for one fucking second that having a baby could be the answer to doing heroin."

I ran to the bathroom and threw up. I was under attack and my entire body went into a panic and convulsion. Paul followed me and stopped ranting as he said, "Irene, having a baby will make me want to do more heroin, not less," and he walked away closing the bathroom door behind him. When I came out of the bathroom, I saw that our bedroom door was shut. I walked past it to the living room where I sat alone on the couch. I wished Paul would come out and talk to me, but he didn't. I just sat there. I was afraid to be yelled at again so I didn't go to the bedroom and approach him either. I turned off the record player and sat by the candlelight. Nothing was the same as it was when I had lit that candle in the long ago illusion of hope. Now it was like I had descended into hell. Everything was ugly and it was still Thanksgiving. I didn't want to throw up again, so I put on the kettle to have a cup of mint tea and I lay on the couch in silence. I looked over at my new album, Melanie's,

Candles in the Rain. I opened the album cover and read the words, "Let the white bird smile up at the ones who stand and frown." I don't know what it was in those words that helped me shift, but my mind seemed to grasp onto something new. I think it must have been the image of the white bird. It reminded me of the Dove of the Holy Spirit and I felt reconnected to God. The image actually seemed to suck me out of this helpless hell I was in and gave me clarity.

I walked calmly into our bedroom. Paul was lying face down on our bed with his face buried in a pillow. I spoke softly, as I did not want to cause any yelling; I needed Paulie to stay asleep. "Paul, you are right, I was a complete idiot," I said. "Sandra down the hall told me that if I ever needed an abortion that she knew of a really good doctor in New York. I'll get the number tomorrow, I am sorry; I will take care of it." I shut the door and left. I slept on the couch that night, listening to album after album, trying to get solace from the music, but for the first time, music was not able to help me. There was not a song, a note, or a beat that could erase the vision of a baby girl sitting in a seat on the kitchen table, while my sisters and I dunked bread in the gravy.

Chapter Ten

Choice

THE ONLY STATE IN OUR NATION WHERE ABORTIONS were legal was New York and fortunately it was only a three-hour drive for me. I called the 206 phone number that Sandra had given me and made an appointment for December 17th. The cost was $300 in cash. Since I was less than nine weeks pregnant, the nurse said the procedure would be relatively simple. The address of the doctor's office was on Park Avenue, so I felt confident that this would be a medically safe experience.

Paul and I did not have $300 so I had to figure out how to get the money. It was not as if I could ask a family member and I did not want to tell anyone what was really going on. When I confided the whole truth to Gwen, she suggested that I go to my bank and ask for a loan. She said to just tell them that I wanted to buy some furniture to establish credit. I went to the bank in my least hippie looking clothes to practice my hand at telling a big white lie. Within a week I had the money, and I just had to get someone to drive me to New York. Paul offered to go with me but by this time I was absolutely sure that I did not want to spend all that time in the car with him. I just needed a girlfriend to go with me, someone who loved me. I immediately knew it was my sister Teresa. She was in nursing school but I was

Irene Isobel Carver

sure she would take the day off to help me. Teresa said she would drive me and sleep at our apartment on the 16th because we would need to leave my house by 6:00 a.m. in order to be on time for my 11:00 a.m. appointment on Park Avenue. Paul was going to call in sick to work and take care of Paulie for the day. It was only a three-hour drive, but we wanted to give ourselves extra time, since neither of us had ever been to New York City, and we figured we had enough stress without the pressure of being lost or late.

I thought I had all the bases covered, until I awoke to the 5:00 a.m. alarm and looked out the window and saw about four inches of snow on the ground with huge white flakes falling at a fast rate. I shook Teresa awake and said, "We've got to hurry Tee, wake up, it is snowing hard out."

"Holy Shit," Teresa said, as she joined me at the window. "Well, no time for showers, unless you think that this is a sign that we shouldn't go," Teresa added, as she pulled on her jeans. "Tee, it is a sign that we'd better move fast; I'll fill the thermos with tea" I said, heading to the kitchen, "we can stop for a muffin along the way." We ran combs through our long brown hair, splashed water on our faces, and I grabbed a pack of saltines off the counter to ward off my morning sickness. I scribbled a quick note saying, "Had to run, see ya tonight," and left it on the kitchen counter as I closed the door quietly and down the hall we ran to the elevator. The elevator took us to the underground parking lot; at least we didn't have to shovel the car out of the snow. Teresa jumped into the driver's seat and said, "Thank God dad bought me all new tires in October; boy, am I grateful now." I lifted my eyes to heaven, chanting thank you God and daddy, as we drove out of the garage and into the blowing snow. There were barely any other cars on the road, but there were snowplows and that is what mattered. I turned on the radio to see if we could get a weather report, and I said, "Teresa slow down a bit and remember what Mr. Whiting taught us, that if you skid, drive in the direction of the skid." Teresa laughed, breaking the tension and said, "Remember how his toupee slid off his head every time we took a sharp curve?" I joined her laughter at the memory of our high school driver's education teacher.

As we pulled onto Alewife Brooke Parkway, Teresa drove slowly behind a plow, and I kept my eyes peeled for an open store to get a muffin. But mile after snowy mile through Cambridge and Bridgetown, nothing was open. No busses or trolleys were running and we just stayed behind one plow after another until we got to Newton. Then the last plow took the turn into Newton Center and we inched onto the entrance to the Massachusetts Turnpike. Fear welled up in both of us; we could see that the road before us had not been plowed. Teresa rolled down her window and stuck her head into the storm to see where she was going. The snow was falling faster than the wiper blades could keep up; it was becoming a full-out blizzard. My stomach erupted with bile and I stuck my head out my window and threw up. The wind blew the bile into my hair and I quickly closed my window. I grabbed a sweatshirt from the backseat and wiped my face and hair. I took a swig of tea to rinse my mouth, and then spit again out the window. I looked over at Teresa. Her hair was covered in snow and her face looked frozen as she strained to see the road ahead. "How close am I to that rail on the right, Renie?" she asked me without taking her eyes off the road. I looked for the silver rail and said, "Looks like you have about two, three feet, Tee, just go slowly so even if we bump, we'll be okay." And then, like a guiding light from heaven, we saw

Irene Isobel Carver

the bright headlights of a snowplow coming up behind. As he barreled past us, he gave a loud honk and we honked back with delight. "We've been saved," Teresa yelled. She rolled her window up and shook the snow off her hair and I burst out crying. Everything broke open at once as the news report on the radio station informed us that we were driving away from the storm and not into it. We cheered and clapped and then, like manna from heaven, we saw a Howard Johnson's ahead. That red-lit open sign in the window looked beautiful.

Teresa pulled into the snow-covered parking lot right next to the walkway that an employee was shoveling. He had his scarf pulled up over his face.

"What the hell are you girls doing out in this mess?"

"Don't ask," Teresa answered, as we walked past him. Inside, we snuggled up in a booth to recover and when no waitress arrived, we went to the counter and yelled to no one, "Any chance of pancakes?"

"No way ladies, you're out before the griddle is hot, how about oatmeal?"

"We'll take two with brown sugar, raisins, and cream."

"And toast for two, please," Teresa added. Then we both headed to the bathroom, feeling like we had just crawled onto the shore from a marooned ship.

When we got back on the road, it was 7:30 a.m., and there were a few other people on the road. No one would have been in a car that morning, unless they had to and, well, I had to. I was not having any second thoughts about this decision, and Teresa wasn't offering any wishy-washy opinions either. She could see I had made my choice. Once I had seen clearly the predicament I had gotten myself into, I was moving full-bore into getting myself out of it; no blizzard was going to deter me.

There was no hint of snow in New York City, and we easily found our way to the address written on the envelope, with $300 in cash in it. Teresa dropped me off right in front of the building, and said she would go find a place to park and then come and join me. The nurse greeted me when I entered the third-floor office. I sat in a formal leather armchair, filled out a medical form, and paid at the office window as I turned it in. The same nurse came to me with a small cup of water and a muscle relaxer.

I was called into the doctor's office promptly at 11:00 a.m. and the nurse sat next to me and held my hand. She explained the procedure to me as I lay back on an exam table, with my lower body undressed and covered in a warm cotton sheet. The nurse said the abortion would be done by a simple suction method, since I was less than nine weeks along, and it would not be complicated to remove the small mass of cells that had formed. She was a very gentle, middle-aged woman, and she asked me about my family as the doctor proceeded with the suction. When I told her I had a two-year-old son, she assured me I had plenty of time to have more children and not to worry, that this procedure would not affect my reproductive ability at all. A half-hour later, the procedure was over; I had been awake the entire time. I felt no discomfort. As I was taken to a recovery room I noticed I was a tiny bit woozy from the muscle relaxer. I was told I would have to lie down for two hours to make sure that there was no hemorrhaging and then the doctor would check me. At this point the nurse left and I fell asleep, exhausted; it had been quite a morning.

When I woke up, it was because I heard Teresa's voice. She was standing next to me. I looked at the clock; it was just 3:00 p.m.

"Can we go now?" I asked.

"The doctor is on the way in to check you; then we can. How are you feeling?"

"I'm good, ready to get going; what have you been doing all this time?" I was feeling more lucid.

"Well, when I finally found a parking garage, there was a bar right next to it. I saw a sign in the window saying the drinking age here is eighteen, so I figured I'd go in and pass some time."

"Wow, what did you drink?" I was rather surprised.

"I had a couple of beers and played a game of pool with some chicks."

"Beer, yuck, that sounds awful. I guess I'll be driving home."

"No, that was over an hour ago, I only had two, I'm fine," Tee said.

Just then, the doctor came in and examined me and said I was fit to go. The nurse brought me my coat, gave me a prescription for an antibiotic, and we left. We walked three blocks to the parking garage on that crisp and sunny December day and I felt perfectly normal. "Tee, I'm serious, I would really rather drive home. I like to drive and it will keep my mind off of things. Plus, you had a heck of a drive down here, you deserve to lay back." "Well, okay, if you're sure. I'll be in charge of keeping good music on the radio," she said as she put her arm around me. "Good job, sister; you did good," she said as she kissed my cheek.

We managed to get out of New York City before rush-hour traffic began and were soon cruising home on highways that were now all plowed and clear. We traced our path back and stopped at the same Howard Johnson's restaurant. This time we each had a bowl of warm clam chowder with lots of bread. I didn't want to see another cracker for a long time. While waiting for our check, I realized that I was completely happy. What a relief it was going to be not to wake up with morning sickness, and I felt a deep internal strength that I had been able to solve this problem by myself.

"What are you thinking?" Teresa asked.

"I was just wondering what a girl my age would do if she lived in Kansas or someplace far from New York and found out she was pregnant by stupidity."

"Click their heels three times and have a baby, I guess," Teresa said with a light-hearted grin.

"I'm serious Tee; we were able to drive here; that is the only way this happened. I would have lost control of my life or who knows what."

"Well, I guess you just would have had another baby, or borrowed more money from the bank and flown here. I don't know, let's get going; we've got miles to go before we sleep," quoted Teresa, as she grabbed the check and headed out, not wanting to philosophize this day.

It was about 8:00 p.m. when we pulled into my apartment complex. We could hardly believe our eyes when we walked to the elevator and there was a sign that said, SORRY, ELEVATOR TEMPORARILY OUT OF ORDER, USE STAIRS. We stood there and read it aloud a couple of times, letting it sink in. It was really hard for us to believe we had to walk up nine flights of stairs after this incredible day that had begun at 5:00 a.m. It just seemed so unfair. Teresa still had to drive to Boston to her dorms and I told her she didn't have to walk up with me; she could just take off and I would be fine. But like the wonderful sister she is she said, "No way, I can use the exercise after all day in the car." So up we climbed, chanting the words from a Beatles song, "Number nine, number nine, number nine."

When I opened the door to our apartment, the sound of a party going on hit me like a slap in the face. I looked in the living room where Paul sat with about five other people. I took a sharp right that went down the hall to our bedroom, my anger finally rising at Paul. Teresa followed me into my bedroom and as I undressed I asked her to go tell Paul to get everyone the hell out of our house, that I was not in the mood for an abortion party. Teresa said she would and then she would leave. I kissed her pretty cheek and thanked her for being the best sister and friend in the world. I went into the bathroom and ran water in the tub. While I was lying in the warm water by candlelight, Paul came in and said everyone was gone. He sat down on the toilet seat and asked me how we had ever made it through that blizzard. "Determination," was all I had the energy or desire to say. I slept deeply that night and woke up feeling changed inside. Something in me had shifted. I knew I had made an important choice in life and there was no point in looking back. Somehow I knew the elevator had broken just for me. It was so life affirming for me that I could hike up all those stairs after the day we had.

A week later it was Christmas. Santa managed to get Paulie a fire truck that he could sit inside and peddle, and a cowboy hat and holster. Paul and I got each other nothing; I could not muster up any spirit and apparently, neither could he. One afternoon, I let Dora babysit Paulie and I found myself walking around Harvard Square in a daze, pretending to be Christmas shopping. I ended up buying myself a book, *The Greening Of America*, which was on display in all the bookstore windows. I had been hearing how good it was and I needed something to inspire me.

I went in the Wursthaus, a restaurant as old as the Square itself, and slipped into a tall mahogany booth and ordered a pot of tea. I stared at the book cover, savoring the words on the cover. The three words, "change political structure" went straight to my heart and I felt hope that the information in this book could help me out of my funk. In *The Greening of America*, author Charles Reich said a revolution was coming. On page one he mentioned our hometown of Larchmont, Massachusetts. On page three he said, "At the heart of everything is what we shall call a change of consciousness, this means a 'new head,' a new way of living, a new man."

Right away those words made me smile. We hippies called ourselves "heads" because pot was changing our consciousness. I felt a surge of hope seep into me along with the warm tea. I read on, "This emerging conscious-ness seeks new knowledge of what it means to be human." I felt myself breathe, almost as if I had been holding my breath all week. I finished my tea, tucked my book in my coat pocket and walked back into the crowded streets of Harvard Square feeling a little less sad. "War, corruption, and hypocrisy must go," wrote Mr. Reich, and I was fully ready to let him sweep me away into a revolution that did not require violence to succeed. "Amen," I said to myself as I hopped onto the trolley car back to Larchmont.

When I arrived home later that day, I called Gwen who had asked a few days earlier if Paul and I wanted to come down to their apartment for dinner and a New Year's Eve party. I told her I didn't know what we were doing. As soon as I hung up the phone, I realized that for the first time I didn't care one bit what I did on New Year's Eve. I had no desire to celebrate anything. I had never been depressed before in my life so it took me awhile to realize the symptoms. I was experiencing what it felt like to be awakened from illusion, from the death of a dream, and it sucked, especially during the holidays, when I would have to pretend to be happy. I told Gwen we would come to her New Year's party and I would bring some Mateus wine and a hors d'oeuvre. I laughed at myself, observing how quickly I could shift.

"Well, Mr. Reich," I said as I placed my new book on my bed stand, "this new human is going to put aside the hippie ban on alcohol for New Year's Eve and dance!" I may as well start the dancing right now, I concluded, and I put on the album, *Déjà Vu*, by Crosby, Stills, Nash, and Young. I danced Paulie around the living room to the song, "Carry On." I sang along with the song, "a new day, a new way . . . we have no choice but to carry on." Paulie laughed as I tickled him and sat him down on the couch so I could begin cooking dinner. *I'm back,* I thought to myself. "I have to disagree with you guys," I said to the stereo, "we do have a choice." I could carry on in depression or carry on in hope and joy; it was my choice and I chose dancing. When the song "Helpless" came on, I picked the needle off the record and placed it back "Carry On." I just didn't want to hear Neil Young sing his sad song about big birds flying across the sky leaving us helpless. I refused to feel helpless. I had just made it out of a state of illusion and I was going to build myself a new Happy New Year's scene. *Fuck this sad shit, man*, I told myself as I chopped carrots.

For the first time in our marriage, there was no dispute over what to do on New Year's Eve. Paul and I both felt comfortable going downstairs to Gwen and Randy's and we could bring Paulie and let our two-year-olds play until they fell to sleep. I rang in 1971 in wearing maroon suede bellbottoms with a matching top that had flared sleeves and silver beads lining the pleats. I wore an emerald green beaded choker with matching earrings. I was feeling strong and confident. I was planning to go back on birth control pills as soon as I got my next period and I hoped Paul and I would be able to patch things up as this New Year began.

I am sad to say, the fun and relaxation of that New Year's night was short lived. As the year progressed so did Paul's addiction to heroin. Paul kept going to work and then on the way home he would stop in Central Square to cop his smack. If I made any comment he would get angry and say he was working, the bills were paid, so what was my problem? I was completely confused. I knew this was not okay, but felt helpless to affect his thinking. Those big birds that Neil Young referred to in his song were casting shadows on our lives after all.

I noticed I wasn't happy when I woke up in the morning. I would find myself sitting on our balcony watching the sky, feeling lonely while Paul would get home later and later after work each day. Paul was living in a different world from me and the isolation was getting to me. One night Paul walked in and held out his hand with a little white envelope in it and said, "This is the purest smack I have yet to score, so if you ever want to try it, here is your moment." I had always told myself I would never try heroin. I would never put a needle in my arm, but that night the loneliness and isolation had gotten to me. With Paul's assurance of the purity of the drug, I realized I wanted to escape my feelings and join Paul in his world, so I justified trying it. After we put Paulie to bed for the night, I joined Paul in the bathroom where the ritual of my first and only heroin experience began.

Irene Isobel Carver

Paul told me to sit on the closed toilet seat and to roll up my sleeve to above the elbow. He instructed me to turn my arm with palm up and to make a fist, causing the main vein in my arm at the elbow, to bulge out a bit. I did as he told me and then closed my eyes. I wasn't afraid at that moment; I had surrendered to the fact I wanted the experience and trusted Paul. I felt Paul tie a piece of rubber around my bicep, and then I smelled sulfur burning from a match. I felt a needle prick my arm and it caused me to open my eyes. I saw the syringe fill up with my blood and then a nauseous feeling came over me. Paul took the needle out of my arm and I leaned over and threw up in the sink.

My very first thought was how it didn't feel yucky or bad to throw up like it usually does. It was just throwing up with no bad feelings attached. I was a bit surprised at this and calmly rolled down my sleeve and walked to the living room in a trance-like state. As if I had this all planned, I opened the storage closet and took out our camping cot. I set it up right next to the couch and put a soft blanket on it. I lay down on the couch and Paul lay on the cot next to me. Not a word was said. Paul put on a Moody Blues album, and for many hours we just lay there listening and floating in and out of consciousness. The music floated around and through my mind. Our makeshift bed felt like a cloud. I was drifting through space and time. The experience definitely gave new meaning to the word relaxation. I felt like I didn't even have a muscle in my body to relax. When I got up to go to the bathroom, it wasn't like I was walking; it was like I was drifting. We lay together enjoying the feelings of kissing without any further desire for sex. No tension was possible, no stress, just peace, perfect peace.

Chapter Eleven

Still Catholic After All These Years

WHEN I WOKE UP THE NEXT MORNING, I GRADUALLY became frightened as the numbness of the heroin wore off. I figured any drug that made throwing up seem like a good experience was definitely dangerous. As I reflected on the night before, I could see how a person could get completely lured into not feeling, especially if there were things you didn't want to feel. I looked at Paul with a deeper understanding. I could see now that he was using heroin to block the trauma he had gone through in Vietnam. Paul was choosing to live in a world of not feeling and I was really afraid for him now; I was afraid for us.

I looked at the tiny red dot in my vein where the needle had gone in and I shuddered. *I really had "shot up" heroin*, I thought to myself, and the part of me that would always be Catholic knew I had sinned. I had sinned against my body and I was ashamed. I decided that on Saturday I would ask Dora to babysit, and I would take the train into Boston to the Arch Street Church. That is the church that Catholics go to with their worst sins so there was no chance their parish priest would recognize them. I told Dora I needed to go to Jordan Marsh to return a Christmas gift. I went out into a

Irene Isobel Carver

snow-covered, yet sunny Saturday to see if I could return my sin to God.

When I got off the trolley car in Harvard Square, I stopped and looked around. I did so wish I was just there to return a Christmas gift. I looked down into the subway entrance. The dark stairway went down and away from the winter sun that was reflecting off the three-foot-high snow banks that lined the street. I was glad I had worn my calf-length beaver fur coat. I could feel it protecting my heart as I grabbed each elbow, hugging myself and forcing my feet down the subway stairs. The roar of the incoming train filled the tunnel and I ran with my token in hand, hurrying through the turnstile booth. At the first stop I turned my face to the window, which looked out at nothing but a black wall only inches away; there was not even any graffiti to distract me from my thoughts.

Okay, calm down, Irene; it will be over in a couple of minutes once you get there, I told myself, and tried to breathe deeply to calm my stomach. *All I have is one sin to tell the priest, and I'm sure this is mild compared to all the sins happening in Boston every day,* I pep-talked myself. On and on my brain babbled, almost as fast as the train that was speeding along on its underground tracks, now slowing as it approached Kendal Square. I watched as rows of billboards came into focus. The train came to a complete stop right in front of an ad for the Red Cross asking to donate blood, with a picture of a mother holding a baby. A teenage girl squeezed onto the seat next to me, and I suddenly felt trapped between a young girl, a mother, and a baby. *Oh, my God,* I held my breath for a couple of seconds. *Should I be telling the priest about the abortion, also?* The thought froze my mind. The parental monitor in my head said, *Of course you should.* I thought to myself, *Who says I should? The Church Says, that's who,* said a voice inside. *Well, that is precisely why I don't go to church anymore,* I retorted to myself.

I found a few minutes of peace from my thoughts as the train rushed on through time and space. Then a blast of light shot into the darkness as the train came out of the underground tunnel and onto tracks suspended over the Charles River. The train came to a stop and the doors opened automatically, letting in a rush of cold air and red-cheeked people clamored for seats. The air felt different to me. I didn't feel judged anymore by some force greater than myself. The train doors closed while the last passengers squeezed into every available space and the train sped back into the underground tunnel. Once again I let myself sink into an internal debate. *Okay, Irene, defend yourself. Just why do you think shooting heroin is a sin, so much so that you are speeding through dark tunnels on a perfectly beautiful Saturday, but having an abortion never entered your mind as being a sin until this moment?* I had no answer; I just felt amazement at myself. When the train came to the next stop, Park Street, I decided to get off and walk across town to the church. I needed daylight shining on this question brewing in the depths of me. As I ran up the subway stairs and the cold air hit my lungs, I became aware of things in my subconscious that I had never before seen. I immediately knew I was free to live by my own standards and I could make them up as I went along.

I walked around Boston Common three times waiting for four o'clock, when confessions began. I had to remind myself not to mouth the words that were going through my head, lest I look like one of the many crazy street people who were waiting for the missions to open for the night. When I finally walked up the steps to the church, I had settled my internal debate. *Here is the answer,* I summed up to myself. *It is about* feeling *and not thinking. Heroin felt like a sin to my body and to my spirit,* I told myself. "*The abortion did not feel like a sin to me on any level; it felt like pure freedom, which gave birth to new parts of myself.* That was the day I knew I would always listen to my own body for information on how I would experience life as right or wrong. *This is what a conscience is,* I decided. Furthermore, everyone has a unique conscience; therefore, what is a sin for one person may not be a sin for another. *If you think it is a sin, then it is.* "Aha," I yelped, as I detoured past the swan boats in the Public Gardens to think about this. *Life is a personal experience, not a group one,* I surmised.

I looked up at the spires of the church before me and thought, *Hey, this is where the word inspire must come from,* and I ran up the steps to the church. I kicked the snow off my boots as I pulled open the heavy wooden door. I took off my new Christmas gloves and blessed myself with the Holy Water in the brass bowl hanging at the entrance. The stillness of the church flowed through me like a warm wave and the arched cathedral ceiling seemed to hug me as I walked forward and knelt on the padded kneelers in a pew right next to the confessional booth. There were only a few people ahead of me in line, so it wasn't long before I was in the tiny confessional, reciting the old familiar words, "Bless me, Father, for I have sinned. It has been three years since my last confession. I have sinned, Father," I blurted out.

"I shot heroin into my arm a few days ago and I am truly sorry, Father." There was a silence, and when I said nothing more, the priest said, "Well, at least it has brought you to your knees, my child, and back to church. Is that the only thing you would like to confess?"

"Yes, Father." I added confidently.

"Don't wait another three years to confess your sins, child. Remember, Confession is a Sacrament that gives you the Grace to help you withstand the temptations you are facing."

"Thank you, Father, I will try to come more often," I said, "for the Grace and not the sin, I hope."

"For your penance, say the rosary every day for a week. You may go and serve God, in the name of the Father and of the Son and of the Holy Ghost, Amen," he concluded as he crossed himself. I bowed my head and blessed myself along with him. I left the cubicle and walked up to the statue of the Blessed Mother, and kneeling, I said the rosary. I chose the Sorrowful Mysteries, as I wanted to meditate on Jesus being crowned with thorns, carrying the cross, and then being crucified. I really did want to do penance, and asked Jesus to help me carry my burdens with more strength. The beauty of the stained glass windows comforted me and I lit a candle at Mary's feet, asking her if she would please bless Paul.

When I walked out of the church into the setting sun and sparkling snow, I tried to reason with God, pleading that if he would help us stop this stupid and senseless war, people like Paul wouldn't be needing heroin and my husband wouldn't be fading away from me, from our son, and from life. As the train sped towards home, I vowed never to sin against my body like that again. I began wondering if my soul was a part of my body, actually permeating my cells, or did it have a separate spot all its own? I tried to access the Catholic dogma from high school. *Well,* I thought, *the soul does live on after the body dies, so it does have a separate force, but does it have a separate place? There is just so much yet to learn.* Pondering all this, I closed my eyes and tried to look into my heart.

DIVINE PLAN OR SERENDIPITY?

If nothing happens by accident then here is a divine plan for you: In March Clare called me from work telling me that the company she was working for as a secretary had chartered a plane for its employees to go to Portugal for a week, and two people had to cancel at the last minute. For any two people who could quickly stop their routines of life, it would only cost them $200 apiece, which included air fare, a luxury hotel, and two meals a day! Hmm… *I could do that*, I thought. I told Clare to give me an hour and I'd get back to her. I called Gwen and told her about the offer. She said, "Hmm… I could do that. Give me a half hour and I'll get back to you." We both called our in-laws and asked if they could babysit for a week and we both got yeses. I called Clare and confirmed before either of us asked our husbands. When our husbands got home from work, we told them the plan and they both happily forked over the $200. Hmm… double hmm…If there was something wrong with this picture, I wasn't seeing it. I weighed the options, "Let me see, waiting for Paul to get home from work every night, or a week in Portugal?" I was going and happily. Gwen and I raced into Boston the next day and got passports; all the ducks just fell in a row. I had no clue that my life was about to change forever.

Gwen and I experienced culture shock in Portugal. For me it was mostly the food, and for Gwen it was the language. She immediately bought an English/Portuguese dictionary and spent most of the week trying to figure out how to ask for things. I spent most of the week trying to figure out how to fill the tuna fish sandwich and hamburger gap. All the food seemed complicated to me. All I wanted was an English muffin for breakfast and the hotel managed to turn that into something with sauce and spices that my bland taste buds could not relate to. I told Gwen to look up "muffin" and say it for me; I got a roll. But fish, there was plenty of. There were kinds I had never heard of, but they were never just simply baked. I think one night an actual yellow fish was stuffed with liver or some organ with sprigs of tree or something. I swear, if I thought Gwen's Italian cooking was a new experience, I was now totally out of my league and I began dreaming of a juicy hamburger on a bun with lettuce. I missed America and now knew what "American as apple pie" meant and how much it meant to me. Lord, give me a BLT, I yelped one night as I tried to fall asleep.

By the third day the gorgeous Mediterranean weather got my full attention. I watched a foot- tall parrot with a blue chest and bright yellow wings fly right over my head. My first thought was that it had escaped from a pet store or something, then I realized it was as native to Portugal as robins are to Massachusetts. That was my most memorable visual of the trip; parrots are quite psychedelic in color and amazing to see in the wild. On another day we walked to the fish market on the coast, about a mile from our hotel, and just watched as the boats unloaded nets of fish and workers gutted, iced, and sold the fresh fish by the wheelbarrow full. "Now if they would only deep fry it with some fries and tartar sauce," I whispered to Gwen. "God, wouldn't a Coke be like heaven," Gwen added.

One night Gwen and I decided to go out on the town and see what the nightlife was like. We located a street that had a few clubs, and following the music, we entered one. We sat at the bar and ordered the local wine. "God, this is strong" Gwen said, "It tastes like my grandfather's home-made stuff." I ordered the same wine and soon we had a man sitting on either side of us. When I saw one of them put his hand on Gwen's shoulder, I realized I didn't feel safe. I motioned Gwen to come to the ladies room with me and we slipped out the door and ditched those two suave men who spoke English so well and who wanted to take us "sight-seeing." After that night out, we didn't feel safe on our own, so we spent the evenings in our room reading the novels we brought with us and shared all the good things about our husbands instead of the bad. We talked about all the things we were looking forward to going home to because stepping briefly out of our lives made us appreciate all that we took for granted. We both missed our two-year-old sons the most; we missed being mothers.

A week later, when our plane arrived at Logan airport, Randy was there waiting for Gwen but Paul was nowhere to be seen. Gwen and Randy took off; I assured them that Paul would be right along. I stood alone for about ten minutes and then decided to go to the luggage terminal and get my suitcase where I continued to wait. Trying not to panic, I took my suitcase to the outside curb wondering what to do. Just as I was about to ask a cabbie how much it would cost to go to Somerville, Paul pulled up to the curb. I threw my suitcase into the back seat and, jumping into the front seat, my fear screeched out, "What the fuck happened to you, I've been waiting over an hour!" And very casually he said, "Oh, I just figured I'd give you time to get your luggage and meet you outside; I never planned to park and come in, that's a waste of time."

My fear turned instantly into sadness that caused my heart to fall into my stomach with a thud. Paul said nothing to me; he didn't ask about the trip, he just kept his eyes on the road. Finally, more frightened than I wanted to admit, I asked him how his week went and he just mumbled, "Same as always, work." By the time we pulled into our under-ground parking space, I could feel that something was very wrong. When we got into bed that night, Paul turned away from me, and by this point I was just too shocked to react to his coldness. I was too stunned to even cry; I just lay there wide-eyed and hurt until I finally got up and made a peanut butter and jelly sandwich. I poured a glass of milk and looked around my living room, scanning my plants. I held up a limp leaf on my Wandering Jew and finally, I cried.

Paul got up early the next morning and left for work. There was no note, he didn't say goodbye; he was just gone. I went downstairs to see how Gwen was and to have a cup of coffee with her. She was all happy; when I asked her if Randy had mentioned anything that might have gone on around our apartments while we were gone, she said she didn't have a clue. I left and drove over to Paul's parents' to pick up Paulie. It was hard to talk about my trip and act as if everything was fine, so I quickly got Paulie's things together and made up an excuse of why I had to get going.

That night, when Paul got home from work, he was cold and uncommunicative. When I asked him what was wrong, he said, "nothing" and walked away. I followed him down the hall and began yelling at him to tell me what the hell had happened while I was away. He finally turned around and looked me right in the eyes and said, "I'm in love with Natalie Rogers." I seemed to be standing there in space watching his words float from his mouth to my ears and ricochet off the walls. Like a robot, I put Paulie in his pajamas, got him a bottle of warm milk and put him in his crib. I heard myself saying to myself all the while, *In love, in love, what the hell does he mean? We have been together since I was fifteen years old; we have history, we have a child. You can't fall in love with someone else in one week.* I felt like I was in a trance as I closed the door to Paulie's room. Paul was in the living room with the television on. As I stared at him, I felt a deep need to be alone. I picked up the car keys, grabbed my coat, and left the house, giving him his own medicine of silence.

I drove to Harvard Square and parked the car along the Charles River, and walked into the heart of the bustling crowd with the March wind waking me up. I went to Nini's Corner to buy a pack of cigarettes and there, on a circular rack of postcards, I spotted a book that drew me in. "Find out who you truly are by your birth date," the cover stated. I bought the book and went right to a café, opened my Newports, and ordered hot tea.

That little hand held-book told me my sign was Cancer, ruled by the moon, a water sign. I am maternal, love home and family, and I am a homebody. I chain-smoked and realized that all the basic qualities of my birth sign had just been shattered. There was something about this information that kept me sane that night. It helped me see the world and myself from a broader perspective than my little world in 9N. I looked up Paul's sign of Virgo. It said health and service to others. Already, my limited knowledge of astrology showed me Paul was veering way off his course. He was not paying any attention to his health, in fact, he was slowly killing himself, and now he was about to destroy our little family. As I drove home I was oddly soothed, in the midst of this trauma, by this new information. *I can handle this,* I told myself as I took the elevator up the nine floors. I straightened my spine and whistled as I walked down the corridor, with an old song sustaining me. "Whenever you feel afraid, just hold your head erect, and whistle a happy tune and no one will suspect you're afraid." Just my blue lava lamp was aglow when I got in the house. I tiptoed into my room and there was Paulie, asleep in our bed with Paul. I gently moved him to his crib and slipped into his warm spot on my side of the bed, exhausted.

I awoke, and it being a Saturday morning, Paul didn't have to get up for work. Suddenly the tables were turned and Paul wanted to talk to me. Surprisingly, I was without words for what I was feeling, or I was not allowing myself to feel. I silently went about making coffee and settling Paulie with a bottle in front of the TV to watch morning cartoons. Paul followed me around, talking, and strangely enough, he was acting like I was just a friend. He was saying how much he loved Natalie; how he had never felt like this before, and how he hoped that now he wouldn't need heroin. He didn't seem to know that his words were like daggers. It was altogether bizarre. Then, just as strangely, I poured a cup of coffee and said "Who the fuck is Natalie Rogers? By the fucking way."

"Oh, I thought you knew who I was talking about. She's at Danny's house a lot—straight blonde hair, skinny, in school."

"Well, seeing that I'm at home with Paulie, I've not been at Danny's hanging out enough to meet her but obviously you have," I said as I walked to our bedroom to be out of earshot of the baby.

Paul followed me and said, "I'm sorry it happened this

way; I didn't see it coming either. You were gone, Paulie was gone, and I crashed at Danny's a few nights and all of a sudden we were in bed together."

My heart hit the floor. "In bed with her" felt like a kick in the stomach, but a higher force stepped in and said, *chin up,* and looking into my coffee cup, I said, "Yeah, love the one you're with, I get it but 'in love' is really dramatic isn't it?" I sat on the edge of our bed and tears filled my eyes.

"I don't know what to say, Irene, it's just different, it just happened, we fell in love."

"Are you serious about the heroin thing? You think if you are with Natalie you could stop using heroin?" I could barely get those words out as they caused such a sting in my heart. "You mean I am the reason you use heroin?" I mumbled in disbelief.

"No, no it's not you, it's just that I feel trapped being married. Sometimes I don't think I can breathe, and I feel too screwed up to be a father." Paul was sitting next to me on the bed with his head between his hands. I actually felt sorry for him as I stood up and said, "Well, here, let me open your cage," and I took off my wedding band and dropped it in the wastebasket as I walked out of the room.

Paulie had fallen back to sleep with his bottle on the living room floor, so I slipped out our front door and walked down one flight to Gwen's apartment. When Gwen opened the door I said, "Paul is in love with Natalie somebody and I don't know what to do." "Well, get in here and have some coffee, for starters," Gwen said, closing the door behind me. "Got a joint? Oh never mind, I can't get stoned now, the baby is upstairs asleep, and who knows what's gonna happen next. I better stay as sane as I can, 'cause right now I feel like an earthquake is just beginning. Help me make a plan, Gwen; I need help thinking. I'm fucked. I don't have a job or training at anything except being a mother. Oh, my God, I'm terrified." I blubbered into my coffee and I finally let myself cry in my friend's arms.

Irene Isobel Carver

Chapter Twelve

The Cruelest Month

April is the cruelest month
Breeding lilacs out of dead land
Mixing memory and desire.

—T.S. Eliot

IT NEVER CROSSED MY MIND TO ASK PAUL TO LEAVE
the apartment and I would stay. The apartment must have
wanted us to leave it. There must have been someone on the
waiting list whose turn it was to live in 9N. Change had to
happen. On the first of April, we gave our one-month notice
to the apartment manager and we began to make separate
plans as to where we would move.

Paul easily got a room at Danny's apartment in Boston
and I had an interview at a large communal house in Brookline. The house sounded beautiful in the newspaper ad; it
was one room in a mansion of ten bedrooms on two acres
of land. When I arrived for the interview with Paulie at my
side, a man and a woman answered the door and proceeded
to give us a tour of the house. While I stood mesmerized by
the enormous fireplace in the bedroom that was for rent, the
woman kindly took my arm and told me not to get my hopes
up; she was pretty sure the commune board had decided
not to allow children. I picked Paulie up in my arms and

quickly walked back to my car feeling disheartened. I *had* gotten my hopes up and now they were dashed and I only had two weeks before I had to move. As I drove down the long driveway I knew I could not take any more rejection and, as if on automatic pilot, I drove to my parents' house; the house where my roots were so deep that they could call me from many miles away.

When we arrived at my parents' house, they were both in the kitchen having tuna fish sandwiches and tea with the Red Sox spring training news blaring on the television in the living room. My mother quickly wiped her hands on her apron and Paulie ran directly into her arms, obviously happy it was lunchtime at the home of the never-ending Toll House cookie. My face must have been a dead giveaway since all the action stopped and my father asked, looking right at me, "What happened?" My mother took Paulie to the living room and set him up with a TV tray and a sandwich so we would have some privacy to talk. When she came back to the kitchen the three of us sat at the table. I just let the whole long story of Paul's heroin addiction finally pour out of my heart. I said I could no longer live with his addiction and that I had to leave. I left out the painful part of Paul's new love; I just didn't think I could bear saying that out loud, admitting it and making it even more real. Then I asked if I could move in with them temporarily while I figured out what to do. I could see my mother arranging the bedrooms in her mind to accommodate us while my father looked deeply disappointed.

Mother calmly poured us all some more tea and said, "Of course, you and Paulie can stay here while you try to figure this mess out, but there has to be a time limit. We'll

Irene Isobel Carver

give you until July first, that's two months. That should be enough time for you to find your own place." Her stance echoed a line from a poem she used to quote to us, "Let me lay down and bleed a while, then I will get back in the battle again." Dad got up, not offering any opinions, and escaped to the living room to watch the Red Sox with Paulie. I took that as my signal to leave as well. There we stood at the kitchen stove, on the battlefield of life. I took my mother's hand and said, "Thanks, Mum. I'll call you soon, but you can expect us on April 30th. My friend Robbie has a van and he said he'd help move me. I'll have some stuff to store in the basement for awhile also, if that is okay?" "Of course," said my mother as she squeezed my hand in support. I gathered Paulie up in my arms, with a chocolate chip cookie in his hand, and my mother went back to listening to her beloved Red Sox. On the drive home I began to feel a sense of relief, I had a plan. At first, my mother's words had felt a bit harsh to my already wounded heart, but now they seemed to put some structure around my falling apart life and I felt like I could breathe again.

LICKING MY WOUNDS

As Robbie and I chugged up the tree-lined street of my childhood in his overworked 1962 Dodge van, I was comforted by the protective arch that the maple trees made as they canopied the street. Robbie looked at me as I quietly quoted one of my favorite poems. "I will go back a little while and be with old untroubled things, no peril can befall them; they are part of everlasting loveliness and fold their peace around the far returning heart." He chimed in, "For your sake, I hope it is just for a little while, I sure don't think I could live at my parents' house anymore." I swallowed hard as we pulled into my parent's driveway, wishing he hadn't said that.

Paulie spent the night at Dora and Ed's house, so I could make this move with as little confusion as possible for all of us. After Robbie, my parents, and I unloaded the van, I had the privacy to go to my childhood room and begin to unpack my suitcase into the small familiar dresser. I closed the bedroom door behind me and sat cross-legged at the end of the twin bed that looked out over the forsythia bush, which was at the height of its spring glory. My fingers curled around the edge of the mattress; this was the same bed I slept in all through high school. The top bunks that Teresa and Brigette slept in were now gone. My eyes filled with tears as I remembered how I used to sit right here by the window, writing in my journal when life was so simple; this had always been my spot. Even when there were four of us girls sleeping in this one room, I always managed to get this spot where I could curl up next to the window in every season, and watch the trees and the sky go from icicles to apple blossoms to fall leaves. Here I was again after three years on my own. *How did this happen?* I wondered, hoping the forsythia would have some answers.

In the separation of possessions, I kept the car and Paul got the stereo and records, the only two things either of us cared about. After a quick shower and a sandwich, I drove to Dora and Ed's to pick up my most prized possession, Paulie, my soon to be three-year-old. As he ran into my arms, I tried not to notice that Dora looked as if she had been crying. Managing my own feelings was going to be challenge enough; I just could not acknowledge her suffering over her son's pain, at least not now. I quickly gathered Paulie's overnight bag and headed for the door.

"Irene, I just read that the circus is going to be in Boston all month, and I'd like to buy you and Paulie tickets, if you think you'd like to go," Ed said.

"Wow, Ed, that would be great, it could be Paulie's third birthday present."

"Call us when you get settled in, Irene, and we'll decide on the date for the tickets." I put Paulie down and walked back to their kitchen and looked at the calendar.

"How about the Saturday before his birthday if tickets are available."

"Alright, I'll call and reserve them and let you know later, for sure," Ed said. I picked Paulie up again and said to him, "Paulie, the circus, this is gonna be a blast!" I slowed my pace now, not so afraid, and kissed both Dora and Ed on their cheeks. "Call me," I yelled back as I headed down the front steps to my car.

Our first week at my parents' house was peaceful and routine. Breakfast was at 8:00 a.m., lunch was at noon, and dinner at 6:00 p.m. on the noggin. In between our balanced meals, Paulie and I explored the parks and libraries, and I showed him my childhood penny candy store, Hardy Spa, where they still sold my favorite Bulls-Eyes and red, chewy money. At night after everyone went to bed, I would call Gwen and see how the rest of my old life was doing. Gwen said they hated it at the apartments without us there and she and Randy were looking to move to an apartment in Newton where her family lived.

My heart ached all the time. Some days, I wanted to call Paul so badly I thought I'd throw up, but I was terrified that Natalie would answer the phone, so I just bit all my finger-nails off instead. When Gwen heard me crying one evening over the phone, she asked if I wanted her to bring me some pot. I thought about it a minute and then, remembering I often got emotionally volatile when I got high, I told her no, I was afraid that if I got high at my parents' house, I would totally lose it. I needed all the equilibrium I could muster during this earthquake of my life.

On a lovely Saturday afternoon, while Paulie was taking a nap, I went outside and watched the bumblebees pushing their fuzzy heads into the tiny bell-shaped opening of each of the forsythia blooms. I was filled with calmness and I wondered where it was coming from. There was no logical reason for me to be so calm, and yet, I was. I thought of the picture that hung in my bedroom of the guardian angel watching over the children as they crossed the bridge, and I wondered if angels really protected us. *Had my angel felt me cry myself to sleep last night?* I walked back into the house, and as I climbed the stairs, I saw my mother sitting in a chair in the sun parlor saying the rosary. She was doing what she had always done, asking and trusting that the Blessed Mother was watching over me and that I would be helped by her prayers.

Back in my room, I sat at the vanity remembering how my sisters and I used to fight for space at this coveted spot while we got ready for school. Only Brigette's eyeliners and four-inch rollers remained now that she had gone off to college. I looked into the three-way mirror and saw my reflection in the glass. I tried to look away but I was drawn to my own eyes. I noticed, for the first time, as I peered closely into the glass, that my brown eyes had a golden hue in them and how pathetically short my eyelashes were. I rummaged in the tiny drawer hoping to find an old tube of mascara, but there wasn't one. I took the eyeliner and lined my eyes like I used to in high school, a long black line on the top lid above the lashes and a black line along the bottom flesh of the lower lid. I made a cat meow at myself in the mirror and then threw the eyeliner in the trash.

I plopped down on the bed and stared up at the ceiling. I felt odd, like I was floating, and I realized that I was really confused. It was totally surreal to suddenly be in my old life, like I had drifted back in time. Blessedly, the spring breeze coming in the window lulled me to sleep. Hours later, I awoke to my mother knocking on the door and saying, "Renie, come on down and watch the Lawrence Welk Show with us, it's just starting." I looked out the window and it was night. *What? I slept through dinner?* I was amazed my mother would let that happen. Then my mother's words hit me like a sledgehammer, shattering the calm of the day that had put me to sleep. "Lawrence Welk," I repeated out loud as I peeked in Paulie's room where he was sleeping. I rounded the staircase and sat down on the third step from the top where I could see down into the living room. I could see the TV through the white rungs of the banister and there were the bubbles rising as Lawrence Welk and his orchestra began their music. "And tonight we have the Lennon Sisters," I heard him say, and I tried to shut down my senses but it was too late. I began to cry as I realized it was Saturday night. My role as a wife was over, my apartment was gone, and I was at my parents' house with the Lawrence Welk show on. Right there on the third step from the top of the stairs, my identity shattered. I felt like the Wicked Witch of the West when water was thrown on her and she melted. I could feel myself shriveling inside and I was paralyzed as I looked at the wallpaper of my childhood, pulsating before my horrified eyes, mocking me. *You're at home on a Saturday night with your parents and Lawrence*

Welk; you have made your bed, now lie in it, taunted some mean girl in my head.

My mother walked into the hall and saw me sitting there. "Did you have a good rest, dear?" I guess my stunned hysteria didn't show as she didn't wait for an answer, but kept going to the kitchen to put on water for tea. The sane part of me stood up and followed her to the kitchen and, acting perfectly nonchalant, I said, "Hey, do you think it would be okay for me to take Brigette's bike for a ride to Harvard Square? I could really use some exercise." "Sure, it's okay with me, just use the lock; that bike was expensive, and don't be out past midnight." "Okay," I answered, as I grabbed my sweater and wallet. I sprinted out the back door and onto Brigette's bike with an urgency to escape as if the driveway itself was going to engulf me.

I sped down the hill towards Harvard Square, letting the evening air blow all the scary thoughts from my mind. I slowed the bike just a bit when I went past my childhood church. I waved to the plaster statue of the Blessed Mother on the lawn and called to her, "I could use some amazing grace, Mother." I peddled downhill as fast as I could until I came to the Mount Auburn Cemetery where I slowed to a coast. I felt the blood pulsating through my muscles and the air pumping in my lungs, giving me the breath of spirit that I so needed. I waved to the dead people in the cemetery and yelled with outstretched arms, "I'm alive." By the time I got to the Longfellow Monument, I was filled with a sense of freedom. I sat down on the marble steps for a rest and asked, "Okay, Longfellow, got any words of wisdom for me tonight?" I tried to remember a poem by him but all that came to mind was our childhood joke, "I'm a poet and I know it cause my feet are longfellows," which made me laugh.

I walked my bike the rest of the way into Harvard Square so I could watch people and decide where to go. I made my way to the entrance of the Harvard Coop, where a lone violin player was taking advantage of the acoustics in the entrance way and attempting to collect a few dollars in her hat. I stood listening with a handful of others and thought, *Okay, I have to move out of my parents' house as quickly as possible. How am I going to do this? I need a plan.* I let the beautiful music of the violin take me higher and thought, *I can't let myself get depressed, I've gotta have a place of my own and I need help.*" I looked up to the sky with pleading eyes for an answer as I maneuvered my bike around the crowds of people out enjoying the spring evening.

I made my way to Charlie's Kitchen, thinking I could use a beer and I locked my bike outside on a tree. I spotted a seat at the end of the bar and hopped onto a stool. I had never been in a bar alone. When the bartender asked me what I wanted, I really didn't know, so I looked at the bottle of the person next to me and said, "Michelob." The woman with the Michelob looked at me kindly and said, "Hi, I'm Rita, watch out for Jake, there," her head nodding at the bartender, "he sees you're alone and he'll try to take you home, unless you want him to, that is," and we both laughed. "No, keep me away from men," I said as Jake poured half of my beer into a glass, wanting him to hear that. "I've got a big problem to solve and a man got me into it," I added after Jake walked away. "Maybe I can help you think," Rita said, "want to tell me what's going on?" She signaled Jake for another beer and as we clicked glasses I began to tell her how I ended up at my parents' house with a three-year-old son and how I needed to find my own place to live as quickly as possible. Rita smiled and said, "Well, that's easy.

Just go to the town hall and apply for public assistance. You will qualify for money, medical, and food stamps because you have a child." I was amazed. I had not thought of that. I stood up and swallowed the rest of my beer. I thanked Rita for her advice and slipped out of the crowded bar; I had my answer.

I walked the bike all the way down Mount Auburn Street to steady myself and to think about Rita's idea. *She's talking about welfare.* I realized. *Hmm, why don't I just get a job and have Paul give me child support?* I thought. As soon as I had that thought, I realized I would not be able to count on Paul for anything anymore. Rita was right; I needed to apply for assistance. I thought about what I read in the astrology book—that as a Cancer sign, home was the most important thing for me to thrive; I knew I needed my own home if I was going to stay sane. I walked the bike all the way home with renewed energy. This time I went over to the statue of the Blessed Mother and I thanked her for the Grace she had sent to me in the form of Rita, and I said a few Hail Mary's.

The next day I felt so relieved, I decided to show Paulie how I could climb the apple tree in our back yard to the highest branch. "This was my airplane," I told him when I reached the highest point on the tree. "None of my sisters ever dared to climb this high," I bragged. I think I was really trying to prove to myself that I could still climb to the top and I hoped to absorb a tiny bit of the hawk's eye view of life my airplane always gave to me. I shook the limb wildly, making Paulie laugh and beg to come up, too. "Go look for the fairies in the bushes over there," I yelled down to him, "this is too high for you." He did as I suggested. I looked through the tree branches into the billowing clouds above me and asked, "Okay, help me know my next step." I talked aloud to the clouds and to myself for awhile, "I don't want to go to Bridgetown town hall for welfare assistance. Everyone in this town knows my dad, it would embarrass him." I shifted my body to lean my back on a branch and I took a deep breath. "I know, I'll go to the Larchmont town hall and give Dora and Ed's address as mine."

Wow! Excellent plan, Renie, I congratulated myself, and with mission accomplished, I began my not-so-graceful descent down the tree. I stood on a big lower limb and dramatically quoted more of the poem I loved, "Then fearlessly, I will face whatever storms may come, having been home." I sat down on the limb and watched as the sun began to set where it always did in May, behind our clothesline and over the tips of the lilac bushes. A flash of my old life rose up and I sang to myself a Moody Blues song, "Isn't life strange, just the turn of a page. "God, I need my music," I yelled and I jumped from the last tree limb to the ground and headed over to the bushes where Paulie was busy turning sticks into swords.

Saturday, May 13th was a beautiful spring day; it was the day we were going to the circus. Paulie and I had to take the train further into Boston than I had ever gone. At the train's end we had to take a trolley to the North Station. My fear of being this far from home alone with a three-year-old caused me to feel like the biblical Jonah swallowed by the whale. I was in the bowels of Boston squeezing the hand of a three-year-old for support. The exciting part came when we walked right into the magical and colorful world of the Barnum and Bailey Three Ring Circus! The usher took us to our fifth row center seats and the next thing I knew we had popcorn and Cokes in our hands. *Ed must have paid a lot for these tickets*, I thought as I looked around the enormous Boston Garden Stadium. I took a deep breath, thankful that we made it here.

As we took in the sights, from clowns to multicolored acrobats swinging in all directions, Paulie suddenly asked, "Where's daddy?" I pretended I didn't hear him because I had to; it felt like there was a knife in my throat. I looked around us. I guess he had noticed families with mothers, children, and fathers that were here together. This was the first time he asked about his father since we had split up. "Paulie look," I pointed to the entrance where horses were prancing in with women dressed in wondrous costumes riding on their backs. It worked; Paulie let the question float away as the animals and nonstop action carried us away for the rest of day.

I put on a great act, like the rest of the circus players. I laughed and clapped and held back a torrent of fear. Occasionally Paulie would grab my hand, afraid because we were too close to those huge lion heads and mouths. We didn't leave our seats until it was time to go home. Then, along with hundreds of other Bostonians, we got onto trolleys and trains and traveled back into our old worlds with new dreams.

Irene Isobel Carver

Chapter Thirteen

A House Of My Own

In the month of June, I learned that I would always get the second house I loved. The first house would be my test of faith. I followed Rita's advice and applied for public assistance in Larchmont and was easily accepted. The next day I took Brigette's bike to the store and got the Larchmont Herald to begin looking for my apartment. I parked my bike and went into Brigham's and sat at a booth. I ordered a vanilla Coke and spread open the newspaper. My eyes darted to the words, cute and cozy, two-bedroom on Beech Street. I went outside to the phone booth and called the number listed. The woman told me I could come right down and see the place; it was available on July first. I folded the paper, sucked down the Coke, and hopped back onto my bike. I was at the door of the rental within five minutes and after leaning my bike alongside the house, I knocked on the door.

An older gentleman answered, and when I told him I was there to see the house, he ushered me in and immediately asked, "How many of you are there in your family and where do you work?"

"It is just for me and my three-year-old son," I answered, as I fell in love with the circular front windows that allowed the living room a full blast of sunlight.

"And work?" he raised his eyebrows in question.

"Um… I am getting a divorce and I have been accepted for public assistance. I plan to get a job as soon as I can," I said as I walked towards the kitchen.

"I am sorry," he said stopping me in the hall, "there are two other people interested in the apartment they already have jobs."

"But I have a lead on a job, and an interview actually," I lied as I looked longingly down the hall.

"Well, call after you get the job and if it isn't rented you can come back," he concluded as he walked me back to the front door.

I stood next to my bike and leaned my forehead against the house, tears pouring out of my disappointed eyes. "Damn," I said aloud as I sadly realized I had gotten my hopes up that this was surely my house. I walked the bike down the street and rounded the corner at Greer's Fish Market. I stopped and stared into the lobster tank trying to hide my feelings from the world. "I better get a job," I said to the lobsters and began again to push my bike up the hill to my parents' house.

At dinner that night, as I cut my pork chop with stewed tomatoes on it, I told my parents about my experience and tried to not sound so naive about not getting the very first place I had looked at.

"What do you think you would like to do for work, Renie?" my mother asked.

"Well, I loved waitressing when I worked at McManus' in high school," I said, feeling a spark of hope. "I loved getting tips right on the spot."

"What are tips?" Paulie asked, as he dipped his pork chop in applesauce.

"Tips are money people leave on the table for you when you serve them their food," I said, happy to make conversation. I was afraid my father would say, "Too bad you never finished Katie Gibbs, you could get a job as a secretary." But he didn't; my dad just excused himself from the table and went to the sunroom where he liked to make evening phone calls.

Paulie took his chocolate chip cookie that grammy offered him and went out to sit on the back step to eat it and watch the evening birds fly about. While my mother and I cleared the dishes, she said, "Don't get discouraged, Renie, I am sure the right place is waiting for you. Chin up, just keep looking in the paper and think about restaurants that you can apply to for a job. Now you can look in the help wanted section, too," she said smiling; she was being optimistic for both of us. I joined Paulie on the back stoop with a cookie as well, and mum joined dad in the sun parlor with tea.

Oh, yeah, jobs, I said to myself and stood up to go get the newspaper I had bought that afternoon. But my dad intersected me in the kitchen and said he had called a friend who managed an upscale restaurant in Cambridge, named Rosario's. He said I had a job interview the very next afternoon at three o'clock. I threw my arms around him and said, "Thank you, daddy, thank you for not rubbing it in my face that I didn't finish Katie Gibbs" My worst fear just came blurting out of my mouth. "Well, I thought about it," he said, "but time has taught me to be silent," he added as he moved me out of our embrace. "Now don't embarrass me. Be on time and, well, be very appreciative to him; he's doing me a favor, not you." "Okay, dad, I'll use every manner you ever taught me and all the big classy words too" I joked as I ran out to the apple tree. This merited another climb to the top.

The job interview went well and I was told I would train the following Monday afternoon and then I would be given a schedule. On the way home, I stopped at the drug store and bought the weekly Herald. Sure enough like a dream come true, there it was: Two-bedroom duplex on a private cul-de-sac. I went home and called the phone number listed. A young woman answered the phone and told me the address; she said I could come right down and see it. When I turned onto the alleyway the house was on, I was very excited, but warned myself not to count my chickens too soon this time. The woman who had taken my call lived in the other side of the duplex with her husband and two kids. Her father-in-law was the landlord.

She interviewed me first and if she liked me, she would call her father-in-law, and that is what happened. She showed me around the house, asked for my work and financial situation, and then she called Mr. Costa, my soon-to-be landlord. Minutes later, he drove into the cul-de-sac in his boat-like Lincoln Continental. There was barely room to open his door in the narrow driveway. He managed to step out of the front seat with his big belly in tow and looked right at my bra-less chest. I stuck out my hand to shake his and told him what an exceptional spot he owned in this lovely town and I would love to rent it. I didn't want him to judge me immediately as loose and wild because I didn't wear a bra, so I put forth my most adult and educated persona.

He looked to his daughter-in-law for her approval nod and when she gave it he handed me a rental application and told me to bring it back that evening with a deposit check of one month's rent of $165 and if my references checked out, I could move in on July first.

Irene Isobel Carver

I ran into my parents' house and sat right down at the kitchen table to fill out the application. My mother came in and said, "Dad said he will loan you the deposit but he wants to go back with you and see the house and meet the landlord." "Oh, ma, I am so excited and afraid, what if I don't get it." I stood up, my energy rushing. "This house is more than I could have hoped for. You should see the kitchen; it's so big I can put a couch in it. It's like a dance floor," I spun in a circle. "And being on a cul-de-sac, I don't even have to worry about Paulie and cars." I plopped back down in my seat.

My mother looked down at my application. "Well, you have a good steady reference from Clarendon Hill for two years, I don't see why you wouldn't get it," she added, patting my head.

"Let's say a prayer," mum said and she sat down next to me. I watched as she bowed her head and said as she held my hand, "Dear Lord, if this is the house you have set aside for Renie, then please let it all happen smoothly and easily, Amen." I was so grateful for a short prayer as I folded the application and called to my Dad that we should probably go right back down with it. He yelled down the stairs, "Give me fifteen minutes, Renie." I sat on the front stoop and whispered, "Please Lord, let it be mine."

On July first, four days before my twenty-third birthday, Paulie and I moved into 12 Thayer Street in Waverly Square. This house gave me wings! There were no parents and no husband with a monkey on his back, just me, my three-year-old son, and my new job. When Dora and Ed came to see my new house, they noticed right away that I could use a rug for the living room and took me to Lechmere Sales that very day and bought me a brown shag rug, which I loved. It seemed to give the whole house a hug. The loving support of Dora and Ed was such a comfort, especially because I hadn't heard a word from Paul since we split. It had been two months and he never called to even ask how Paulie was. I chose to think he was ashamed to call my parents' house, rather than feeling that he and Natalie were just so happy that he forgot all about us. To survive, I had to avoid that painful possibility.

Truthfully, I wasn't giving Paul much thought either. I was busy decorating my new place. It was like having a house, not an apartment, as I had an upstairs with two bedrooms and a big bathroom. Downstairs there was a smallish living room with two windows that looked out onto trees and shrubs, not neighbors. The kitchen had knotty pine wainscoting, which was met with wallpaper of tiny flowers. It looked like someone who longed for New Hampshire had built it. There was a four-foot dividing counter built in the center of the room, which was a perfect mini-office for paying bills and making phone calls. My kitchen table and chairs were made of solid maple and fit perfectly. Paulie sat right down and spread out his Disney paint set and began painting Goofy; it seemed as if life had never skipped a beat for him. To make it perfect, there was a back door that opened out to a fenced yard, just waiting for flowers to be planted.

Dora and Ed continued to be my child-sitters. They loved having Paulie stay overnight with them when I went to work. My schedule was to waitress Thursday through Sunday nights, from 5:00 p.m. until closing at 10:00 p.m. I would pick Paulie up each morning around 9:00 a.m. and we would have all day together to go to the park and library or just be at home. Paulie was very much into his

Big Wheels that summer and I'm sure he felt as much like he had wings as I did. He would put on his red superman cape and peddle as fast as he could and soon he learned to do donut spins. We were happy.

There was one problem I needed to solve. Paul had taken our stereo when we split up our belongings. I had taken the records that were specifically mine and now I needed a record player. I hinted to my parents this is what I really wanted for my upcoming birthday. I told my sister Teresa to help my parents know how to pick out the kind of speakers, amplifier, and turntable I wanted; not the furniture style cabinet ones. She agreed to this and my wish was granted. My parents invited all my sisters, brothers, and their spouses over to their house for a Fourth of July cookout and they royally presented me with this treasured item.

I bailed out on going to the fireworks on the Esplanade, which is a Bostonian tradition, with Arthur Fiedler conducting the Boston Pops orchestra on the Charles River. All I wanted to do was go home and set up my new sound system and blast it. Ever since the Lawrence Welk trauma, I had been waiting for this moment. Once again I got my wish. Paulie went off with the rest of my siblings to the fireworks and I went home to find out just how hard it is to assemble a stereo system. I spread everything out on my beautiful shag rug and began reading the directions. After ten minutes, I burst into tears and surrendered to needing help. I called my friend Tim LePasse and begged his assistance. He said, "Okay, seeing it's your birthday, I will come on over, got a joint?" "Ah, no, actually, do you think you could find me one of those on your way, too?" I laughed. *This is when you find out who your friends really are*, I thought to myself as I hung up the phone.

I sat on my rug going through my albums as I waited for Tim, optimistically deciding which one I would play first. "Let's see," I talked to myself, Janis's *Pearl* album, Rod Stewart, Gasoline Alley, Blind Faith, Jimi, Midnight Lightning, Traffic, Melanie, Dave Mason, Carol King, Cat Stevens," and then Tim walked in. "Groovy, my very first guest, my first party, my birthday," I announced as he entered. "And voila, a joint," Tim said, holding up a thick, old spliff, and he lit it right up. And you know what? The party never stopped. There was a tremendous spirit of love through music that summer that found its pinnacle in the Concert for Bangladesh, which was held at Madison Square Garden, on August first. George Harrison and Ravi Shankar organized this concert to raise money for the relief of the refugee children of Bangladesh. Bob Dylan and many others also joined in to make this a consciousness-raising experience for us all. The cover of the album that was recorded at the concert had a photo of the check for the proceeds, which was $243,418.50. Spreading love on earth through music seemed to be the balance to the continuing Vietnam War. I didn't get to go to the concert, but the spirit was contagious. I had a friend who was producing concerts on Cape Cod at a Club called The Abtrex, and when I could afford to take a weekend off, I would carpool to the club with friends. This is where I met my first boyfriend in my new life, Jeffrey Harris.

They say that in relationships, we see what we need to about ourselves and I found this to be true. Jeff was a handsome and happy twenty-three-year old young man who had the misfortune to fall head-over-heels in love with me. He loved that I had a child and he was ready to play a substitute dad. I, on the other hand, saw things quite diferently. One night after Jeff and I had gone to Harvard Square to hang out, he just naturally began to act like he would be staying overnight. I didn't even know how I felt until I saw him sitting there taking off his shoes. I realized how much I wanted to be alone. I had to stop him quickly. His shoes looked like an enormous neon sign that said *moving in.* I caught my breath; it felt like a scarf was just pulled too tightly around my neck, and I said, "Hey Jeff, I think it would be better if you took off tonight; I really need some alone time."

He looked up at me completely surprised and said, "Alone, to do what?"

And just as surprised, I said, "Well, that's the thing about being alone, you know you need it but you don't always know why."

He looked at me like he had just heard a foreign language and I realized, *Oh my God, he wants to settle in and play house.* He walked past me to the door, trying to act casual, and said "Call ya, tomorrow," and he kissed me on the cheek.

Now I really did need alone time, I thought. I watched Jeff get into his car and I wondered why I wanted him to go. We were having fun together, what more was I wanting? I sat on my shag rug and listened to Cat Stevens sing "On the road to find out." I sang with him . . . "So much left to know." I turned on my lava lamp, put a pillow under my head, and lay back on the rug. "What are you doing Renie?" I yelled into the lonely air. I wished the Wandering Jew hanging by my front window would reply but instead, Cat Stevens did. His voice suddenly sang out, "The answer lies within, so why not take a look, pick up the good book, now."

Man, it was a bit eerie, like I was just ordered about. I stood up and went to my bookshelf. Yup, I had it. There was my small, black Bible that I was given in high school. I sat down on the couch, turned up the three-way light, and randomly opened it. I read a couple of sentences and twice it said, "fear this or fear that," and I immediately closed the book. "Sorry, Cat," I said to my record, "I'm just not going into any fear conversation, I don't believe in it, I believe in healing by love and music, not fear." I turned up the volume and let *Peace Train* blast. "Now that's more like it," I said, as I walked to the kitchen to make tea. I looked at the clock, it was only eleven o'clock and it seemed like forever since Jeff had left. I was exhausted from thinking. I took my chamomile tea and my Ayn Rand novel, locked both doors, and turned out the lights. As I headed upstairs I said to myself, "I'm calling it a day world and, hopefully, *Atlas Shrugged* will have a bit of wisdom for me."

I awoke at ten o'clock in the morning with the phone ringing; it was Jeff. Wide-awake and cheery, he said, "So, did you get enough aloneness? Want to go for a walk up to rock meadow?" "You woke me up," I said, "Can I call you in an hour?" And I hung up annoyed. I talked to myself all the way to the kitchen. *Damn, too bad he didn't get it. I wish he had waited for me to call him.* I flung open the back door realizing it was going to be a hot, August day. I boiled water for tea anyway and picked up the phone to call Dora. I wanted to get Paulie home before it got too hot. Then I realized it was Saturday and I had to be to work at four-thirty. Ed answered the phone and said right away, "We were hoping we could just keep Paulie all day and overnight while you work. Christine and the girls invited us over for the afternoon."

"That would be great, Ed. That will give me time to go and look for a book. Can I say hi to my Paulie, first?" I asked.

"Ma, I'm not coming home," the small but determined

Irene Isobel Carver

voice said to me on the other end of the phone.

"Yeah, that's what grandpa said. You are gonna get to play with your cousin and that's okay by me. Have fun and I will see you in the morning, I love you."

"Love you too, mummy," he whispered in a tiny voice as the phone clicked off. I took my tea to the back yard and sat under the shade of the birch tree. I reminded myself that I was supposed to call Jeff back. I knew that was the word I didn't want to feel—*supposed*. I went back in the kitchen and dialed his number to get it over with. He picked up on the first ring.

"To answer your question, no, I don't think I got enough alone time because all I want to do today is to go back to Harvard Square and look for a book." I said without preface.

"I've got a lot of books, want to come over and check my library?" he said with a surprisingly sexy connotation in his voice.

I took a breath and softened my tone. "Thanks Jeff, maybe another time, I would like to see your collection, but for now, I really want to just float about the square and see what happens."

There were a few moments of silence and Jeff said, "Is there something I'm not getting here, Irene? Are you trying to get rid of me?"

"No, not rid of Jeff, it is just that I just left a relationship in May and I need some room to breathe."

"Okay, then, call me when you have had enough air," he said as he hung up, obviously hurt.

I went into the living room and put on my new Carol King album and blasted it as I happily ran up the stairs feeling the freedom I was craving. While I got dressed in my jean shorts and my green paisley tank top, Carol was singing, "I feel the earth move under my feet, I feel the sky come tumbling down." *Yeah, my thoughts exactly*, I thought as I took the needle off the record, flung on my backpack, and headed for the bus stop.

I have four whole hours to myself, I thought. *Okay, angels, lead me to just the right book to teach me; I really want to know something about this being alone thing*, I dialogued to the invisible. When I stepped onto the bus, I realized how incredibly happy I was. I had come so far since that torturous Lawrence Welk night. "You're as beautiful as you feel," I smiled and quoted Carol King to myself as I took my seat.

REMEMBER—BE HERE NOW

When I got to Harvard, I headed for the Sphinx bookstore. Right there, displayed in the front window, was the book I was looking for. It had a purple cover with a wicker chair in the center of a circular web. All around the circle it said, "Be here now, Be here now, Be here Now, Be here Now," with the word *Remember* blocking it in. The author was Dr. Richard Alpert, later to become known as Baba Ram Dass. I had recently heard of this book but had not yet seen it. In the bookstore I began to flip through the pages. As soon as I read that the author had been thrown out of Harvard, I bought it, noting the interesting price of three dollars and thirty-three cents. I put it in my backpack and stopped to buy an ice tea because the day had deepened into one hot August afternoon. I headed to the Harvard Yard and found a shaded bench under the towering sycamore trees.

The first page said, "Made in love for love." I was ecstatic; it touched my heart and feeling humbled, I remembered my off-hand angel request. I read all the white pages and then realized I better get the bus home since I only had an hour and a half to get to work. On the trolley, I continued reading the brown pages, printed on coarse paper in large, uniquely designed print. On page one was the Bible quote, "Except ye be converted and become as little children, ye shall not enter the Kingdom of Heaven." The author interpreted that line as "Unless you start again, become that trusting, open, surrendered being, the energy can't come in; that is the kingdom of heaven."

By the time I got home, I was in love with the book; I felt changed. *This is like a Hippie Catechism,* I told myself. I wanted to call Jeff to see if this book was in his collection, realizing it would have been nice to share this moment with someone, but all I had time for was a shower and to slip into my uniform—a black skirt and a white tailored blouse. As I gazed into the mirror putting on my lipstick, I paused a moment; I felt different, which made me wonder if I looked different, too. I put my face right up to the mirror and looked square into my irises. I noticed again that there was a blonde quality to the brown. I added a line of black liner to the bottom lid and kissed my reflection in the mirror, leaving the pink imprint of my lips.

The hot days of August began to let go of their grip and a cool breeze wafted in every so often and along with it, that deep feeling of change that only September can bring. Teresa had finished her two-year nursing program and with her dormitory living over, we quickly set up a second-hand, single bed in my large kitchen against the knotty pine wall. It was a great relief to have Teresa with me; we needed each other in many ways. I was confused. I had never really let Jeff into my heart and life, even though I was lonely. What the book *Be Here Now* had shown me was that all I could do was be right where I was, no matter if I understood it or not. I needed to be alone with myself to figure things out. On page thirty-seven it said, "Life is like the big eternal ice cream cone, always melting. Just be present with what is." So I let Jeff slip out of my life with a painful tear here and there, and Teresa slipped in.

On Teresa's first night at my house, we bought a bottle of wine to celebrate and she almost immediately let slip out the hot-off-the-press gossip that Natalie had left Paul two weeks before, when she finally realized how seriously addicted to heroin he was. She used school as an excuse and scurried back home to her parents. Teresa watched my face for a reaction as she said, "Sorry Renie, I didn't mean to just blurt that out." "That's okay, Tee," I said, "I'd rather hear it directly from you, than some beating-around-the-bush bullshit." I went into the living room to change the record. This called for The Moody Blues. Teresa just let me lie on the living room floor and listen to music while she gave Paulie a bath and read him stories until he went to sleep. When she walked back into the living room, I said to her, "You know, Tee, I realize I just don't feel any anger towards either of them. I feel like Natalie opened a door and I was let free. It's weird how calm I feel," I said, and lay back down on the soft shag rug. "Speaking as a nurse, I'm guessing you're in shock," Teresa said as she poured herself more wine.

I lit up a joint, sucked in two deep hits, and as I blew the smoke out into her face, I said, "Hey, I'm just a melting ice cream cone, and when I come out of shock, there will be a puddle of me like the tiger in *Little Black Sambo*." She put her hand on my forehead, pretending to take my temperature and we both went into a great laughing fit. "Oh my God, I live with a fucking nurse," I said, as I laughed my way to the bathroom. "Now I have you and Gwen tracking my symptoms; at least we live close to McLean's Psychiatric Hospital if you two decide I've gone totally bonkers." Another album dropped onto the turntable and we let Carol King lull us both to sleep.

Chapter Fourteen

The Tie That Binds

I HAD MY FREEDOM UNTIL ONE OCTOBER DAY, WHILE I was in the front yard raking leaves, and Paul simply walked up with flowers in hand and said, "Happy Anniversary, four years, right?" He leaned in and gave me a kiss on the lips and it felt as if he had never left. "Your nose is still cold," he said, "I've got to find you a nose bootie." This is what he had told me when I was fifteen and he gave me my very first kiss. By ten o'clock that night, Paul was asleep on my living room couch, and by Friday he was asleep in my bed. *So this is why I couldn't let Jeff into my heart,* I told myself, *Paul still occupied it.* I had just let him go on a long leash so I could rest and grow.

In the morning, as I showered, I thought, "*All the world is a stage and my heart is writing the script.*" I commanded my mind to be still. Paul lured me back by telling me that he was now in the VA methadone clinic program and he would be going to downtown Boston every morning to get his daily dose of methadone. He said this would keep him from needing heroin. His mood was consistently cheery. He said he was ready to get a job and he was hoping we could begin again. Paulie hadn't seen his father in six months so it took him a few days and a bit of new toy coaxing for him to relax into us being a family again. I easily rationalized it

Irene Isobel Carver

would also make life easier for me with Paul there to babysit when I worked nights. We allowed ourselves to rest into the comfort zone of the known, as the music of Crosby, Stills, Nash and Young comforted our hearts with, "Carry on, love is coming to us all." And with the depth of our kisses, we avoided the questions of this song, "Will you bring me happiness or will you bring me sorrow?"

VIRGIN ISLANDS HERE WE COME

Paul and I could talk now that he wasn't filled with urgency and desperation. We would stay up late into the night and talk about what had happened to each of us during our tumultuous six months apart. We never fought and I felt no fear, I was just relieved to have my marriage intact and I began to feel a level of tense responsibility lift from my shoulders.

Paul began to make leather belts and suede pouches, which he would sell each day at the clinic. Teresa was paying rent and I was waitressing, so we began to save up a little money. Just at that affluent moment our friend Leonard wrote to us and invited us to come visit him in Saint Thomas, Virgin Islands. He was living in a large tent just outside of town where he had a maintenance job for a local business. The timing was perfect since the restaurant business slowed down quite a bit in the winter and they were glad to give me the month of January off. Teresa was suffering from a broken heart and so was happy to have a winter escape plan. She said there were plenty of jobs in nursing homes and she could easily find a job again when she got back, so she gave a two-week notice at her job. Paul asked the clinic to begin cutting back his daily dose of methadone so that in a month's time, he would also be free to go away.

I waitressed on New Year's Eve while Paul and Teresa stayed home, packing and preparing the house for our departure on the second of January. When I walked through the front door, in time for the midnight countdown, Teresa and Paul were blasting Joe Cocker and drinking shots of tequila. They handed me a shot, which I threw back and headed up the stairs to shower. "Wow," I hooted, 1972 is gonna be far fucking out."

My brother, Alex, picked the four of us up very early on the morning of the January second, because we had to be to the airport by 8:00 a.m. Paulie looked so cute wearing his small army issue backpack that we had found at a Salvation Army store. When Alex dropped us off at the departure curb, we took off our winter coats and boots and left them in his car. We slipped on sneakers and sweaters and prepared for a full month of warmth. The airplane was huge. The upper level had a full bar. We took turns going for a drink as children were not allowed. I heard myself telling the bartender that I had never been to the tropics; in fact I had never even been to Florida. He filled my glass full and said, "Boy, are you in for some fun."

It felt otherworldly when I stepped off the plane and breathed in the moist, warm air of Saint Thomas. Paul put Paulie on his back and as we descended the steps of the plane, I watched the backs of their heads as the sun shone on their strawberry blonde hair. Teresa grabbed my hand and said, "Oh, my God, Renie, thank you for taking me with you guys." Leonard picked us up at the airport in his Jeep and took us to his campsite. His home was a twenty-foot tent on top of a wooden platform. His area of work had a chain-link fence around it, which Leonard had beautified by planting tropical vines that climbed the fence and flowered into morning glory type flowers. He had moved his belongings into one corner so we could spread out our mats and sleeping bags. He didn't have running water but he had a rain barrel to collect water in for bathing, teeth brushing, and cooking.

It rained every single afternoon. It was amazing, just like clockwork; the sunny day would suddenly cloud over and warm rain would pour onto us. It was exhilarating. We would strip off our clothes, soap up, and if the shower didn't last long enough to rinse, we would throw buckets full of rainwater over each other. We were having a blast. We had a two-burner camp stove and two coolers. We would go to town every other day for ice and spend the day sightseeing or hanging out on the beach making sand castles. About a week after we arrived, I woke up to find Paul gone. He had left a note on the cooler saying, "I hitchhiked to town; someone pick me up at the corner bar later today." Leonard was out in the fields doing his maintenance work so I went and found him and showed him the note. He said, "Yeah, I talked to Paul when he got up. He asked to take my Jeep but I said no 'cause I figured he was going for alcohol and I didn't want him to drive."

"Do you mind if Teresa and I go to town and get him?" I asked.

"I'd rather you wait for me. I'll be done here by 1:00 and we can all go and get Paul and head to the beach for the rest of the day."

"That sounds cool; we'll be ready when you are," I said, but I wasn't feeling cool at all. An old anxiety was creeping into the tropical bliss. Paulie and Teresa were still asleep, so I looked through a crate bookshelf that Leonard had in his corner of the tent. I pulled out a small blue paperback,

Siddhartha, by Herman Hesse. The image of the Buddha on the cover drew me in. I sat in the yard on a lawn chair and let the Buddha calm my worried mind. I was captivated by the book, so when Leonard walked up and said, "Okay, let's go to town and find Paul," I was quite surprised. I looked around for Teresa and Paulie and saw that they had spread out a blanket near me and were reading *Winnie the Pooh,* one of the books we brought with us for Paulie. We quickly stuffed our backpacks with bathing suits, towels, and sunscreen, and hopped into the open-air Jeep.

Paulie boosted himself up on one of the tall stools that lined the outdoor cabana bar. The first thing I noticed was that Paul was laughing and talking to a cute hippie chick and her friend. A wave of jealousy and fear flooded through me, a flashback of Natalie, and I looked away. I avoided eye contact with him and sat next to Paulie on a stool. "Two Orange Julius'" I said to the bartender, "one for the little guy here and one for me with a shot of rum on the side." Paul came over to us, carrying a plate of fried plantains and took my hand. His eyes were pretty blood shot and he had a drunken grin on his face.

"Rene, I met these two chicks from Michigan; come on over and meet them, they are super cool," he said as he grabbed the bar stool for support.

"Are they as smashed as you are?" I asked when I looked over towards them.

"No, actually, they are the vegetarian and pot smoking types, you'll like them. Then one of the chicks came over to us and squeezed in next to Paulie and said, "You must be the little Paulie I've been hearing about."

Paulie was dipping the fried bananas into his Julius and slurped a messy, "Yup."

Irene Isobel Carver

Next thing I knew, Michigan Cindy was eating the plantains with us, and Leonard chimed in and suggested that we all go to a burger joint. Teresa came walking up to us with a beer in her hand and said, "Oh my God, I just found the most far out thing, a fucking beer machine!" Paul held up his beer and clinked cans with her and she went off on a rant about how amazing it was to see not a Coke machine, but a fucking BEER machine. Finally, even little Paulie said, "Okay, Auntie, we hear you, beer not Coke, yippie." We all turned and looked at him in surprise. He was not quite four and had just expressed himself in such a socially savvy way that we all burst out laughing.

Over burgers, I got to know Cindy and her friend and we liked each other; but there was an air of sadness around me now as I watched Paul eating his burger, half unconscious and about to pass out in his food. *He's not really okay*, I thought. *He is just replacing methadone with alcohol. He has to numb himself.* I wondered if I had made a mistake going back to him. We never did get to the beach that day and on the drive home in the Jeep, I had to hold onto Paul's arm to keep him from falling out.

The next day, I overheard Paul and Teresa talking, and Teresa was telling Paul that she had some Valium pills with her if he needed any to get to sleep. His answer was, "I need something when I'm awake and I'll take anything you've got." I pretended not to be eavesdropping but I asked Teresa later that day why she had the Valium. She said she began taking them after Greg broke up with her and she was having trouble sleeping. One of the doctors at the nursing home gave her a prescription for them and told her they were not addictive but would just calm her nerves. When she ran out of the Valium, she realized her body was craving them and she told the doctor. He changed her prescription to Librium. When those ran out, she felt the same thing. The doctor told her that at twenty she was too young to be taking them, and wouldn't prescribe more for her. "After that, I just began to take any extra ones patients didn't use and started storing them up," Teresa said, as she held up a plastic pill bottle full. "That's it, that's my stash, guess they will have to last till I get home." I asked Teresa how many she gave to Paul. "Only about ten, and I told him to just save them for at night, 'cause we can't get more," Teresa said, as she tucked the bottle in the bottom of her backpack.

It had become a routine for Paul to be gone when we woke up in the morning, and if we didn't go to town to pick him up he would find other places to crash for the night. Leonard and I talked about Paul's drinking one day, and he told me that he thought Paul should go home early and get back into the methadone program. We had a family powwow the next morning and we stopped Paul before he headed out to hitchhike to town; we confronted him about his drinking. Paul agreed he was doing badly without methadone, and he also thought he should get back to the clinic. It turned out that we all couldn't change our ticket dates without a large fee but we were able to get a medical permit for Paul to go home early. Paul left two days later, looking forlorn and beat. Teresa took one look at me as we left the airport and said, "Are you alright, Rene?" "Fuck, no, I'm not alright," I said, way more harshly then I meant to, "are you?" I was scared shitless for all of us. "Rene, take it easy; Paul will get back on methadone and we are going snorkeling tomorrow." "Can you give me one of those sleeping pills, Tee? I really need to relax," I asked holding out my hand. She opened the plastic container and took out one pill and handed it to me. I noticed how very close to empty it was and said, "Never mind, you keep it, Tee; I might like it too much; one of us better stay tense."

I was really glad Teresa and I had planned a snorkeling day trip the day after Paul left. Even though I was relieved that Paul and his problems were far away, I felt a deep sadness that I really didn't understand. Even Leonard took the day off from his chores and carried a cooler to the cove we found and settled in under an umbrella with his book; he too was relieved. Teresa looked adorable with her long black braided hair and big square sunglasses, but I sensed heaviness in her rounded shoulders, so I handed her an ice tea and a tuna sandwich as soon as our blanket was spread. "Hey, I even brought potato chips to put in the sandwich," I said, hoping to remind her of our childhood days at Nantasket Beach with mum.

"Oh, God; did you have to remind me of Clare and her perfect legs when she would do a hand stand in the water," Teresa shot back with a pained grin.

"How the hell do you get Clare's legs out of potato chips?" I said, confused. *I guess she's not going to let me cheer her up*, I thought. I picked up Paulie's shovel and pail and headed to the water's edge, where Paulie was sitting and letting tiny tropical, blue waves wash over his legs.

"Look mummy, I found a shell with a hole in it," he said squinting up at me, trying to see through the tiny hole.

"Let's walk down the beach and look for more," I suggested as I swung his pail. I was amazed that with every step we found translucent shells, so thin they looked like fingernails and each one had a tiny hole in it.

"We can make necklaces out of these," I told Paulie. "We

will buy some string at the store and make them tonight for Dora and Grammy,"

"Let's make one for my cousin Annie too," Paulie said with new enthusiasm. I looked back over my shoulder and saw that Teresa was on the blanket sunbathing with a beer in her hand. I watched my feet as I walked, noticing how incredibly white the sand was. I stopped abruptly and sat in the sand. "Let's stay here and build a castle, Paulie." I did not want to go back to our blanket and I didn't want to walk further, either. I had no idea how deeply I had immersed myself into the sand until I heard Teresa's voice behind me saying, "Oh, my God, you two, look at that high rise castle you have made."

Paulie stood up, yelling "Wow!" He too, had lost track of how deep we had dug a moat around our tower. He jumped into the moat and slapped both hands on the top of our castle. "Oh, be careful, Paulie, let's decorate it before we stomp it," I said, as I began to empty our bucket of shells on the top. Then Teresa and I began to neatly make steps down the side of the three-tiered castle with the shells. "Number Nine, Number Nine," said Teresa and we both flashed back, laughing about the night we had to climb nine flights up to our apartment. Paulie found a couple of pieces of drift-wood and stuck them on the top and we all stood back and admired our work. "One, two, three, jump" Paulie yelled, as he landed right on top of the whole castle like a giant in control of the world. He began to spit the sand out of his mouth, which caused us to run back to our blanket for our Cokes and tuna sandwiches. "Wait, the shells," Paulie yelled as he spit. "We'll get them after we eat," I said, as we ran.

This is how the days passed and once again I began to feel the sense of freedom I had forgotten I was missing.

One afternoon, Teresa stayed at the beach with Paulie and I rented a bike and cruised around the town. I bumped into Cindy and her friend and I pushed the bike as we chatted. When they started to say that they were sorry to hear about Paul, I stopped them and said, "Hey, have you heard of the book, *Be Here Now*?" "Yes," they said excitedly; they had both read it. "Well then, let's practice it. Paul has gone to help himself and I am here now." I needed to believe that. I waved goodbye and hopped back onto my bike.

God, how I have missed having alone time, I told myself as I sped through the alleyways, sweeping past mothers holding their paper umbrellas over their heads while their little ones huddled against stoops and calypso music resonated from open windows. I breathed in the salty air and headed for a park that was in the center of town. As I got closer I heard the sound of steel drums. I got off the bike and walked slowly into the crowd. There was a large table full of food and I realized I had walked into a wedding party. I leaned my bike against a tree and locked it. Everywhere I looked there were baskets of fruits and flowers. Everything was dripping with luscious color, especially the swirling skirts of dancing women. The men's shirts were vibrant lime green and orange. I made my way closer to the band of steel drums, maracas, and dancing people. The warm tropical air and the spirit of the music moved me to dance and my hips started swaying to the rhythm. A shiver went through my body. I started to understand why I needed to be on my own; the freedom and solitude I was craving is what my spirit needed to grow and expand. I danced until I was sweating like the others and then grabbed a mango; I knew it was time to go.

Chapter Fifteen

Crossroads

I stand at the crossroads
Where three roads converge
A place of choice
All paths lead to the crossroads
But only one can you travel
Choice creates endings
And all beginnings come from endings
Which way will you go?
The choice is yours.

—From the Goddess Oracle

PAUL

Paul stood shivering in jeans and a tee shirt on the curb
outside the baggage claim at Logan airport waiting for
his ride to pick him up. He rubbed his arms vigorously,
"Damn, I forgot about the cold," he talked to himself and
pulled a pack of Winston cigarettes out of his pocket. He
sucked the smoke extra deeply into his lungs, hoping the
tiny head of the lit cigarette would warm the air around
him. Paul's old using buddy, Drew, showed up quickly
and when he saw Paul coatless, he hopped out of the car,
threw open his truck and heaved an army fatigue jacket
over the car hood to Paul, calling, "Hey, buddy, get the

hell in." "Holy shit," Paul said, as he huddled around the heater vent. "I forgot I was flying into fucking winter. Can we stop and get coffee somewhere?"

"I got us something better then coffee," Drew said as he patted his chest pocket. "I got us something to help us forget we even have a body." Paul opened to the memory of the exquisite comfort of heroin in his veins and he lay against the headrest, taking a deep breath of anticipation. "God, I haven't shot up in over two months," Paul said. "Thanks man, this will tide me over till I get to the clinic in the morning." "That's just what I was thinking," Drew said as he paid the toll and headed into the Sumner Tunnel. An hour later, after shooting up, Paul rolled his sleeve down, and made his way to a couch in Drew's warm apartment. "This is more blissful then tropical anything," Paul mumbled to himself as he floated in and out of consciousness. His head nodded into his chest as all tension left his body; even the effort that it takes to hold his head up was gone.

When daylight came, Paul awoke in a crash pad full of junkies, male and female, all planning how to score their next bag. Paul wandered into the kitchen and found a loaf of bread and some peanut butter. As he made a sandwich he noticed how his body still felt relaxed from the night's clean white powder. Drew came into the kitchen and said, "So, man, that chick Rachael, the one with the tattoo of a vine on her forearm, she just asked me how married you are?" Paul looked up at Drew, "Well, married enough to have a ring on my finger, but I don't know, what's her story?" "She says she can get you two enough money to stay high for a week *if you're into it," Drew said, playing messenger. Paul clenched his fist and looked at the vein in his arm. His blood would be craving something soon and methadone just doesn't hit that vein.*

"Well, actually I happen to be unmarried for a week. Irene and Paulie won't be back from the islands 'till next Thursday. Tell her to come in and talk to me." Then, for just a second, as he slipped off his wedding ring and put it in his pocket, Irene's long black hair floated around him on a pillow and he started to feel guilty. Quickly his need to not feel anything pushed that vision away and he told himself he had never been with a woman with a tattoo, and what the hell, we could all die tomorrow with this bullshit world we've got going. It's all bullshit anyway; his body convinced his mind, as his old lover heroin seduced him. Rachael walked into the kitchen, and, without a word, entwined one of her legs around Paul's and whispered as she put her tongue in his ear, "Let's get out of here."

Meanwhile, I stood in a phone booth in the tropical sun. I hadn't had any contact with Paul since he left the island four days earlier, so I thought I'd call his parents' house and see how things were going. When Dora answered the phone, she told me she had not heard a word from Paul and had no idea he had returned early. I was immediately filled with fear and I had to swallow and clear my throat to continue talking. I could tell Dora felt the same fear and asked in an aggravated voice, "Why did Paul come home before you, Irene?" It was the first time I had felt judgment from Dora, and I heard, *why did you let him go again Irene, I thought you'd know better?* I loved Dora, and I knew it was the same fear I had that made her sound the way she did so I lied to comfort her.

"Paul got an infection of some kind and we thought it better if he could go to the VA for treatment. I think it's from that jungle rot he's had on his feet since Nam."

"Oh, well, when do you get back, Irene, we miss our Paulie a lot?"

"We'll be flying in on Thursday morning and my brother is picking us up, so I'll call you as soon as we are home safely, okay?"

"Okay, be sure to call right away."

"Will do, Dora, love you," I said as I placed the receiver on the hook and wiped the perspiration from my brow. As I walked back to the Crawfish Café where I had left Teresa and Paulie, I just knew Paul was using again. *What will I say to Teresa; how can I hide this tension in my chest*? I looked up at the perpetual blue sky, wishing for a cloud to give me some dimension.

"So what's up?" Teresa asked, "How's the homestead?"

"I called Dora, and," I stammered, "she hasn't heard from Paul at all; he never called from the airport."

"Shit, that's not good, Renie."

"I know, damn it, Teresa…" but I stopped as anger arose in me; I didn't want Paulie to hear me. I couldn't protect Dora endlessly or Teresa but I could protect my Paulie from knowing about the devastating effects of this drug and how it has affected his father, and I would. I decided right then; no more, he's out.

"When he resurrects from his smack pit, he can pick his clothes up and hitchhike to hell and see if I care." My heart ranted on as I ate fried plantains and a Coke quickly while my thoughts and anger arose.

Teresa grabbed my hand, "Renie, slow down; we don't know what's going on; don't go picturing the worst."

"I know, Tee, trust me, I know," I said with prophetic assurance.

Alex picked Teresa, Paulie and me up at the airport, and our winter clothes were still in his backseat for us to wrap up in. The first thing out of Teresa's mouth was, "Alex, you wouldn't believe it but there are beer machines on the streets!" I saw from the glint in Alex's eyes that he felt the island spirit we brought home, imbedded in our tanned skin. As we sped along the frozen banks of the Charles River, we sang in unison, "Love that dirty water, Boston you're my home."

The house wasn't even warmed up yet when Teresa called the Regency Manor nursing home just down the street from us. She hung up and said, "See ya, I have a job interview in a half hour." "Way to go, Teresa," I said, only half meaning it. I was glad she was diving right back into work but also afraid her motivation was more the valium than the money. "Want me to drop you off at the place? I'm on my way to the Laundromat," I asked as I stuffed my laundry basket full of our happy summer clothes. "Sure, I'll go warm up the car," Teresa said. "God, it's great to be home isn't it?" she said, not waiting for my answer. My heart cautiously smiled with her.

When I went back to work the following Monday, I still had not heard a word from Paul. I drove Paulie over to Dora and Ed's house to spend the night, and the sadness in their faces was hard for me to see. I was blocking all my feelings and hopes I had about Paul and our resuming a happy life together. I had put a wall around my heart and I didn't want Dora's sadness to penetrate it. I was late on purpose so I could just drop Paulie off and run.

Irene Isobel Carver

When I walked into work at Rosario's, I knew I looked really cute in my white blouse with my tropical tan and even the bus boy, Jose, whistled when I walked by. I enjoyed the obvious lust of the Latin men; *at least they were authentic*, I thought, observing an opinion I didn't even know I had.

That night, I had a dream that shattered the wall around my heart and I awoke in tears. Paul was sitting on a park bench, dripping in sweat, and when I touched his shoulder to get him to look up, he said, "Leave me alone and let me bleed to death, please." The next morning I called Dora and asked her if she could keep Paulie all day because I needed to go look for Paul. "Where are you going to look?" Dora asked. "I'm going to the methadone clinic and see if anyone knows where he is," I answered. "OK, thank you, Irene. Let us know, we are very frightened, too," Dora said and we both hung up. *Oh, my God, she can feel my fear over the phone*, I thought as I hopped on the trolley for Harvard Square. I sat in the trolley seat with my eyes closed, hoping that people couldn't tell the panic I felt; I pretended to be asleep. *God, if you can lead me to a book, I know you can lead me to Paul; please help me, please help Paul* was my internal prayer as the trolley clacked and clattered along on the metal tracks.

The clinic was at the VA hospital in Jamaica Plain, which was complicated to get to, but I managed to get there. I stopped myself from running when I saw a group of men milling around outside the huge building. I pulled my hat down around my ears and walked up to the group of men. "Hey, I am Paul O'Connell's wife; I was hoping someone would know where I could find him," I blurted into the cold February air. A black dude looked up at me and I could see truth in his eyes. "Ah, I think he's shacked up with some rich chic from Gloucester, Rachael, or something like that."

I burst into tears, all my fear erupted, and I sat down on the wall that edged the courtyard. The black guy came and sat next to me and said, "I'm sorry to tell you that, but I could tell you wanted to know. It's not like he digs this chic; it's just that she takes the train home to Gloucester every weekend and steals enough money to keep her and Paul in smack all week."

"Has he come to the clinic at all?" I asked

"No, I saw him over at this cat, Drew's house, last week. He looked like shit. I was bummed out that he isn't making those nice suede pouches anymore."

"If you see him again, will you tell him to call his mother; she's worried," I said angrily.

"What about you, you have a little boy, right? You okay?"

"Yeah, I'm fucking great, thanks for asking." I hurried back to the trolley station, shivering as much from the coldness of life as the thirty degree temperature and the harsh wind.

When I got home I put on Joni Mitchell and let her sing to me, "It's love's illusions I recall…" "Well, you have that right, Joni," I said back to her as I put on water to boil for rice. The words Gloucester and Rachael bubbled up in my face with the steam. I stood over the pot of water and let the warm moisture envelope me. *Love's illusion*, I said to myself. I knew I needed to call Dora and let her know what I had found out about her son. I thought, *Shit, how can I sugarcoat this news*? So I sat down with a bowl of rice to figure out my next white lie.

I had the night off from work, so I drove up to Dora and Ed's house after I ate to pick up Paulie. It was a great comfort to have my happy three-year-old run into my arms and drag me to the kitchen to see the picture he had finger painted, which hung on the refrigerator. Both Dora and Ed looked at me longingly wanting to know something so I said, "Hey, Ed, can I talk to you in your office? Paulie, let go of my leg, honey; I have to ask grandpa a business question." Ed and I went into his office and he shut the door behind us. I sat in the rose upholstered chair and he sat in his desk chair. "I took the train to the VA clinic." "There was a group of vets milling around outside so I told them who I was and asked if anyone had seen Paul. One black guy said he had seen him at his old drug-using friend's house and that Paul hadn't rejoined the methadone clinic, as far as he knew." I leaned back into the curve of the chair, relieved, with some of the weight of truth off my shoulders.

"So, he is back to using heroin, is what you are saying?" Ed looked down as he shared my pain. "That is what it looks like, Ed." I reached over and put my hand on his. "So, he's not calling any of us 'cause he's a mess and he doesn't know how to tell us." I decided it made no sense to give them any of the Gloucester details. That was my personal pain; I didn't need to spread it to them. Ed walked into the kitchen and lit a cigarette. Dora took a look at us and poured a small glass full of bourbon. I gathered Paulie's bag of clothes and we all hugged goodbye; none of us wanted to infect Paulie with our sadness, so I left in relative silence.

That evening, I was sitting by my lava lamp still listening to Joni Mitchell, when Teresa came home from her evening shift at the nursing home. She sat next to me in her white nurse's uniform and I told her about my day trip to the VA. She pulled a small vial of Valium out of her pocketbook and asked if I needed one to help me sleep. "Yes, I would love to take one, Teresa, but I'm too afraid to. Someone has to stay together here. I'm afraid of what could happen to

Paulie. His father is a damn junkie and I have to work to keep this house together; I'm afraid, Tee, and I'm afraid for you, too. What the hell are you doing taking those pills? Do you take them every night?" My voice shook and I could no longer hold back my tears. "No, not every night," she lied, "and they are not like heroin, Irene, so don't take your fear out on me. I've got my own shit to worry about and I need a shower; here, take one," she said and threw the vial to me and went upstairs.

I sat and looked at the tiny blue pills in the vial and said to them, "I don't trust you, you tiny chemical things; I'm gonna have a shot of whiskey, *that* I trust." I went to the kitchen and, like Dora, I poured myself a pretty glassful of golden liquid and belted it back, *no sipping tonight*, I thought. The whisky soothed the pain in my head and brought me into my heart. When Teresa came downstairs after her shower, I let all my sadness about Paul sleeping with another chic cascade out of me. "Renie, if he's using every day, he probably can't even get it up to have sex; he is sleeping with heroin, not Rachael," Teresa wisely said. But it didn't help, not really, as the hope of being married again, of camping, and of family holidays was vanishing before my eyes and it was so painful. Teresa unwrapped the towel from her head and began running a comb through her hair. She gave me a hug as she picked her vial of valium up off the floor and, kissing my cheek, she headed to her bed.

Alone with whiskey surging through me, I remembered the dream of Paul wanting to bleed to death; it was too real, and an energy around my heart began pulsating in pain. At first, an overwhelming sadness seemed to shrink me; my shoulders and heart caved in. Then I felt a bolt of anger shoot up my spine. "Fucking War," I yelled, and I witnessed

178   Irene Isobel Carver

a dense blackness surrounding my heart as I rolled onto my side. I couldn't stop myself; I searched behind the blackness and got a glimpse of my pain. I closed my eyes. I knew this blackness wanted to stay hidden, where it could suffocate me, so I took a breath and asked into its depth, "Can I manage you?" "No," the blackness said, "you will fall apart, too." I heard an echo. *Paul wants to die, Paul wants to die, let him go.* "No, I can save him, I'll pray," I yelled into the void as I got onto my knees and begged God," Where are you? Help me." Then Teresa flashed through my mind. "What was wrong with my Teresa?" I cried and coughed until my head hurt from all these questions. I finally collapsed onto the couch, exhausted from weeping. At one point in the night, I felt Teresa stroking my hair and whispering, "Shh, Renie, shh." And then mercy came and I slept peacefully.

When I woke up, emotionally hung over, I needed something, someone. I almost called Jeff to ask if I could come over and look through his library, but I didn't. What if he, too, rejected me; I just couldn't take it. So I took Paulie to the library and asked the librarian if she had a section on love. She walked me over to the Psychology section and sarcastically said, "Good luck." I looked her in the eyes and we both smiled weakly, sharing an intuitive knowing. I left the library with a book called *The Art of Loving* by Erich Fromm and it scared the shit out of me even more. I had to put it down almost immediately; I was not ready to read what Fromm wrote about family dysfunction. I went back to the library and this time I asked God to guide me instead of the librarian. I was led again to the gentle author Hermann Hesse and got his book *Narcissus and Goldmund*. It was perfect; I would learn in a monastery, not a psychiatric ward.

March, in its usual fashion, rolled in like a lion, my

tropical tan fading along with it. Memories were not turning Winter into May like one of my favorite poems promised. Instead, I was in the "winter of discontent." I could see there were two distinct sides to me: the Irene who loved freedom and alone time, and the Irene who wanted to be all curled up in the coziness of marriage and family. I was glad I had put down the Erich Fromm book; he would have likely labeled me bipolar. Mercifully, God led me to more esoteric studies, which gave me the lens of astrology. I learned I have five planets in Gemini, the twins; that explained a lot, no wonder I related to both Narcissus and Goldmund.

I found a coupon in the back of a paperback book that offered the choice of any three books for ten dollars. I selected the ones on the I Ching, Palm Reading, and Reincarnation. When they arrived I flipped through them and decided I would study the *I Ching* first because the subtitle was *The Chinese book of Change*. It was change that my life seemed to be about and I wanted a little more guidance. The *I Ching* was fun. It was like Chinese fortune telling with pennies. You make patterns or hexagrams according to how the coins land when you throw them, heads and tails. I felt like Goldmund's gypsy mother when I bought a special cloth mandala to throw the coins on. The first hexagram I got was number sixty-three, which was called "After Completion." The layout was a broken line, then a solid, then a broken, and finally a solid line, all stacked up on top of each other; there were six of them in all. I didn't even need to read what the book said because the layout of solid and broken lines gave me a good picture of my relationship with Paul; broken, together, broken, together. I laid the book down and contemplated the hexagram. After we were broken, some emotional elastic band seemed to draw us together

Irene Isobel Carver

again, and then life broke us apart. The book said, "Good fortune at the start, disorder at the end." I closed the book and put it on my altar with the question, *How do you know when it's the end? When it feels like total disorder*, I thought. *Well, it felt like total disorder when Paul took off with Natalie, then that disorder settled into the solid-line configuration for awhile. Oh God, I'm going to make myself crazy.* I took my earl grey tea to my sunny kitchen as Bonnie Raitt played in the background.

Dancing is what I need, I counseled myself, so I called my pal Tim LaBlanc to see if he knew of any parties happening. "It just so happens there are a bunch of jocks throwing a party on Beacon Street Saturday night. I'll be happy to escort you if you want," Tim said, and I could tell he had a crush on me.

"No can do, dear, gotta work till ten, can I show up after that with a work friend?"

"Sure, it's 1155 Beacon Apt. 33; is your friend cute?"

"Not as cute as me!" I teased.

"Ya, but you're all taken," he said.

"Taken by who?"

"Irene, can't you even see it? You can't let go of Paul."

"Just watch me," I said and hung up startled to be so transparent.

On Saturday I brought a party outfit with me to work, ready to find out more about this illusive love thing. The elastic band of my emotions was now stretched far from Paul and I was relieved to be free of the emotional heaviness of his life.

I was twenty-three years old and my next illusion of love, Dickey Sweeney, was at the party that night, ready to teach me. I walked into the circular living room in the third floor apartment, with my royal blue beaded earrings dangling, right into his arms. He was a smooth dancer and an elegant gabber. When he told me he was a Gemini, I knew we were going to have a lot of fun together. He brought out the part of me that was my parent's daughter—the politician, the public relations manager—and we made a date for the following Friday as I kissed him goodnight on the corner of Beacon and Exeter Streets.

On Friday, Dickey showed up at my house carrying the book he was reading, *Hiroshima Mon Amour*. He asked if I would like him to read a bit of the book to me before we went out. So we sat and he read from this book about a love affair between a Japanese architect and a French actress in Hiroshima. What a smooth move that was on Dickey's part, for by page ten, we had our arms and legs wrapped around each other, making out on the couch. I loved the fit but tried to slow the pace a bit by asking him if he wanted some tea. Instead, he returned to his car for the bottle of white wine he had left there in a cooler. I was levitating in Dickey's presence. It was the exact opposite of being with Paul and his need not to think. Dickey wanted to philosophize about the book he was reading, about life, and about love. I could feel my mind expanding as he read, and I began to breathe more deeply than I had in years. His reading tone was oxygenating my soul. I was in love, or love's illusion, that is. Fortunately, I had already dropped Paulie off at his grandparents' house because Dickey and I never made it out that night. The sensually real photography in the book soon led us right upstairs to my bed and the intense love affair of the Tufts first-year law student and the married woman began.

Dickey woke up at my house on the morning of April

Irene Isobel Carver

first, walked up behind me and cradled me in his arms as I turned the calendar page to April. I had always loved the ceremony of changing to a new month. I shared with him how amazed I was that it had been exactly a year since Paul and I gave notice on our Clarendon Hill apartment. Dickey spun me around, all six feet of him, and his curly blonde hair, still wet from the shower, dripped on me as we kissed.

"One year, huh," he said coming up for air, "is that all; have you filed for a divorce yet?"

God, I didn't see that question coming and my only answer was a blunt, "No." "Well, speaking as a soon-to-be lawyer, my gut tells me it would be a wise move." He casually breathed the words into my neck that seemed to have no charge for him, but they were paralyzing me. I turned back to my calendar, and attempting to sound as casual as he did, I said, "Way too intense conversation for the morning." I held the next month's calendar page up and with a Scarlet O'Hara-like impertinence, I said, "I'll think about that in May."

Dickey was on a rugby team and on the third weekend in April, I drove with him and his sister to New York to a Saturday afternoon game. Late that night his sister drove us to Dickey's downtown apartment to drop him off, and I got out of the car with him. I could see the surprise on her face that she wasn't driving me back to my own house. The next morning Dickey was driving me home and telling me how he goes to his parents' house every Sunday for dinner and martinis. Suddenly he turned to me and said, "I think you should come with me; have a martini and meet my folks." I was speechless at the abruptness of his suggestion. I flashed on the wealthy people that I served at Rosario's. They were Larchmont's upper crust; many of them came in weekly and ordered martinis. The women were dressed in mink coats and most of them ordered the same thing every week—baked stuffed shrimp—and their husbands ordered prime rib. After the first martini, the phony politeness would disappear and they would start to bicker.

What if I recognize his parents? I thought, as I looked in the rear view mirror and checked my hair. Dickey looked over at me and while touching my hand with his he said, "Aw, come on, they'll love you, and I want them to meet you." I looked down at my jeans, they were clean, "I suppose I could pass a parent inspection," I said, "but I can't stay for dinner, just a drink and then you'll have to take me home. I only have a babysitter until one o'clock." That turned out to be one of the most terrifying decisions I had ever made. His house had a circular driveway and two lion statues at the front entrance. I thought for a second that a doorman would step up and open my door, and tension flooded over me. *Shit, why had I said yes?* I thought as I got out of the car.

Dickey shut off the engine, walked around the car, and opened my door. I had officially entered another world, and it wasn't going be a good one, I ruminated, as I walked up to the front door with Dickey holding my hand. Dickey's mother greeted us in the foyer. I didn't recognize her but I could see the surprise on her cosmetically-layered face when she saw me.

"Dickey, darling, you didn't tell me you were bringing a guest," she admonished.

"Sorry Mum, it was a last minute idea," Dickey said as he kissed her cheek. "We went to New York to a rugby game yesterday and I just thought I'd bring Irene up to meet you before I took her home."

"Well, lovely. Irene what?" she asked.

Irene Isobel Carver

"Irene Adams," I said as I held out my hand to shake hers.

Dickey looked over at me questioningly and I realized that I had automatically given my maiden name. I suppose I was subconsciously hoping that she would recognize my dad's name from politics and not judge me too harshly for coming unannounced. Dickey's sister entered through the door behind us and with an even more surprised look said, "Irene, hi, I didn't know I'd see you again so soon." She hung her coat on the large brass coat stand and continued into the kitchen. I heard her say rather loudly, "Quick, a martini, Berta, this is going to be uncomfortable." Dickey and I joined his sister in the kitchen and I watched as their maid poured several drinks from a pitcher into identical stemmed glasses. Everyone stabbed an olive and then walked in unison to the black leather couches in the living room, which were arranged around the fireplace. As soon as we sat down, the questions began.

"So, Irene, what college are you going to?" asked his mother. Dickey tossed down his entire drink and answered for me, "Boston State," he blurted and stopped in his lie. We both immediately knew this had been a bad idea. So I spoke up and said, "I was at Boston State College, actually, a while back. When my boy friend came home from Vietnam, I got pregnant," I could feel my shame as I lowered my eyes and said, "so I had to drop out of school." I wanted to drain my martini glass, but I knew I didn't want to be part of this class status conversation, so I said "Yes, Mrs. Sweeney, I have a four-year-old son and now and I really must be going home. It was lovely to meet you. Dickey, could you give me a ride home please?" I stood, leaving my barely touched martini on the glass coffee table and walked back to the foyer. I stood staring at the marble floors as I waited for Dickey to join me.

Dickey sped down the driveway while I sat in stunned silence; there were absolutely no words to convey how I felt, and if there were, I wasn't about to share them. When Friday rolled around and Dickey hadn't called, I decided to mail him a card. I wanted him to know I wasn't mad at him for putting me in such an embarrassing situation. *Live and learn*, I thought, but he never responded to my card.

I felt broken-hearted and I needed someone to talk to about the situation, so I called Clare to get her perspective on the situation and she very quickly gave me her analysis. She said his parents obviously convinced Dickey I was a very bad risk, that girls like me would try to trap him by getting pregnant because he was such a good catch, becoming a lawyer and all. They most likely convinced him I would trick him and he would have to drop out of law school. I was utterly amazed at how insightful Clare was. What she said made perfect sense. I hung up the phone and paced around the house ranting. *Fine preparation for becoming a lawyer, Dickey; you are cutthroat and cold. Well, Mr. Lawyer Prick, you didn't even have the courage to be honest with me, you slithered away like a worm. Guess lawyers aren't exactly known for honesty, anyway; you're probably going to be a good one.* I was steaming mad. The situation struck me as so wrong. So I got out the Ajax and began to scrub the tub and from there I went to the kitchen sink. Finally, I sat down exhausted and lit a joint, I needed a perception shift and this always did it.

When I woke up the next morning, my anger was replaced with sadness. I made a pot of tea and stood staring at April on my calendar. "I guess I don't have to think about divorce," I said to the beautiful picture of apple blossoms on a country road, and I found myself wondering what Paul

Irene Isobel Carver

was doing just then. I took my tea to the backyard and sat in the morning sun, understanding that Dickey had chosen his family over me. With that thought came the memory of how my father had wanted me to go to Trinity College in Ireland. If I had followed my father's desires, people like the Sweeneys would have probably approved of me. I looked up through pools of tears in my eyes at the sun flickering through the leaves on the sycamore tree and contemplated the martini-drinking phoniness of those types of people. I told myself that I valued honest communication more than status and that I would be a little bit more careful about giving my heart away in the future. I put on a Joni Mitchell album and lay on the floor, relating to her music; I did know something more about love and its illusions. I was sad but I was okay. I was in the game and learning how to play it, I pep-talked myself.

A few weeks later I saw Dickey at a party. He started to walk over to me with a drink in his hand and a big grin on his face, but I turned away and walked over to another crowd of people, avoiding eye contact completely. He was a phony, that I knew, and I had already busted though the illusion of status years ago. I was going forward not backward; I didn't want to waste another minute on him. Before the night's end, I danced a long and deep dance to Grace Slick's "White Rabbit" with a cool and genuine guy whom I sat with on the couch afterwards. He told me about the book he was reading. It was the next book that would change my life, *Autobiography Of A Yogi,* by the East Indian guru, Paramahansa Yogananda. April had proved after all to be the "cruelest month," but that cruelty helped me to grow. May arrived with crocuses and daffodils. The arrival of spring helped everything, especially my jilted heart.

Paulie's fourth birthday was on the twentieth of May and I had not heard a word from Paul in four months, which was sad for me. Dora, Ed, and I had a silent pack; none of us mentioned Paul, it was just too painful to acknowledge our helplessness. When I asked Paulie what he wanted for his birthday, he said, "A big pack of G.I. Joe men, all of them." I winced at the thought of allowing my little boy to play at war. It seemed to me that playing war could be part of the problem with our world. "Is there anything else you can think of that you would like?" I asked. He shook his head no, and handed me his superman cape to tie around his neck. I noticed how golden brown his eyes were as I knelt to his level to tie the cape. I kissed his soft, freckled cheek, and my little superman turned and flew out the door to ride his Big Wheels. I would be twenty-four in July. As I watched Paulie run outside to play, I wished that my parents could give me a gift that would give that same kind of joy.

May first was a lovely spring morning. I took my *Be Here Now* book and sat on the front stoop to be with Paulie while he zoomed up and down our alleyway practicing spins in the loose gravel at the corner of the street. His lips would automatically flutter making the sounds of car engines and mufflers that boys seemed to be born knowing how to do. I browsed through the book and stopped at a big picture of a butterfly. Around the picture, Ram Dass explained in words how first the butterfly is a caterpillar and how he has to live in his caterpillar-ness, not longing to be a butterfly or even knowing that he will be a butterfly, but is just content to be a caterpillar. I felt the tension between my shoulders relax. I smiled at Paulie as he skidded up to me, and I thought, *just be a caterpillar Irene, and hopefully, on your birthday you'll land on a luscious green leaf somewhere.*

Irene Isobel Carver

May and June proved to be a tranquil cocoon for my heart. Between waitressing shifts, I dug up a four-foot by four-foot plot of earth in the backyard, and planted my very first vegetable garden. I put in four small tomato plants and next to them planted three rows of corn. The package said to plant three rows of corn in order for them to pollinate, so that took up the whole garden. It was a good start.

Chapter Sixteen

Becoming A Butterfly

MY LUSCIOUS GREEN LEAF TURNED OUT TO BE A CLUB on Cape Cod called the Abtrex. My pal Tim called and invited me to drive down with him on July third and camp, because the band Seatrain was playing and they were getting rave reviews in *The Phoenix* newspaper in Boston. I asked my boss for the time off since it was my birthday, and of course Dora and Ed said they would love to have Paulie stay with them.

What an amazing twenty-fourth birthday I had! Tim gave me a Quaalude as a gift and he and I went on a magically high experience like no other. Where acid took your mind on a multidimensional trip, Quaaludes took your body on a sensually ecstatic journey. As we danced to the bluesy ecstatic music of Seatrain, my body felt like it became each individual instrument. There was a woman dancing on stage with the band and I felt sure she had taken a Quaalude too; either that or she was naturally free, and I knew that that would be my new goal. I burst out laughing at one point and said to Tim, "To be or not to be this eternally stoned is actually the question that Shakespeare forgot to finish."

Our campsite was on the ocean and after the concert we went for a moonlight swim. It was a good thing there was a roped-in area, because I was so high that I just wanted to swim out and become one with the ocean itself. Tim told me he had heard Quaaludes were actually horse tranquilizers. "Wow," I said, "horses are lucky if they get these after a race or before an operation." As I spread out my sleeping bag Tim hushed my words with a kiss on the lips. We both stepped back appalled; we felt like we were kissing a sibling, not a lover, and we collapsed in a puddle of laughter together without having to say a single word. There seemed to be a form of Quaalude telepathy between us and we were forever grateful for that. We held hands as we fell asleep and I said, "We're just a couple of caterpillars; thanks for helping me find my perfect birthday leaf." Tim squeezed my hand and began snoring.

Autobiography Of A Yogi was my next class in caterpillar-ness. It was through this book I learned to meditate and to chant the word AUM. The author, Paramahansa Yogananda, taught that Aum is the sound of the Holy Ghost, the invisible divine power that upholds all creation through vibration. I was immediately enthralled. It felt like a divine connection that a Yogi from India spoke of the same Holy Ghost I had been taught of in the Catholic Church in Bridgetown, Massachusetts. In fact, Yogananda quoted the Bible throughout his book, comparing verses to the Eastern texts. This made it easy for me to extend my spiritual thinking to include chanting. When Teresa saw me reading the book, she asked me questions and a few days later she came home with a blue crushed velvet Indian print mandala for our coffee table. It was soon moved to a corner table and turned into an altar where only holy objects were allowed. Each night after Paulie was asleep, I would light a candle and incense and call on the "Blissful Comforter," as Yogananda called the Holy Spirit. Just saying the words

"Blissful Comforter" calmed me. I found myself praying for Paul and wondering where he could be and why he didn't call us.

It was now six months since we returned from the Virgin Islands and I felt like a different person in many ways. Between public assistance, waitressing, and having Teresa as a roommate, I was able to pay all my own bills. I was grateful for this but the more I meditated, the more I became aware of a deep place in me that was afraid, and no matter the length of time apart, I still felt connected to Paul and his pain. One stifling hot August morning when the humidity was dense by 10:00 a.m., I reminisced about an August camping trip with Paul to Franconia Notch, New Hampshire, and how the cool mountain air had felt. Suddenly I was angry and began to pace the kitchen talking out loud to no one, "What the hell happened to my life, to my family, where is Paul?" Tension rushed through me and horrible thoughts burst into my brain. I was filled with rage and I yelled out loud to no one, "Fucking war, fuck the government," and then I stopped myself; it was as if a hand touched my shoulder and I knew just what to do. *It's August,* I told myself, *I will drive up Rt. 2 to Concord. The farm stands that line the highway will all be open and filled with the summer's harvest. The lush countryside always fills my spirit.* I took a deep breath and relaxed. Driving always made me feel so free. I coaxed Paulie off his big wheels and told him we were going to the country to buy corn on the cob for everyone. "Everyone in the world?" he so innocently asked. "Everyone we love," I told him as I hurried him into the backseat of our Toyota. With windows open, hot air blowing my hair all around, and the radio blasting, I called over my shoulder to Paulie, "Look at the crows, Paulie, they are following us," and I pointed out of my window to the sky. Then I burst into song, already feeling the freedom I craved. "The corn is as high as an elephant's eye," I sang at the top of my lungs, "and it looks like it's growing clear up to the sky." Over and over I sang 'till Paulie chimed in.

I pulled in to the first farm stand we came to. There was a wheelbarrow full of corn with a sign that said "Ten ears for one dollar." I pulled back the husks on a few to check for rot and then said to Paulie, "How many people do you think we love?" "Two hundred million," he answered as he tried to pull back a husk also. I took his little hand and led him to a huge oak tree where we sat down in the shade and counted our people. We looked around the tree for some small rocks and sticks to count with. I listed all the aunts, all the uncles, grandparents, and then Paulie said, "And daddy, too, don't forget." Immediately, sadness engulfed me as I realized that was exactly what I was trying to do, to forget.

We cruised home more slowly on the back roads that were lined with stone walls and pastures with horses. Our bag containing thirty ears of corn was on the seat next to Paulie. I allowed tranquility to overpower the pain in my heart. Once again I had been saved from the harshness of life by its beauty, its gifts, and my little son. When I pulled into our driveway, my friend, Danny, was sitting on our stoop. He stood up and blurted out, "Fucking Nixon, man. While we have people trying to negotiate for peace in Paris, he is now dropping fucking bombs on Laos!" "Danny, don't start. I just bought thirty ears of corn to block this existential rage that is erupting and I just can't do it." I spoke emphatically as I walked into the house with my brown bag overflowing. "Under my altar; go help yourself," I said, nodding in the direction of my pot stash. Ten minutes later

Danny walked into the kitchen smiling. "Thank God for the holy herb. You know what I'm gonna do?" he rambled on, "I'm gonna drive up to New Hampshire and volunteer to help in the McGovern campaign." "Yeah, I'd go with you, except I've got to stay home and work and all," I said buttering and salting an enormous ear of corn. "McGovern's whole platform is about ending the war and he says the second he wins he's pulling out all the troops." Danny joined me at buttering corn.

"You got The Band, *Music From Big Pink* album?" he asked as he went for his second ear.

"No, Paul took that one. I'll put on Blind Faith," I said. I went into the living room, calling over my shoulder, "I'll put on 'Sea of Joy.' We need a sea of joy today." I put the needle down on the record and picked up the joint where Danny had left it, determined not to let the world bring me down.

REALITY SUCKS

Instead of a sea of joy we got a tidal wave of trauma. In September, Arab guerillas stormed the Olympics in Munich, killing two Israelis and taking ten hostages. I never knew why. I hated listening to the news; the headlines were enough to make me want to escape reality out of self-preservation.

In November the Presidential elections took place and Richard Nixon won the Presidency in a fucking landslide. Those of us who so desperately wanted an end to the Vietnam War were crushed and heartbroken. Our collective loss of hope was horrifying. It was pretty cool that our state of Massachusetts was the only state out of all fifty with a majority voting for McGovern, but it did nothing to help towards our goal of ending the war. It mattered little really;

it wasn't a matter of pride, as we were begging for peace.

The following Sunday, I abruptly sat up in bed at 7:00 a.m. The morning sky beckoned me. Teresa and Paulie were fast asleep, so I quickly put on jeans and a sweatshirt and began walking into the angelically painted sunrise. Cat Steven's song, "Morning Has Broken," began to ripple through my mind and I felt my first moment of hope since the elections. I wished I had brought a camera with me as I stopped to admire a white-steepled church with the heavenly colored sky as a backdrop. I looked at the bulletin board in front of the church, which said:

Sunday Sermon: Fear God

I turned away from those words and began walking briskly towards Waverly Oaks. Those words, "Fear God," made the world seem colder. *Why would I fear God?* I asked myself as I walked. *Why would ministers want to tell us to fear God when they also teach that God is good, God is love; it just seems so contradictory.* I pulled the strings on my sweatshirt a little tighter around my neck. As I walked I remembered what I was taught in Catechism classes. Yes, the Old Testament was full of fear and a vengeful God. But wasn't that why Jesus came to earth. He came to teach us to put all that aside and to love one another as he had loved us, and to pray to our loving father in heaven to help us.

I headed to Andros' Diner for a warm cup of coffee. As I swung open the door to the diner, I had the thought, *Why is a Christian minister still preaching fear?* A waitress stood behind the front counter with her ordering pad. She just held her pad, poised to write, not saying a word. I suppose she had to conserve her words for the long day ahead, so I followed her mode and said flatly, "Large coffee, regular, to go." Then, I felt my caterpillar-ness tickling me, so I smiled and said, "I'm so glad you are open early, thanks, you made my day." She snapped a lid on my coffee cup and took my crumpled up dollar. "Keep the change," I said, and this time she smiled back at me, putting the fifty-five cent tip in her apron pocket.

It's not good to be so serious, I mused, as I sipped my coffee and walked down to the bridge that crossed over Beaver Creek. I leaned over the bridge and stared into the shallow water. *Be still and know that I am God*, I thought. Then I felt a nervous spot in my stomach and I recognized it was fear. I sat at a picnic table with my coffee and dissected the feeling. I concluded that I wasn't feeling fear of God; I was feeling fear of man. Some children ran across the bridge; the world was waking up, it wasn't all mine anymore, so I headed home. When I got close to the deceivingly cute church, I crossed the street. I didn't want to be near any of their "fear thoughts." Yet, I stood transfixed and watched as cars pulled into the church parking lot. They were all the cars that we hippies called "American pig cars"—those gas-guzzling Cadillacs and Chryslers, the cars of the establishment. I watched ladies in fur stoles being escorted into the church by their husbands who were wearing suits. I became tearful as I realized they were the people who voted for Nixon; those who chose to keep the war going, and now they were here to listen to a sermon on fear. *Is it fear that keeps the war going?* I wondered, looking at the sky. *It's the capitalists protecting their money* was my inner response.

I remembered the story of Jesus walking into the temple and turning over the tables of the moneylenders. I felt angry, and a part of me wanted to run through their church ranting, "How dare you bomb our brothers and sisters in Vietnam," but the rest of me just blinked back tears and headed home to my people, now fully knowing what FDR meant by his statement, "The only thing we have to fear is fear itself."

DON'T LET IT BRING YOU DOWN, IT'S ONLY CASTLES BURNING—*Neil Young*

I was determined not to let the painful politics of America bring me down. I couldn't join Abbie Hoffman and be a revolutionary, but I could keep myself from being squashed by the heaviness of reality. So I sat in the sun on a Saturday morning reading the *Real Paper*, a local alternative publication, when I saw an ad for a concert. Bonnie Raitt was going to be at the Harvard Square Theatre. I ran upstairs excitedly and woke Teresa up and told her I was going down to the Square to buy us tickets to the concert. "Okay, I'll stay here with Paulie; how much are they?" she asked sitting up. "Doesn't matter, my treat," I said, thrilled to have a babysitter and a fun plan to look forward to. I had Bonnie's album, *Give it Up*, and I loved it; she sang to a woman's heart, she was one of us.

The night of the concert, Teresa and I spent some time getting as cute as possible, which was actually quite easy in those days. All a girl needed was a pair of bell-bottoms, a cute top, and—for me—my beaded choker. We could pull all that off stoned, which was the real requirement. We stood side-by-side at the bathroom mirror lining our eyes with a jet-black pencil. We each chose an eye shadow. Mine was a yellow/mustard and Teresa's was green, of course, to accent her gorgeous green eyes. Bonnie was serenading us in the background and then, as always, Teresa and I turned to each other for an inspection. We pinched each other's cheeks to bring the blush to the surface, like our mother had taught us. We laughed at ourselves as we relit the joint that had gone out in the ashtray. We were so happy that the concert was right in Harvard Square; that meant we would only need to take one bus and have no worries about parking. I stared out the trolley window from under my adorned, stoned eyes at the maple leaves that were in their last days of beauty. We were silent as the trolley clattered along on the old metal tracks while the anticipation of going to a live concert welled up inside me. We were unaware that the universe was about to deliver us an unexpected gift.

The concert was open seating in an old and lovely theatre, with chandeliers hanging from the ceiling, and velvet-lined balcony coves. I imagined Bonnie chose this venue because it was small enough to be intimate but large enough for a performer who was rapidly becoming well known. As we all got settled in our seats, the emcee came on stage and announced there would be an opening band from New Jersey and would we please welcome **Bruce Springsteen And The E Street Band.** After about three chords, the entire audience jumped to their feet and started dancing, and we never once sat down. The experience was so unexpected that it held a mystery all its own. It was like the birthday gift you never got but always wished for; it mended a shattered dream or two, and if you were still pining over missing Woodstock, it erased that longing. I think only New Jersey knew of their hometown boy until that night in Cambridge, when Bruce Springsteen was forever put on the world stage.

Poor Bonnie Raitt! She had to walk onto a stage that was on fire and we knew she wasn't sure she could pull it off when she came on and said, "Oh, my God, how do you follow that?" She did, though, because we had all come to hear her and most of us knew all the words to her songs. She sang her heartfelt blues and rocked our souls and soon the crowd was yelling, "We love you, Bonnie," and her amazing gift of music and love continued till after midnight. I wish someone could have videotaped the busses and subways of Boston that night. On our trolley the party just kept going. There was absolutely no putting a lid on the energy that was pouring out from everyone who had been to the concert. Joints were lit the second we hit the street and no one even thought about the police. We knew we were elevated way beyond their vibration and if they *could* see us, our energy would have turned them right away. We were electric!

The next week was Thanksgiving, and when I asked Teresa if she was going to come to the Larchmont/ Bridgetown football game with me she said, "Hell no; I would run into that jerk Greg, with his new girlfriend." I could feel how Teresa was still suffering from his rejection. "Well, maybe we'll both run into some new guys to flirt with," I optimistically answered. "Screw men, I don't trust a damn one of them," Teresa said. Her pain was obvious and she wasn't about to let me cheer her up. After the Thanksgiving morning football game, all seven of us kids converged in our family home for the traditional turkey dinner. Our mother coaxed us into expressing what we were grateful for that year. Teresa stood and as she left the table, she quoted the movie *Bambi* saying, "If you can't say something nice, don't say anything at all." I chimed in quickly so no one would have a chance to comment, and said, "I am grateful to have a house of my own." And then I reflected privately, that I was grateful to have a door to shut behind me so I could weep in privacy. I knew my privacy was a gift but I wasn't about to admit out loud that I was still so sad.

December brought more sadness; I could feel I was

starting to lose Teresa, my Tee, my little sister by three years, my friend and roommate. I had known since our time in the Virgin Islands that she was taking sleeping pills, but I had no idea how much of a hold they had on her, until the day I came home from grocery shopping and she began to help me put the food away. I watched in disbelief as she put the milk in the canned goods cabinet. I grabbed her hand and turned to look into her eyes. Her lids were heavy and she looked at me as if from a great distance and said, "I'm just tired, Renie, don't make a big deal of it." But it was a big deal. We stood looking at each other and she was caught, not by me, but by reality. I took the milk from her hand and put it in the refrigerator and then, robotically, we put the rest of the groceries away in silence. There were no words for our sorrow.

Two nights later, after her swing shift at the nursing home, Teresa came speeding down our driveway and slammed her car door. I was sitting in the living room reading an Ayn Rand book when Teresa threw her purse on the floor and said to me, "What the hell do they care if some of their precious pills are taken? They don't even bother to count them, and they give them out like candy to all the old people, keeping them numbed out." When she stopped for a breath and hung her coat in the hall closet I said, "What the hell happened?" "Got a joint?" she asked, implying that the story could not be told without some form of medication. I put my book on the floor, reached under the altar, and pulled out the wicker tray that held my baggie of pot, rolling papers, and matches. Teresa's hands were shaking as she tried to put the pot into the thin paper, so I took it from her and quickly handed her a loosely rolled joint. "Here," I said, "tell me what is going on." She

Irene Isobel Carver

lit the end, sucked in deeply, and on the exhale said, "I got caught taking Valium pills tonight. I got suspended from my job. Oh fuck, this is the worst, this is no fucking joke; I could lose my nursing license for this." She let her head fall between her crossed legs and I scooted over next to her and began to rub her spine.

"How many pills did you have when you got caught?" I asked trying to stay calm.

"Man, what a jerk I am, I was thinking that the weekend was coming up and I should grab a handful, and just as I put them in my pocket, Nurse, fucking, Ratchet comes around the corner and catches me red handed." Teresa rolled onto her side crying, "I can't believe I was so careless."

"Had you already taken any pills during your shift?" I carefully asked still rubbing her back. She continued to cry as she nodded yes.

"Tee, don't freak out, Gwen just told me the other day about a rehab in Brighton that is helping people get clean from all kinds of drugs."

"Don't freak out; you must be kidding. I can't lose my nursing license. That is who I am; if I'm not a nurse, I'm nothing. Plus, I need those damn pills to get to sleep. I'll be up all night pacing the house; I can't bear this shit anymore," Teresa sat up and blew her nose into the tee shirt I handed her.

"Tee, this is what rehab is for. They have counselors who will help you deal with why you need pills. I love you Teresa, and I don't love you 'cause you're a nurse, I love you 'cause you dance to Rod Stewart with me and 'cause I... I need you. I miss you Teresa, when you are on those pills it feels like you're gone and I want you back." I lay down next to her and as I cried, she began to rub my back.

Rehab

We tried the next day to get Teresa into rehab but nothing was available for six days so she was still at home with me. That first night without medication, I found her sitting in our living room at 3 a.m., biting her fingernails. I sat down next to her and gently pulled her hand from her mouth and held it in mine. As I stroked open her hand I saw that she barely had any nails to bite. "What are you thinking?" I asked, as I rubbed her hand and put pressure in the middle of her palm rubbing deeply.

"I am thinking I am completely fucked," was her answer.

"Hold on," I said as I went to get my Palmistry book from the shelf. "Let's just see what a palm reading will say about how fucked you are," I said, hoping to make us both laugh. I turned to a page that had a picture of the palm and searched for the "lifeline." I had no idea what I was doing or seeing, but I said, "Well, too bad Tee, you're not getting out of this early or anything, you have a very long lifeline, so buck the fuck up."

"Oh, yeah, I have some Nyquil in the bathroom, want to try that?" I said.

"Get it, I'll try anything," she said as she pulled her hand from mine. I tiptoed upstairs not wanting to wake Paulie; I needed to be alone with Teresa right now. When I handed her the bottle of Nyquil, which was three-quarters full, she guzzled the bottle of sticky, green liquid. She calmly handed me the empty bottle and when she saw my mouth hanging open, she said, "What, don't worry; I've drunk whole bottles of that before, it's not dangerous." The Nyquil worked and she was asleep on the couch in minutes. I covered her with an afghan and sat down on the floor next to her. I wanted to cry but I was afraid to let my guard down and I was afraid to wake Teresa up. I pushed myself up from the floor, straightening my spine. I could feel the Macalister in my cells, and the Scottish side of my genetic pool saying, *Renie, it's going to be a long haul; it's no time to be Irish.*

Teresa had only been in rehab for ten days when she showed up at my door with Charley Duffy. I was mashing bananas to make bread for a Christmas party I was invited to, when they came swooping into my kitchen like a flash of fire. "Renie, this is Charley Duffy. We were in rehab together, which is bullshit by the way. We don't need to be locked up with a million restrictions. We just need to get the hell out of this town and away from all the old haunts; get a new lease on life, so we're going to Florida for the winter."

Teresa rummaged through her box of clothes she had stored underneath her kitchen bed, while Charley leaned against the kitchen counter and kept pushing his long, straight, dark hair behind his ears; a nervous habit.

"Charlie, what drug were you in rehab to kick?" I was trying to slow down Teresa's frantic pace. "Just Jack Daniels, but I don't need that shit anymore now that I found Teresa." Teresa stopped rolling up tee shirts to go over and kiss him on the lips and she turned to me and asked, "So where are the keys to my car?" Her eyes darted around the kitchen counter looking paranoid that I might try to stop her. "They're over there on a hook by the fridge. I got sick of looking for keys so I made an official spot," I said trying to sound calm and casual as my thoughts raced; I didn't want them to run away and be on the lam.

"So do you have any gas money?" I asked

"I've got some bread stashed at my parents' house," Charley answered, still fiddling with his hair. Then Teresa tossed her backpack over one shoulder, kissed me on the cheek, and whispered in my ear, "Don't worry, Renie, we're going to be good together." I walked them out to the driveway and stood there in the wake of their escape as their two brown heads came together in a kiss and the yellow VW bug disappeared.

I walked back into the kitchen, measured a cup of sugar, and told myself not to worry; at least Teresa had been off drugs for two weeks and it did look like they really cared for each other. Apparently, I hadn't convinced my heart of Teresa's safety, for as soon as I put the banana bread in the oven and set the timer, I went straight to my altar and picked up my rosaries; I needed help and I wasn't ready to call my mother and tell her this tough news. My mother and I had been saying a Novena of Rosaries for Teresa, and our hopes were high that rehab was going to cure her, but disappointment was back, making hope a harder job.

It was the week before Christmas and in an attempt to quell my anxiety over Teresa's whereabouts, I retreated to the sanctuary of my kitchen to make lasagna. I found myself layering noodles and ricotta with anxiety; it wasn't working but I was committed to the project. The winter sun flooded my kitchen, which helped my mood, so I kept making the lasagna, trying to figure out what had happened to Teresa to get her so dependent on pills in the first place.

As I grated Parmesan cheese, I flashed back in time. Just before we left for the Virgin Islands, Teresa's boyfriend, Greg, had suddenly broken up with her. I figured that was where it started. *Why did she take it so hard? He was a good guy and all but he could be so serious.* I layered tomato sauce with astrology, remembering what my book said about Libras doing best when in a partnership. *So Teresa, being a Libra, would need a man more than some other sign would, I surmised.* I recalled how Teresa and I had joined The Women's Liberation Movement early on by getting on birth control pills when they became available. I thought about the weeks following her breakup with Greg and I recalled her being happy she had met a cute blonde guy at Fathers II, a local club. She didn't come home the night and she waited for the phone to ring all that week hoping, he would call. When he didn't call, she looked so rejected. This scenario happened a few more times to her. I abruptly slapped my wooden ladle on the counter and became angry as I thought, "*This is the downside to the 'free love' thing.*" It felt like a huge Aha. The problem was Teresa was looking for love and the birth control pill was giving *free sex* to us, not *free love.* I wrapped tin foil over the top of the lasagna, feeling relieved that I figured out what I thought happened to Teresa. She got caught in the downside of a changing world and her self-esteem took a serious blow. I concluded that because Teresa was a nurse, she was able to get the pills that blocked her pain, which led to her emotional collapse. I wiped my hands on my apron and with a deep breath I told myself that I could now call my mother.

Two days later the doorbell rang at 9:00 p.m. My heart fell to the ground when I opened the door and saw Paul standing there with a large box, gift wrapped for Christmas. His strawberry blonde hair was dirty and scraggly. I stepped backwards making room for him to enter as he said, "This is for Paulie for Christmas." "Paulie has already gone to bed," I said, feeling like I was looking at a ghost. I was shocked; it had been almost a year since I had seen Paul and his face looked gaunt. He walked into the living room and placed the gift under the tree and then sat down on the couch. "Let me have your coat," I said and reached out as he handed it to me. "It's late, why don't you sleep in Teresa's bed in the kitchen; she is in Florida right now. You can give Paulie his gift in the morning?" This was my automatic response of compassion as I looked at the weariness in the face of my friend. I was surprised I could actually feel my heartstrings being pulled.

"Sure, I'll stay. I'm beat from riding the bus and all," he said as he took off his shoes.

"So, would you like some lasagna?" I asked, beginning to relax enough to breathe normally.

"Yeah, I would, but do you think I could take a shower first?" He didn't look at me.

"God, yeah, sure; I'll put out a pair of sweats and a tee shirt with a towel for you," I jumped into action. Paul reached out and pulled me to his chest. My heart began to weep before my eyes did, and then I let myself collapse into his slight chest. A year's worth of tears flowed out of me. When I finally pushed myself out of his embrace, I was embarrassed and felt as fragile as he looked.

The next morning when Paulie woke up and saw his father asleep in the kitchen, he came into my bedroom, shaking me and saying, "Mum, come quick, I think Santa Claus brought daddy here." I was instantly alert and frightened. I hopped in the shower and lectured myself. *Irene, don't let him near you. Those strings to your heart are dangerous, cut them now, quick. Remember, he left you for some chick from Gloucester. God knows what he's been doing for eleven months. Do not let him hug you; you will just turn to mush again. STOP IT, RENIE!*

Irene Isobel Carver

When I got downstairs, Paul was up and dressed and Paulie had already opened his gift. It was a plastic boxing ring with two muscle-bound men that you could move with levers and they would punch each other. There they were, two boys being boys, and I felt the well-worn patterns of my soul resting for just a moment in another time—a time that didn't exist anymore—and I stiffened. Not wanting to show my reserve, for Paulie's sake, I said, "Who wants pancakes?" They both raised their hands in unison and I tried to shake off the comfort zone of that vision. *It is not real,* I told myself as I cracked eggs into the Aunt Jemima mix.

When I called them into the kitchen to eat, I went to the living room and put on Crosby, Stills, Nash and Young's *Déjà Vu* album. The words to "Teach Your Children" became altogether too real for me—"Their father's hell will slowly go by." I poured maple syrup on my cakes as I looked up at Paul to see if he had heard those words and I could tell that he had when he looked me in the eyes and said, "The War is still going on, Irene." Then he seemed to look deeper at me as if I was a traitor. "That's what's wrong with this whole fucking country," he said as he stood up from the table.

"Paulie, why don't you go to your room and get your new Speed Racer car to show dad," I said, and Paulie ran excitedly from the room. Paul continued talking. "Just because I'm home—one person's son—doesn't mean we should all just forget and go on with life. Someone just had their fucking leg blown off Irene and why? What the fuck for? The fucking government is evil." Exhausted, he sat down on the kitchen bed where he had slept and put his head between his hands like he was trying to keep it from exploding. Paulie ran into the room with his race cars and began to line them up at his dad's feet. Paul reached down and tussled Paulie's hair and said, "Cool cars, man, I've gotta get going, don't ever forget I love you." Paulie held onto his dad's leg trying to keep him from walking, so Paul picked him up and hugging him deeply looked over Paulie's shoulder and mouthed to me, "take him please." I tickled Paulie to get him to let go and said, "We gotta go too, Paulie. Ed is waiting for you to come up and play cards." Paulie looked at his dad, and then let go of his grip, and wiggling down, he ran back to his room to get his backpack. He loved playing with his grandpa, so it was the perfect distraction. I followed Paulie upstairs and stood at the window, watching as Paul walked down my snow-covered driveway. I finished the words to the song on the record player, "Don't you ever ask them why, if they told you, you would cry . . ."

That night I was in a lot of pain as I felt the emotional ties from my heart to Paul's. After I read Paulie a bedtime story, I made myself a drink of hot buttered rum and put on Carol King's album. I sat on my living room rug remembering the I Ching patterns: broken, solid, broken, solid, and I knew I was craving some of the solid. Carol King sang "so far away, doesn't anybody stay in one place anymore," and I burst out crying. "Teresa, where are you? I need you." I yelled as I pulled an afghan around my shoulders. I lay back with a pillow under my head while Carol sang, "if I could only work this life out my way," and I let myself float into a rum-induced vision of Paul and me on a creek in the New Hampshire mountains with Paulie floating his toy men over the rocks. I felt like the water flowing around the boulders of life. I sat up and took the needle off the album. *Carol is even sadder than I am*, I thought. I turned on WBCN and they were playing a Christmas album by Roberta Flack, yeah, *Joy to the World*. I was open to getting sucked into that and I said to my walls, "Jesus, please, joy to my world would be for Teresa to come home."

Chapter Seventeen

1973

CHRISTMAS PASSED WITH MY WISH UNFULFILLED. Teresa never called and no mercy was shed on my heart. New Year's Eve arrived; it would become 1973 and I was grateful I would be waitressing to keep busy and a chance to make a pocketful of cash on this big-tip night. I had plans to go out after work with some of the other waitresses and staff.

I was also grateful for Dora and Ed's willingness to take care of Paulie for me; it was the biggest gift of those hard days of single parenting. Early in the afternoon on that bitter, cold December 31st day, I packed Paulie's overnight clothes and toys and drove him to his grandparents' house. I loved the freedom I felt as I walked back into my own house and put on a Creedence Clearwater album to rev up the New Year's energy as I prepared for my night out.

Christmas had been so depressing that I decided I definitely needed to be kissed and maybe I could end all the fantasies of Paul coming back to me again. *Forget it, Irene*, I would pep talk myself when my heartstrings were pulled by my old patterns. *Paul needs to numb out and forget and you need to stay awake and grow, now move on.* It was as if I was channeling my mother, but it felt right. At the restaurant, Antonio, the busboy, had been flirting with me for months now and I had been ignoring him. I had not

Irene Isobel Carver

been open to him, but now I was, and it was up to me to do the suggesting. So I set my strategy along with my eye shadow and tried not to see Teresa in my eyes as I kissed my reflection in the mirror.

When the restaurant closed, we all decided to go to Harvard Square to the The Far East restaurant, and let other people serve us. I loved going there. They had big tiki glasses filled with rum and vodka, lusciously disguised with juices and fruit. We knew we would quickly get in the New Year's spirit there. I chose my silver hoop earrings to wear out after work, and set my plan in motion to sit next to Antonio so I could initiate a New Year's toast, and hopefully slip in a kiss so I could see how it felt. Now all I had to do was pick the suggestive attire I would wear and I was ready for a new year. Clare had given me a choker for Christmas that was made with red and black beads. It would look great with my black scoop-neck sweater that hugged my breasts so well. *I will be irresistible*, I thought, as I put on the unaccustomed red lipstick just for New Year's.

The working hours flew by in a festive flow of shrimp, martini's, crème brule, and our overstuffed pockets full of twenty dollar tips. After we counted our loot and tipped out the busboys and bartenders, we quickly changed into our party clothes, with our free cocktail in hand from the manager. When I stepped into the kitchen looking lovely, Antonio stood waiting. He asked me if I would like to drive with him and he would take me back to my car after our night at The Far East restaurant. *So he had been strategizing also*, I thought. "Sounds great," I said. I ran through the bitter cold to my car to get my Janis Joplin eight-track tape to listen to on our way to the club, while Antonio warmed up his truck. We drove into 1973 with Janis wailing, "Take it, take another little piece of my heart." Antonio passed me a fat joint and I sucked the smoke deeply into my lungs, silently disagreeing with Janis, for I knew I would be protecting my heart from now on. By the time we reached Harvard Square, we were stoned enough to float right into "Summertime" with Janis, "where the livin' was easy," despite the tiny flakes of snow that were falling and beginning to coat the sidewalks before us.

Twelve of us ordered sweet and sour everything, including dishes that were on fire and drinks that looked like fine art. I got the preview kiss I had hoped for and the person who had made the most tips that night had to pay for the desserts. We sang in the New Year with great joy.

Antonio never took me back to my car. Instead, I woke up on New Year's Day in his bed with a Fu Manchu-faced tiki glass next to my purse. I sat up, partially recalling that I needed a souvenir from the night, and on the way out of the restaurant I had bought a glass. Waitresses always feel rich, at least for a little while. I looked at the clock; it was 11:30 a.m. I watched Antonio sleeping deeply in the fur of his own hairy chest and I remembered him saying, "Don't call me Tony, please, it's too American." And I responded, "That's different, most people coming to America want to be thought of as American," and he had answered me with, "I'm proud of my heritage, and actually I find Americans to be quite lazy." "Be careful," I warned, "I was born on the Fourth of July." I think that is what actually caused our energetic kissing to begin and I laughed at the memory as I hopped into his shower and tried to let more of the night unfold through my Mai Tai-clouded mind.

After I dressed again in my evening outfit, I began clamoring a bit on purpose in his kitchen making coffee, wanting

Irene Isobel Carver

him to wake up. It worked; we wrapped blankets around ourselves and sat on his upstairs porch in the morning sun and drank coffee in the silence of the New Year. "Would you like to go out to breakfast and then maybe to an afternoon movie?" he asked me as we finished our first cup. "Gee, I can't, my babysitters are expecting me at 2:00; they have plans for the day," I lied. I didn't really know why I wanted to go home, but I found myself in a hurry to get back to my own world; I guess so I could sift through all of this. I had hoped for a kiss, but I really hadn't expected to end up in bed with him so soon and I was feeling a little unsure. When Antonio dropped me off at my car and wanted to make a plan to see me again, I moved quickly out of his embrace saying, "I have a busy week with New Year's and all, I'll see you Thursday night at work."

As I drove myself home that first day of 1973, I recollected that Antonio's sign was Virgo, like Paul, but he was so very different. Everything he touched turned into money and that seemed to be what motivated him. Antonio was well off because he was a dog and cat breeder and he made a good profit from that. He made a lot of tips, saved his money, and invested in a three-story apartment house. He was a money-wise man. *Outside of smoking pot, he really wasn't a hippie*, I thought, *he was a capitalist with an American dream*, and I knew right away that he was way too straight for me. In one date, in one night, I could see I had a twisting, turning road ahead of me. It was like Cat Stevens sang, "I was on my way to find out," and even with all the dark, scary corners, I was into the adventure of it.

When I got to work on Thursday evening, there was a gift at my locker from Antonio. He bought me the Joni Mitchell album, *Lark*. Karen, who had the locker next to mine, saw me receive the album and said, "I thought you and Antonio would make a good match." When she saw my expression, she said, "What's the matter with you? Antonio is far out." "Yeah, you'd think I would be thrilled, but I don't want someone to be in love with me, it feels like a fence or something, and somehow I suddenly value my freedom more than anything." "Well, good luck telling him," Karen said, as we raced up the stairs to the kitchen.

Antonio was all over me at work that night, clearing all my tables first and carrying all my trays. It was overwhelming and scary for me and it actually made it easy for me to dump him fast and hard. After the restaurant closed for the night, I asked him to walk me out. I leaned against my car for support and as we breathed the frigid January air I said, "Antonio, thank you for the album, I love Joni Mitchell, and I am sorry if I led you on, but there is just no way I can have a boyfriend right now. I am majorly confused about Paul, in fact, we are still married, and I just need time to be alone and figure things out." I took a huge breath; it was such a relief getting that said. Then Antonio, being the very nice guy that he was said, "Well, okay, then, if you figure things out and you want to go to a concert or something, just give me a call," and he turned and walked to his car. I started my car and as the engine warmed, I stared at the night sky and thought, *You are an idiot, Irene, that man would probably buy you a house.* And the angels of 1973 said, So…

January 1973 was frigid for days on end. At its prettiest, icicles glistened in the morning sun on the eaves of houses, causing prisms of color on the frozen banks of snow; at its ugliest, the snow banks turned black from automobile exhaust, and old people feared leaving their houses, pic-

Irene Isobel Carver

turing broken hips and hospitals. I sat on my front stoop bundled up in a wool coat, scarf, and hat that tied under my chin while I chain-smoked Newport cigarettes. *Thank God for the sun*, I thought, as Paulie spun around me on his Big Wheels, with his superman cape tied over his snowsuit. He kept crashing into snow banks, trying to tip himself over. I kept going over the reasons I had pushed away Antonio. I was finally calming myself with the thought that pushing him away had been a byproduct of meditation and that inside I had a deep knowing that I just needed to be alone.

My next-door neighbor, Nancy, came out and sat down next to me. She gestured at my cigarettes and then helped herself to one, saying, "I used to scratch my head like that when I was having a nervous breakdown." I quickly folded my hands, not even aware that I had been scratching my head. I shifted the focus off of me by asking her when and why she had a nervous breakdown. She told me that right after her first child was born, her husband Larry began racing cars for sport. She was constantly scared he would crash, and she began to fall apart, crying all night long. After about a year of this, her doctor prescribed Valium and told Larry if he wanted his wife to recover he would need to quit racing, at least for a few years. "So he quit and my itchy head went away," she smiled confidently through her frozen cheeks. I sprung off the stoop and announced to Paulie that it was time to go in and have a peanut butter and jelly sandwich. I scooped up my little superman in my arms and promised him hot cocoa, too.

While stirring milk on the stove, I recalled that it was exactly one year since Paul, Teresa, Paulie, and I had flown to the warm Virgin Islands and how nice it had been to have all three of them with me. But now I was alone and there were three months of cold ahead; I thought I was probably having a nervous breakdown. Worst of all, I kept hoping that Paul would somehow become his old self again and come home to me. While spreading peanut butter and jelly on the bread I said to myself, *Irene, you are not having a nervous breakdown, if you were, your hands would be shaking right now*; I rationalized my position for sanity. We sat in our sunny kitchen, dunking our sandwiches is our cocoa, and I noticed my heart was racing. I almost scratched my head, but instead began to tap the tea cup with what would have been finger nails, except I had bitten them all off. *Your nerves are just jumpy, Irene*, I told myself silently, surrendering to the middle path. Paulie finished his sandwich and handed me his red cape to tie around his neck, transforming him back into a superhero; he had a driveway to defend, after all. I began pacing around the house chanting, "What do I do for jumpy nerves, what do I do for jumpy nerves?" I began climbing up and down the stairs, asking myself this question. It calmed me. *Exercise must be good for jumpy nerves*, I surmised, and threw on my jacket.

"Come on, super boy, we are going to the duck pond to watch the geese while we still have daylight and sunshine." He headed for the car and I stopped him saying, "No, lets walk; mummy needs some exercise." He gave me a little pout and then quickly spread out his arms and fake flew down the driveway. I zipped my coat up tight and wrapped my scarf three times around my neck; not so much to keep out the cold but as to keep my fear from leaking out. I didn't want anyone to know I was falling apart; I had to resemble the steady parent of a four year old. *I have to be strong for Paulie.* He was the ballast on my wobbly ship and I knew I wouldn't sink if I had him to keep bailing for. The cold air

Irene Isobel Carver

was stinging my pores but it was also alleviating some of my fear. I could feel the air cleansing my brain. I put Paulie on my back and walked even faster past the playground; I desperately needed to hike up the hill to the tranquil pond. When we reached the top of the hill, I placed Paulie down on the stone wall. Large geese immediately began to come over to us. "Did you bring the bread, mummy?" Paulie asked, reaching his mitten-covered hand out to me. "No, I forgot it, Paulie, I'm sorry; let's remind each other at home next time, okay?" I sounded rather together, and I wondered what stable adult was talking through me.

The geese lost interest in us when another family arrived with bread. Paulie and I picked up sticks from the nearby bushes and poked at the ice that lined the edges of the pond. I was glad it was winter; the cold seemed to settle my nerves. I think if it had been a humid summer day and all I was wearing was a tank top, I may have seeped into the mud along with the duck poop. The well-fed geese walked past us into the water, demonstrating that they knew exactly what they were doing. I so wanted to be a mother goose at that moment. They were the picture of peace and grace as they floated effortlessly around the patches of ice that had formed on the surface. The sun was beginning to set behind the thicket of maples while they swam in unison away from us and most likely towards their nests for the night. I realized that I should follow suit and get us home before dark as well. I lifted Paulie up onto the wall to walk as we headed down the hill and I ran my hand along the stones, hoping to absorb some strength. At the wall's end, I squatted so Paulie could hop on my back. I whinnied and galloped like a horse all the way home, keeping us both warm. When I got to our front door, I was reluctant to open it as if it was the door to my almost nervous breakdown. It was long nights of loneliness behind that door that I was afraid of, but I opened it anyway because my teapot was behind that door.

That week I made an important discovery. If Paulie and I had a snack about 4:00 p.m. and then went to the library until around 7:00 p.m., the rest of the night went by rather quickly. This helped me avoid the loneliness of the dinner hour and kept me away from my bottle of whiskey, which was starting to scare me. *The holidays are over,* I told myself, *no more excuses for hot buttered anything.* Plus, at the library I could research nervous breakdowns before I chewed off all the skin around my fingernails. On the very first night of my plan, as Paulie and I walked into the Bridgetown library, hand-in-hand, I glanced at the headlines on the newspapers stacked at the entrance: **Watergate Investigation Cracked Open.** I digested the reality of this news. *The whole world is screwed up,* I thought, *it's not just me. The President of our country who won by a fucking landslide is a liar and a cheat.* I shook my head and kept walking as I mumbled, "God help us all."

I looked around the children's reading room for another mother with a child; I longed for someone to talk to. I didn't see anyone, so I got Paulie situated with a few books and told him I would be right back; I wanted to go look for a book for me. I walked up to the reference desk and said to the white-haired librarian, "Hi, I am doing a term paper on health issues, do you know where I can find information on nervous breakdowns?" I stood, willing myself not to scratch my head as she said, "Yes, follow me, I will show you; it will be in the Psychology section," and she pointed to the sign above the rows of books. She gave me a tender smile and said, "Anything else, dear?" I shook my head no, and as I

Irene Isobel Carver

watched her walk back to her desk, I thought, *She knows; maybe she had once been a young mother like me and knows the difference a little human kindness can make.* These were the days when a cold shoulder or a smile could make or break my day and I vowed to always smile at people when I could. I opened a thick, hard-covered book and read:

Nervous Breakdowns:

Freudian Psychology says: it is a mental disorder, not of the spine. General public says: a snapping under extreme pressure.

Symptoms are: major depression, lack of interest or pleasure in almost all activities. May have acute psychotic break, thinking paranoid thoughts. Fatigue without physical exertion. Nervous system circuit overload.

I closed the book and marked the spot with my finger as I walked back to the children's section so I could read in more depth. But so far, this information comforted me; I did not feel this list described how I was feeling at all.

Paulie was sitting in a small rocker reading, *Roger and the Fox.* I noticed that I was feeling much less anxious than when we had first arrived. "Let's check out our books now, Paulie; I'm getting hungry, are you?" I watched when another woman with a small child left the room and I thought, *she's probably going home to cook dinner for her husband* and I batted back the tears forming in my eyes. "How about we don't go home, Paulie; let's go and get pizza instead," I said as we stood up with books in our arms. "Pizza, yeah, pizza," Paulie yelled and I hushed him quickly, teaching him about having a quiet library voice. I ordered tea with the pizza and held the cup close to my mouth, letting the steam warm my face. I remembered how when I was small and had a cold, my mother would put Vicks Vapor rub in a pan of boiling water and then put a towel over my head and have me breathe in the warm vapors. As I inhaled this memory with my tea, I felt my loneliness. I was not having a nervous breakdown, the steam said, I was not depressed, I was just lonely and I needed a friend.

A few nights later, God answered my prayer with a double-edged sword when my friend, Tim, stopped over unannounced. It was after nine o'clock, so I offered him a drink of hot buttered rum, observing that I was still allowing myself to be sucked into festive holiday drinking. I rationalized that because it was hot, it was actually medicinal and not just alcohol. I started to put on a record when Tim reached over and put his hand on my knee and said, "You know, it sucks to say this, Irene, but I just have to. I just drove through Central Square and I saw Paul on a corner panhandling," he blurted out. "I got really bad vibes and I felt so sad, I wanted to stop, but I just couldn't; I didn't know what I could say, so I came here instead." Tears filled my eyes instantly and I understood how he felt. It was hard carrying all that sadness alone; it had to be shared to be bearable sometimes. So I put my hand over his and said, "It's probably a good thing you told me so I won't sit around here playing the fool and hoping Paul will come home to me." "You're not a fool, Irene. We all want to believe that Paul is going to make it out of this shit, you just love the guy, that's all." Then we stood up and clinked our glasses together and drained them. We set down our empty glasses and shared a long, deep hug. "Sorry to be such a downer," he said as he looked me in the eyes at arm's length. "Well, it helps to know you're my friend, Tim," I said. "Winter, Spring, Summer, or Fall," he said, mimicking Carol King's song. "You mean, all I have to do is just call," I followed his lead and laughed through my tears, and we hugged again. As I walked him to the door we said in unison, "Yep, I'll be there, you've got a friend." I watched him drive away, like Teresa and Charlie had, and I chanted, "Call me Teresa, call me," as I went upstairs to run the bath water. I just needed something to spill all over me except bad news.

Clare called me on January 27th. As soon as I picked up the phone, she screamed into it, "Renie, President Nixon has signed the Peace Treaty in Paris. The Vietnam War has ended!" "Are you sure, Clare? Do you think we can really believe that lying prick Nixon?" I croaked, afraid to have hope. "It's bigger than Nixon; this is real, Renie, believe it. I gotta go, I gotta call daddy, I love you," and she hung up the phone. Paulie was napping and I was alone in my kitchen. My eyes filled with tears and my heart searched out Paul. "Where are you?" I said to the kitchen bed where he had slept. "I miss you, quick, come home. The war has ended, no more legs are being blown off." My hand reached for the phone. I wanted to call Dora and rejoice, but I couldn't. I felt crazy, my heart and head were exploding. I was rambling aloud, "Paul, call me. Have you heard the news? Where are you?" *No, don't call anyone.* I thought, *I can't talk to anyone. But I'll rehearse my lines in case Paul does call me.* I stood in an odd shocked stillness and then I just plain yelled, "THE FUCKING WAR IS OVER PAUL, WAKE UP, COME BACK, WE'LL START OVER," and I twirled around the kitchen. I scared myself when I slammed into the stove with my hip. *Wash the dishes, Irene,* I told myself, *that always calms you.* I filled the sink with soapy water and

I was scrubbing the inside of a tall glass when it broke and bit a chunk of flesh off the outside of my right thumb. Blood poured into the dishwater. I grabbed a dishcloth and dried my hands, surveying the cut. The flesh was just holding on by a thread so I placed it over the gouge where it belonged and held it tight to stop the bleeding.

No, I will not need stitches, I told myself as I ran upstairs for a bandaid. I held my hand under cold water and mused, *if Teresa were here, she would say I need stitches*. I looked at myself in the mirror and said harshly, "But she's not here, so three bandaids are just gonna have to do it." I held my thumb over my heart and the tears came flooding out. I knelt on the bathroom floor and wept.

The phone rang, startling me. I crawled into my bedroom and picked up the phone; it was my mother. "Renie, did you hear the news?" She asked. "Yeah, Clare called me. Do you think the war will really end this time, mum?" I asked, "God, let's hope so, let's hope so," she said, and I heard a tiredness in her voice I had never heard before. *We are all weary*, I thought and I knew she was worried about Teresa, too. It had been six weeks since she left for Florida, and there was still no word from her. I changed the subject and told my mother how Paulie and I had been enjoying the library these days. She followed suit and told me how she was thinking of running for Library Trustee in the upcoming election. After we hung up, I was glad she couldn't see me lying on the floor next to my bed, holding my thumb over my heart, curled up in a fetal position crying, "Teresa, I need you, come home."

I Felt Like Tinkerbell And No One Was Clapping

Irene Isobel Carver

February arrived and I still hadn't heard from Paul. The groundhog didn't see his shadow, and the first prisoners of war began to arrive home from Vietnam, but still I could not muster up a happy heart. When Chinese New Year arrived, I did a ceremony of cleaning my altar. I took everything off of it and one-by-one dusted and polished each item. I borrowed my mother's silver polish and shined the candle-holders that stood at each corner; no more wine bottles for this spot. I polished the hand-sized brass Buddha, rubbing his belly over and over, as I made a series of wishes and set intentions for the New Year. I used olive oil to polish my wooden incense holder and set a fresh stick of nag champa in the tiny hole. I held my copy of *Autobiography of a Yogi* and stared into the eyes of Yogananda on the cover. I opened to my favorite page and read aloud:

"Aum, the blissful comforter, who reveals to the devotee the ultimate truth." I held the book to my heart, "Ah, the *blissful comforter*," I whispered to myself, "that sounds so nice." Then I got the Windex and cleaned the glass frame around my favorite picture of Jesus. It was a bust of his head on raised white paper. I took it out of the frame and read the back. It read:

One Solitary Life

He was turned over to his enemies and went through the mockery of a trial. He was nailed to a cross between two thieves.

While he was dying his executioners gambled for his clothes

Two thousand years have come and gone and today he is the central figure of the human race. All the armies

that ever marched, all the navies that ever sailed, all
the parliaments that ever sat, all the kings that ever
reigned have not affected the life of man on this earth
as much as this one solitary life.

I clasped the image of Jesus to my heart and told him I
loved him and asked him to help me stay strong. I placed
the picture in the clean glass frame and shook out my blue
velvet mandala altar cloth at the back kitchen door. I surrendered all the prayers and pain of my twenty-four-year-
old heart. I looked up through the bare branches of my
sycamore tree and whispered to the winter sky, "Help me,
teach me, heal me."

"I Wish I Could Find A Good Book, To Live In" —*Melanie*

Help came to me in the form of the book *The Drifters*, by
James Michener. My mother stopped by my house one
afternoon and handed me the book. She said she had gone
to the library and asked the librarian what would be a good
winter read for a twenty-four-year-old. The librarian gave
her the Michener book. I looked at the picture on the back
cover. There were three young hippie kids smiling and
holding hands. I kissed my mother on the cheek and said,
"It looks good mum, thanks." That book saved my sanity.
The restaurant business slowed way down in the winter so
I was only working Thursday, Friday, and Saturday nights.
All those lonely winter evenings were now filled by living
vicariously through six young people who were traveling all
over Europe and Africa, from Spain to Mozambique to Mar-
rakech. I was glad there were almost eight hundred pages,
because I never wanted the book to end. It definitely kept

Irene Isobel Carver

me from pouring that first shot of whiskey in the evening. Instead, I would curl up on the couch when Paulie was all tucked into bed and read until I fell asleep.

The stories of the young people in this book helped me come to terms with the guilt I still felt from disappointing my father when I didn't want to go to Trinity College in Ireland, which was his dream for me. I let myself off the hook of having to do what a parent wants you to do in life as I read the generational tales of these characters. It gave me a new perspective and as I read, I felt myself opening.

As I reluctantly finished *The Drifters*, I turned the calendar to March, and I noticed I was happy. I stared at Norman Rockwell's picture of "The Cold"—a teenage girl curled up in bed with a handkerchief and a flyer for a dance she would have to miss—and it dawned on me that I had made it through the worst of the winter without having a nervous breakdown. I no longer felt there was something wrong with me. I wasn't relying on whiskey to fall asleep and I was allowing myself to grow at my own pace, without any harsh judgment. I knew I didn't want to belong to any church. I wanted the freedom to be led to spiritual books that would teach me. I didn't want to be molded by dogma.

Music was often my teacher. I danced around my house to Cat Stevens' "Peace Train," knowing I was on that train. I usually cooked dinner with the Youngbloods' music playing. Their song *Get Together* always helped me feel connected to myself and to everyone I loved and missed. Memories of Woodstock would float through my mind as I stuffed a zucchini with brown rice, and I could still see Gwen passing out pepperoni to all the stoned people on our blankets. I missed seeing Gwen but she was involved with her new man and the days of our communal apartment living were

ONE GOOD TREE   225

over. I needed a girlfriend that was single. *Better start praying one up,* I told myself.

There were a few shows on TV that kept me company, like *Laugh-In* and the *Sonny and Cher Show*, but my favorite was *Archie Bunker*; it reflected our shifting world in a way that kept me from feeling so alone. Occasionally, when loneliness struck deep, I would pick up the phone to call someone who I thought might be able to tell me about Paul. I would clutch the phone just long enough to feel the desperation of wanting to collapse into the comfortable old pattern of playing house. Then that illusion would morph into the reality of Paul with a rubber band tied around his arm, his head drooping to his chest, and I would hang up before the phone rang.

Irene Isobel Carver

Chapter Eighteen

A Junkie's Life Is Like A Setting Sun

—Neil Young

March 28th was the day Rachael died. Paul and Rachael had just taken the train back from Gloucester and they had money to score the smack they needed for the coming week. They hijacked the bathroom at Drew's crash pad. Rachael rolled up her bell-bottoms, exposing the only vein she had left that could take a needle, which was on top of her foot. Paul got out her bag of works and lit the match to heat up the spoon. Paul put the same amount of white powder in the spoon he had used the day before. As Rachael tied the rubber band over her ankle to make a tourniquet, Paul carefully sucked the cooked powder out of the spoon and into the needle, and injected it into Rachael's vein. She immediately slumped forward and suddenly slid off the toilet seat and onto the floor. "Holy shit, strong stuff," Paul said as he untied the rubber band and lifted Rachael off the floor. Paul was hoping to walk her into the bedroom next to them but she was completely limp. Paul felt for a pulse in her neck and there wasn't one. He picked her up and laid her on the bed. Fear rushed through him as he called out to see if there was any one else in the house. No one answered so he instinctively slapped her across the face. Nothing. "Fuck" he said as he ran and got a glass of water from the bathroom and threw it in her face. Nothing. He put his ear to her heart, nothing. He heard the door slam in the hallway and he ran out to see Drew and a girl entering. "Fuck, man, I think Rachael just OD'd, come help me," Paul yelled, trembling now.

They all raced to the bedroom and Drew started to pump her chest and blow air into her mouth. The girl with him turned and ran down the stairs and out of the house. "Drew, call 911," Paul said as he went into the bathroom to clean up the works. Paul's hands were shaking so badly now that he knew he needed a fix or he would be in deep trouble soon. Quickly he tied his arm off and put only half as much powder into the spoon as he had for Rachael, realizing this batch must have been way purer than what they were used to. As relief flooded Paul, he knew he should leave the works and a small amount of heroin out on the bathroom sink for the medics to find. God, I don't want them to involve me. He wiped off his fingerprints and then quickly hid the rest of the smack in the closet.

When the ambulance arrived, Paul was sitting on the bed next to Rachael's still body, holding her hand. When the medics asked what had happened, Paul told them that when he got home Rachael was passed out on the bathroom floor, and that he had carried her to the bedroom. They went into the bathroom and put the works and heroin into a plastic baggie and then returned to Rachael's body. As they placed her body on the gurney, one of the medics asked, "Do you know her name and address?" He looked at Paul as he covered Rachael with a sheet. "Yes, her name is Rachael Bennett and her parents live at 60 Ivy Lane in Gloucester. I don't know their phone number, though." Drew and Paul watched from the upstairs window as the ambulance drove away. "Fuck man, I've never seen a dead person," said Drew as he walked over and put on a record. "I've seen too many," Paul said, "but never a girl," and he flashed on the rows of body bags that he had seen being zipped up in Nam. Paul slumped into the sagging overstuffed chair next to the record player and listened as James Taylor sang "Fire and Rain." Paul held his head between his hands wishing he could cry, but he couldn't. James sang the next line, "I always thought I would see you again," and it was Irene's face that flashed before him.

Paul stood up, and feeling like a robot, he went to the bedroom and got the heroin from the closet. He put on his winter coat and checked the pocket, clutching the money Rachael had taken from her father's top drawer. As he looked in the bathroom mirror before leaving, he wondered if the police had told Rachael's parents yet and if they would feel some relief that their daughter's struggle was over. Why did they always leave money where it was so easy to find? Paul wondered, as he ran his fingers through his hair. It seems weird, like they wanted her to find it. Paul flashed Drew the peace sign and ran down the stairs.

As Paul hopped onto the trolley car, he felt an odd relief that Rachael wouldn't have her reoccurring nightmare anymore. It was always of the time when she was gang-raped at thirteen years old. The first time Paul and

Rachael shot up together, after the heroin had numbed her, she told Paul her story; how a month after the gang rape, she had to go to Mexico with her mother to get an abortion. When she returned home the family doctor had put her on Librium, but that was never enough to squelch her anxiety, so she began searching for relief. One day, at age sixteen, she discovered the tranquility of heroin and never looked back; she was in love with it. She died with her lover, Paul thought as he got off the bus at the corner of Putnam Avenue in Central Square. I can hang out for awhile at Ron's and get a new set of works, he told himself as he tried not to see Rachael's breathless body being moved onto a gurney.

When Paul opened the door of Ron's third-floor apartment, there was a large group of people hanging out in little clusters. Everyone was talking about the scary strong smack that was flooding the city. When Paul told them about Rachael, they said she was the fourth person they knew of that had died that week from that batch of smack. As the evening went on, a small Puerto Rican guy named Marcel, arrived carrying a pizza. He talked while passing out pizza and Paul realized that Marcel had recently returned from Vietnam. Paul took a chair next to him and they began talking about where they had been stationed and general war stories. Marcel abruptly but quietly asked Paul what he had done with all the money he got while in Nam.

"Man, that was a long fucking time ago now. I was in Tet, what five years ago or something?"

"Sorry man, I heard that was even more hell than the rest of the hell. But didn't you come home with some cash?"

Irene Isobel Carver

"Yeah, I guess so, I was married with a little baby and I think we bought a car."

"Cool man, maybe you can you give me a ride to Dorchester later before we get too loaded?"

"I don't have the car, my wife, ex-wife, has it."

"Man, you got screwed in both directions, that sucks."

"Yeah, I guess that's why I'm shooting this shit up, so I won't feel any of it," Paul said with a fake laugh. Paul felt a rush of anger flood through him. He stood up, took his new set of works and headed for the bathroom. As he tapped some white powder out of the baggie—he took about a fourth of his usual dose—he remembered he was really on his way to Larchmont to see Irene and Paulie. Just in case I die one of these times, I would like to see them again, he thought, allowing a little reality in. And with that thought, he decided not to shoot up at all; so he tucked his new works and stash in his coat pocket and left the house without any goodbyes.

By the time Paul got to Harvard Square, he knew it was a mistake not to have shot up. The tension was gripping his neck and he was beginning to sweat. Oh shit, he thought as his eyes darted around the Square, looking for an alley where he could get a few minutes of privacy. Where is a public bathroom? His mind raced and his jaw clenched in fear as he tried to remember. A bakery by the train station flashed into his mind, but when he got there the door was locked. He fled; his body wouldn't let him wait. He ran out of the Square till he got to the bus stop for Larchmont. There was an alley there, he remembered, but just as he got to the stop the trolley pulled up, so he *automatically hopped on. It was late, he realized, he'd better not take a chance that there would be another bus.*

Paul sat in the back of the trolley clenching his fists. Anger was erupting in his un-medicated veins. Body bags flashed before his eyes. He shook his head. No, not that shit, stop it, and he hit his head on the window; I gotta make it to Irene's. I'll be able to shoot up there and then nothing will matter. The trolley sped through most of the stops; no one was coming or going at this hour. Paul punched his thighs, trying not to remember what happened to Rachael, but he couldn't push the thoughts of her away. He closed his eyes and mentally touched her soft blonde hair; then he imagined her parents viewing her on a cold metal slab. He turned his head to the corner of the bus floor and threw up. Fuck man, this world sucks, he thought. He thought about Paulie and the boxing men he had given him for Christmas. The trolley finally arrived at Paul's stop and he moved forward, throwing change in the box at the exit and he ran to Irene's pad. Paul wiped his mouth on his coat sleeve and spit on the grass before knocking on the front door. The lights were still on. Good, he thought; at least I won't have to wake her up. Paul stood holding onto the door jam and waited.

THERE BETTER BE A GOD

"Holy shit, Paul, what the heck, it's… late," I stammered and once again I backed away from the door so Paul could enter my world. Any hopes that he was making a turn for the better were destroyed as I looked into his fright-filled eyes. "Sorry, it's late, can I use the bathroom?" "Wait a minute," I said standing firmly in his way, "I'm on my way to bed, you can't just show up like this and fuck with my head. What if I had a guy with me right now, Paul; what the fuck are you doing? Paulie needs a father and I… I need a husband."

I sat down on the living room couch, sobbing as anger ripped away the cork that had been damming my heart. I had no idea those words and those feelings were so close to the surface. I was exposed. My anger was like a lightning bolt that ripped through Paul's raw nerves. "Oh poor Irene, sitting here in her cozy world driving *my* car. Give me the fucking keys, I'm taking *my* car back, you can walk for a change," Paul yelled as he walked to the kitchen searching the counter for the keys. I followed him. "Get the fuck out of here before I call the police," I said as I stood blocking the view to my new key rack next to the refrigerator.

Paul pushed me up against the wall and with his hand around my throat, he said, "That is my fucking car. I killed people to earn that car. I watched people die to earn that money, what did you do? Fucking nothing," and he let go of my throat; I flopped to my knees weeping. He reached over my head and lifted the keys off the rack and said, "Now get the fuck up and go get me the title to the car." I stood up and put my hands on his shoulders, hoping to calm him down. I looked him straight in the eyes and said, "Paul, you can't, I need to get to work, I have Paulie, we need a car." "Well, have your boyfriend get you one," he glared at me with a look of such immense pain that I knew I could never call the police on him. I stared into his eyes and it was like I could see visions of hell itself behind his eye sockets, and I surrendered. "I don't know where the title is," I mumbled, turning away from him. Desperation made Paul suddenly clear and he said, "In that shoebox, in your closet." And he sprinted up the stairs to my bedroom. I followed him and watched helplessly as he got the shoebox and lifted out the title as if this moment had been planned forever. I sat on the edge of my bed with my throat closed. I couldn't have spoken if I wanted to. It felt like a terrorizing scene in a movie that just had to be played out. I was a method actor, stunned in place while the director crashed my life to bits. Paul didn't look at me; he folded the title, put it in his coat pocket, and headed downstairs. I heard the front door shut and the engine to my car start and all I could think was, *Thank God, Paulie is at his grandparents' house.*

I looked out my bedroom window; the driveway was empty. I walked down the stairs in slow motion. The clock on the wall said 1:20 a.m. I opened the front door and walked in a daze to the driveway. It was like my mind could not grasp the physical reality that I had no car unless my feet stood in its vacant spot. I was in shock. I looked up at the sky; the stars were in their places. I shivered from the cold March air, turned around, and walked back into my living room. The rug warmed my feet and I sat next to the stereo and put on the Youngbloods' album. Their words could have been echoing from my soul and not a record: "Quicksand, closing in around my mind, forcing me to realize and I'm losing track of time." I found it oddly comforting that I was not alone; whoever wrote and sang that song had been where I am and had felt like I feel. I looked at the album cover. *I will be okay,* I thought, *these guys are all right, they made it. Quicksand doesn't have to permanently devour your soul.* The picture of their mustached faces on the album cover was beautiful and in that moment I loved them. I grabbed a pillow and curled up on the floor and let the music hold me. "Darkness, Darkness" was my pillow and "the emptiness was right now," the lyrics bellowed. Then

Irene Isobel Carver

the music began getting lighter as I heard the words, "When the one who left us returns for us at last."

I sat up, the quicksand let go of its hold, and I said aloud to myself, "I think they are talking about Jesus!" Then an unexpected rush of fear shot through me. The numbing effect of shock was gone instantly and I said to my walls, "Oh my God, how am I going to get to work tomorrow night?" I lifted the needle off the record and shut the player off. The reality of not having a car hit me in the face. Then much to my own surprise, I began to yell at God. The vision of hell in Paul's eyes entered my psyche. I began pacing the house, into the kitchen, up the stairs, to the bathroom, back to the living room. I was like a caged animal, my soul smashing against thoughts I couldn't control. They were too much for the parameters of my body to bear, and they bellowed out a diatribe of pain. *You have got to be fucking kidding me, God. This is a sick world you have created, by the way. You're crazier than I am. What the fuck are you doing creating a world where people bomb each other and then send the soldiers home with minds and bodies blown apart. This is bullshit, God. Fuck you, I hate you. What is this to you, a chess game, and we are your pawns? Is this your entertainment? You go help Paul right now. He is your child, go fucking help him, now! Look what you have created, God: a sick world, lying politicians who keep war going, for what? Fucking money! If you had parents, God, they would be ashamed of you. I hate you. Fuck you.*

I swiped my arm across my altar, scattering all my precious objects upon the rug. I lay down among them, spent of all anger. I was left with just pulsating pain. I rolled onto my knees and picked up the picture of Jesus and held it to my chest. *I'm sorry, Jesus, will you tell God I am sorry? I can't believe I swore at God. Oh Jesus please forgive me, help me. Oh God, help Paul, he is suffering too much. God, forgive me for swearing at you. I don't hate you, but I hate war, please help us.*

I went to the kitchen, got a napkin and blew my nose. I threw water on my face and went back to the living room and began to reassemble my altar. As I knelt, picking up the scattered objects, a calm voice inside said, *It's okay, swearing is allowed, only man makes that wrong. I know you love me.* I could barely breathe. An amazing stillness filled me. I set down the candle I was holding, bowed my head, and spoke to my heart. *Oh God, please be real. I think you just spoke to me. Either that or I have truly lost my mind.* I waited, hoping for an answer. None came so I kept talking. "God, if you are real, if you did hear me, if I'm not crazy, then I need to ask you to help me. I need a way to get to work tomorrow night." I looked up at the clock. It was 3:00 a.m. I went to the kitchen and poured a shot of whiskey, knocked it back, locked the front door, and climbed into my bed, depleted, exhausted, and empty.

My eyes opened to the sun shining in my bedroom window the next morning. I sprang out of bed, looked out at my driveway hoping it had all been a bad dream and that my blue Toyota would be right in its spot, but it wasn't. I felt my throat and remembered Paul's hand there. "Oh, shit, work," I said as I headed to the shower, reality striking fast. The clock said 10:00 a.m., which gave me six hours before I had to leave for work. I went downstairs to make coffee and turned on the television as I went by. I needed some distraction, anything. As I filled the percolator with coffee grounds, I heard a special news report in the background. President Nixon was greeting some POWs who had come

Irene Isobel Carver

home after seven years in a prison camp. I went into the living room and watched the joyful scene and wondered if Paul would ever be set free of the torture that he was experiencing from Vietnam. I poured myself some coffee and wished I could be rejoicing with the families whose sons, brothers, and husbands were free at last, but what happened the night before left me feeling anything but joyful.

I turned off the TV and sat on the couch with the sun on my face. The telephone rang and I went to the kitchen and picked up the receiver, thinking it would be Dora. I was surprised to hear the voice of John, my brother-in-law. "Renie, morning. Great news about the POWs, huh?" Not waiting for me to speak, he said, "Hey, I am thinking of selling my bike; it has a baby seat on it and I thought maybe you could use it."

"A bike with a baby seat on it," I repeated almost in slow motion.

"Yeah, it's a ten speed; I got a ton of use out of it. Missy loved riding on the back, but she's too big for it now so I thought of you, it's just the right size for Paulie, I think."

"I would love it, John; how much?" I asked.

"Fifty bucks sounds about right," he answered.

"Any chance you can bring it over here today before three o'clock?" I asked, realizing this was my ride to work.

"Yep, I have the day free, I'll be over around two, see ya then," he said, matter-of-factly and hung up the phone.

I stood in my kitchen and looked around, expecting to see an actual angel. I began to absorb the deep truth of what had just happened. I poured more coffee and my mind replayed scenes from the previous night. I remembered screaming at God and wrecking my altar. I recalled apologizing to God for my rant and praying for a way to get to work. "I think I heard God talk to me last night," I said aloud, and telling him I needed help getting to work. "John just called and is bringing me a bike with a child seat attached. I can ride Paulie to Dora and Ed's on the bike and then I can ride to work." I spoke to myself in slow motion as if I were in a trance. *My God, this is real*, I thought, *God was in my living room last night, and he did talk to me. I talked to him, and he wasn't mad at me for swearing at him, he just sent me a bike!*

I sat back down on my couch in the sun. I could feel that stillness again. I couldn't move. It was bigger than joy. Joy makes you want to jump up and down or spin around. This feeling was so profound that it took me way past the movement of joy and into stillness. It was bliss; it didn't need to move, it needed to be realized.

"GOD EVERLASTINGLY, WORKS IN SILENCE, UNOBSERVED, UNHEARD, EXCEPT FOR THOSE WHO EXPERIENCE HIS INFINITE SILENCE."—
Meher Baba

When John showed up with the bike, I was happy to see it had a red plaid child seat. I reached out and hugged John, my Italian brother-in-law, and said, "Oh good, it's a Scottish bike," and I pointed to the plaid.

"Leave it to you, Renie, to give it ethnicity. Where's your car?" I took a deep breath and blurted out the harsh truth.

"He took the title, too?" John sadly said.

"Yup, he must be planning to sell it. I'm frightened for him, John, he must have a terrible monkey on his back," I said.

"Want me to call the police for you, Rene?"

"No, John, the truth is it is his car; he did pay for it. I

Irene Isobel Carver

just am glad God answered my prayer with you showing up with this bike."

"Well, okay, I guess I get it. Maybe this will push you into filing for a divorce. You need to protect yourself, Renie; you need to come to a decision," John said in a very parental way. I felt a little nauseous, so I turned and went in the house to get my purse to pay him.

"Hey, keep the money, Renie; it's a gift from your sister and me," John said so very kindly.

"You sure, John? I have enough money; I really am okay," I said turning back towards him.

"Yes, really, just do me a favor; decide. You deserve better than this." And he got into his car and backed out of the driveway and into his logical and planned life.

I didn't have any time to feel sorry for myself as I had to get ready for work and didn't know how long it would actually take me to bike ride there. I called Dora and told her I would ride my new bike up to her house so I could hang out with Paulie for about an hour before I needed to leave for work. I minimized the traumatic way in which Paul had taken the car from me with a huge lie. I told them Paul had called and said it was his turn to have the car and he had brought me a bike to have in its place. I cringed as I lied to my dear in-laws. I loved them so dearly and I just couldn't bear to tell them the truth of their son's condition. Lying was the best I could do and still manage to go on with my life.

As soon as I got to their house and sat in their kitchen with Paulie on my lap, I could see in both of their eyes they knew something was very wrong. Dora told Ed to take Paulie out to the backyard and feed the birds. Dora turned to me and said, "What is really going on, Irene?" My head dropped with the weight of her words and I said, "Paul came over late last night and took the car from me, he even took the title." I felt the depth of that truth stab my heart. "I think we should call the police, Irene," Dora said as softly as I had ever heard a person speak. All I could see was the hell behind Paul's eyes, and I lowered my head and watched my tears plop onto my shirt, as I shook my head "no."

Dora walked over to me where I sat on her red naugahyde stool. She pulled me to her and held my head against her breasts. I could feel her heart beating and I wondered how much hell a mother's heart could endure. I used her apron to wipe my tears away and I looked at the clock. "Dora, I just can't bear the thought of calling the police on Paul, I will be okay; as long as I have you and Ed, I'll be able to manage this and we'll keep praying."

"You are a strong woman, Irene, and we love you like our daughter; you can count on us always," Dora said as she handed me a Kleenex.

"I better go now and get to work. I'll call you in the morning and maybe Ed can drive Paulie home for me. Then I will have the next three days off to adjust to this."

"Tell Ed if you need him to pick something up at the grocery for you," Dora said as she squeezed my hand. "Are you sure it will be all right to ride home in the dark tonight?" she asked.

"Yes, the bike has a really good light on it and the streets are mostly flat and well lit, so I feel confident." We both looked out the kitchen window at Paulie and Ed, who were now throwing a baseball back and forth. Next to the house, I spotted the very first crocus, a purple one. Dora and I hugged and I left for work on my new Scottish bike, which I named Molly.

Irene Isobel Carver

PAUL

After leaving Irene's house, with reminders of his old life welling up in him, Paul pulled into the first parking lot he saw; he had been waiting for this moment all day. When Paul got out of the car to get into the back seat, he recognized the park he had pulled into. A memory of taking Paulie to this park filled him with pain. He saw Paulie, so cute in his tall rubber boots, throwing stones into the water and yelling ker-pow! He shook his head free of the vision as he settled into the backseat and locked the doors. He set up the spoon with the smack in it on the seat next to him while he tied off his arm. Then with his mouth holding one end of the rubber tie he cooked the heroin with the other hand. Within seconds, the drugged blood swirled through his brain, causing his whole body to slump into the peace he sought. The world of pain and evil was gone. Rachael's face passed before him and he heard her telling him that this is what death felt like for her. She smiled, death the ultimate high, and floated away.

Paul drifted in the euphoria of the beloved calm, his friend heroin, his wife, his life. With the pain gone he felt God floating within him. I won't die yet, he thought. No, not yet; Paulie will be five soon; maybe Irene and I will even get back together again. He pulled his arm free of the rubber band and recalled how Irene had slumped to the floor when he let go of her neck. She will hate me now, he thought. No feeling was attached, just a thought. I better get rid of the car before she tries to get it back, he thought, and he floated; but I don't really care what happens. Nothing matters as long as I get the money to keep this high rushing through me. *The money, yes, he felt some urgency. I'll sell the car. I'll be able to stay loaded all summer,* and his thoughts moved through the ethers between worlds for hours until a sliver of sun hit his face. He sat up; the day would need to be faced.

Paul got out of the car and walked over to the creek that boarded the parking lot and splashed cold water on his face. He peered up at the crows calling to each other as they too responded to the early light. An hour later Paul pulled up to the VA methadone clinic in his blue Toyota. Outside the clinic there was a swap meet, a pawnshop, and a trading post forming. A community was growing from the desperation that was masked by the shot of liquid methadone that fooled a person into thinking they could make it through another day. *I can sell the car now, it is mine, I have the title, I earned it,* Paul thought, as he parked close to let everyone see his 1969 well-kept ride. He tried to remember what he had paid for the car but he had no memory of himself at that time. When he came home from Vietnam he was as fucked up as a shit house rat and he had to fake everything. It was just a blur. Irene needed a new and safe car for the baby and it seemed like the right thing to do. He tried to picture going to the car dealership and the bank, but nothing came to mind; he was blank.

So how much do I need for five months of smack to get me through the summer? He walked up to a black dude who was trying to sell a stereo and said, "Hey man, how much will you pay me for this cheery Toyota?" and he pointed to his car. "A car?" the dude squeaked, "Who needs a car man, I've learned to fly," he held out his hand with some small pills in it. "I'll trade ya these for the car." And he laughed uproariously as Paul walked into the clinic.

Paul got in line to receive methadone and when he got to the window the attendant said, "Paul welcome back, but you're not on the list to get any; you've been gone over three months so you'll need to talk to the counselor first." Paul leaned closer and whispered, "I'm not here for a dose. I want to sell my 1969 Toyota, you know anyone who's got some bread?" "No Paul, I don't, and it isn't legal for you to come here and sell things. How about you see the counselor and after a dose you can rethink that idea. When you're not jonesing, you may decide to keep the car and get a job or something." Paul looked at the man like he had heard a foreign language. Keep the car, what bullshit; that meant insurance and registration. It was a world he could no longer be in. He stepped back as anger rose up his spine; he felt like strangling this skinny social worker just for being part of a world that was lost to him. He quickly went outside.

He leaned against his car and lit a cigarette. The nicotine blocked some of his rising rage, so he chained smoked until a car pulled in next to him. A middle aged man got out of his car, threw his cigarette to the ground, not even crushing it, and walked to the things being sold in front of the VA clinic. Paul felt this was his moment. When the man walked back to his car Paul said,

"Hey, I want to sell this car right here, do you know anyone?"

"Got the title?"

"Yeah, right here," and Paul unfolded it from his shirt pocket.

"What year? And how much you asking?"

"It's a '69; how about $1,500?" Paul made up a figure that sounded good.

"Yeah, I know someone," the man said lighting another cigarette. "Can you wait here for a couple of hours and we'll be back with cash?"

"Sure, I'll be right here," Paul answered hoping his body could manage the wait.

By the time the two men returned, Paul was sweating and his stomach was starting to cramp. The man who was going to buy the car was older. He wore a suit and he ran his fingers through his slicked-back hair as he approached Paul.

"So what ya got, buddy?" he asked, as he looked at the interior of the car, which still held Paulie's superman cup.

Paul reached in and took the cup and said, "Me and the old lady need the cash, that's all."

"Let me see the title," he said with hand held out. Paul showed it to him and the man pulled a wad of cash from his suit coat inner pocket and counted out ten $100 bills.

"This is what I got, you want it?" Paul took the bills, counted them and put them in his jeans pocket. The man pulled out a bill of sale from his jacket and they leaned against the car together and filled it out. Paul stood, clutching the superman cup as the man drove away.

April continued to win its award as the cruelest month. I parked my bike in the back of the restaurant each night

Irene Isobel Carver

and watched Antonio get out of his new black Camaro and polish the dirt off of his mirrors. *Damn,* I thought, *life's just gotta rub this kind of shit in your face doesn't it?* I reminded myself how grateful I was to have legs to peddle with. My mother had trained me well for these hard passages in life and for that I was grateful. On the up side, April always brought baseball, and in Boston, that was the elixir of life. The excitement of the season permeated the very air we breathed and no matter what your personal problems were, there was always a game to be watched; and the Yankees to root against.

With the snow officially melted, people came out of hibernation, and driving to each other's houses for parties was a rational idea again. I was ever so grateful for Dora and Ed because they never once said no to my request for a babysitter. It was at one of these spring gatherings in Boston on a Friday night, that I had a big realization about myself. I was drifting around the party house quite stoned on some very good weed when I heard the song *Your Love has Lifted Me* by Otis Redding. There were speakers hung in every room in the house, so as I danced from room to room, I was caught up in stereophonic bliss. Most people I knew prided themselves on the quality of their sound system and this was an amazing one. As I floated past the bay windows in the living room, I saw the almost full moon shining down on me. My hands were raised up to the sky as I sang along with Otis and suddenly I realized I was singing this love song to God. I instantly became self-conscious. I put my hands down and looked around the room to see if anyone was looking at me. Everyone was high and in their own world; they were oblivious of me. I came crashing into my body and decided to go outside for some air.

As I looked up through the Boston skyline, I caught the moon peeking between buildings. A beam of her light seemed to focus on me like a searchlight. "Mother, teach me," I said, feeling a complete connection to the light energy in the sky. "This is why people are afraid," I said out loud. "They don't feel connected to God's love." It felt as if the moon herself had said that to me. I didn't want to go back in to the party; I wanted to be out in the moonlight reading Walt Whitman's *Leaves of Grass*. I needed to tell my friend I came with that I was going to walk home. "Walk? Irene you are in Boston, it's miles to Larchmont, it's dark, it's late, and it's dangerous," yelled my friend. Her words fell on deaf ears. All I could hear were the lines to my favorite Walt Whitman poem, *Song of the Open Road* … "Afoot and lighthearted I take to the open road, healthy, free, the world before me." "Don't worry," I told her, "I'll navigate my way home by the river. I'll be fine, I'll call you tomorrow." I walked back outside, drawn into the moonlight.

I walked up Commonwealth Avenue, which was one big Friday night fraternity party with a gathering on every stoop and laughter coming from every flung open window. I crossed over the Charles River on a stone bridge that led to Central Square. My lightheartedness turned to sadness when I remembered this was where Paul had often come to score heroin. My energy sank as I wondered where Paul could be tonight. What if I ran into him panhandling? My lungs seemed to lose power as fear filled me. Was I safe here? Was this feeling a warning? *Get the hell out of here*, I told myself, looking in all directions. I quickly stopped my spinning thoughts and ordered myself to calm down. *Irene, don't get sucked into fear, what would Walt Whitman do in Central Square?*

Irene Isobel Carver

I must have looked like I had joined the truly insane as I began to stroll down the sidewalk, making up verses I thought Walt would have liked, and chanting them aloud to the moon:

"Oh, you heroin addicts, I salute you, you keepers of the streets, you spenders of your rent money on this white numbing powder. Oh, you panhandlers, I salute your courage to sit so close to the rich and arrogant just down the street. Here, have my waitresses' quarter, add it to you coping bag. It is your life, you may choose to die, to numb; I salute America for the freedom we have to sit on the street and die."

It worked; within three blocks everything changed. *On what number of Massachusetts Avenue does the depression stop and the opulence begin?* I wondered. Bookstores and haberdasheries began to replace pawnshops and litter. I looked over at the arched entrance to Harvard University and remembered standing there as an eight-year-old, holding my dad's hand as he told me and my sister Clare how hard he had to work waiting tables to pay for his books. "I wasn't a Brahmin with a trust fund, I had to earn my keep at Harvard," he told us, and I could tell he was proud of that.

I continued walking, stopping to peer into the window of Wursthaus Restaurant. I remembered how our dad had taken us there and told us stories of his German grandmother, while he ate pig's feet and sauerkraut; we ate hot dogs and French fries. *I'll call my dad tomorrow*, I told myself, *but I won't tell him how I walked home*. At the entrance to the Harvard Coop, a small amphitheater, I heard a song by Crosby, Stills, Nash and Young being sung. I walked over and joined in the chorus of "Don't let it get you down, its only castles burning." I threw a quarter in the musician's hat and then noticed the clock over the entrance to the train station. *Oh shit, it's eleven-thirty.* I ran to the bus stop, hoping I could catch a bus the rest of the way home. The pot high was wearing off and I was tired and hungry. On the bus I looked into my reflection in the window and entertained myself by singing a Crosby, Stills, and Nash song . . ."Four and twenty years ago I came into this life," realizing I only had two more months to be twenty-four. Paulie would be five in May. I put my head back on the seat, suddenly feeling old and lonely.

When I arrived home, I found a small book at my door with a note that said, "The meek shall inherit the earth. We came by tonight to share this book with you, we will come again tomorrow. Jesus loves you, Sue and Jesse." I went inside, made tea and a peanut butter and jelly sandwich and sat down to look at the book. It was smaller than my hand and consisted of cartoon pictures and Bible quotes. The cover said, "Your Spiritual Life and Walk with the Lord: Quotations from Moses David." I couldn't keep my eyes open so I slipped the book under my pillow, recalling that Edgar Cayce said he put books under his pillow to absorb the information as he slept.

In the morning I woke up on the couch, where I had fallen asleep. I put on my Cat Stevens album so I could listen to "Morning has Broken" while I made coffee. I talked aloud to Cat Stevens as I filled the percolator, thanking him for his hopeful songs during all the years of war. I began to review the previous night, trying to remember my "Ode to Central Square." There was a knock at my door and I opened it to Sue's beaming rosy face. Next to her was her man and we all hugged as she introduced us. "Come on in, want some coffee?" Sue replied, "No, thanks, we'll have tea though. We are high on God's word, we don't need stimulants." Sue hugged me from behind as I put the water on to boil. I remembered the book under my pillow and told them what I had done. The name Edgar Cayce didn't seem familiar to them but the second they heard Cat Stevens singing, Sue chimed in. "Listen to the words he's singing, Irene . . . 'Praise for them springing fresh from the WORD.' " She and Jesse hugged each other and in unison said, "He means the Bible. The Bible is the word of God."

I led them into the kitchen and put bread in the toaster, wanting to bring them down just a notch, hoping I had absorbed something from their book. They looked around the kitchen saying, "This is what the book we left you is about, did you get to read some?" Without giving me time to answer, Jesse said, "We call ourselves Jesus Freaks 'cause we are all hippies—hippies who love Jesus—we have been born again and we are going to spread the word of God across the earth in a new way." I joined in their passion and yelled Hallelujah and Amen, as I arranged our tea and toast on a tray and tried to push the words "cult" and "fanatic" from my mind. We walked into the backyard and Sue asked how Teresa was doing. When I told them that she had run off to Florida, Sue burst into prayer: "Jesus, search your daughter Teresa out, bring her to you." I burst in, "And bring her home to me while you are at it." We all laughed and then talked for a couple of hours about our lives. I told them about my kitchen angel who brought me a bike and they got all excited, saying that I had been chosen, and they wanted me to join the Children of God and travel with them. They said they wanted to go to Japan because their leader, Moses David, wanted all his followers to get out of America.

He believed America was an old, ugly, diseased, pompous whore and a capitalistic pimp, exploiting small countries. "She is the epitome of the Great Whore of Revelations," Jesse ranted quoting his teacher.

I was a bit caught off guard. I had heard radical political talk against America, but not radical spiritual talk against my country and I began to feel a little nervous, like I was being trapped. So I redirected the conversation and told them about my realization just the night before that I was singing all my love songs to God. "Oh, come with us, Irene, that's how we live, it's so far out." There was a very lonely part of me that wanted to join them just to have the support of other people who loved God in a new and expansive way. But as I flipped through the pages of their book, I knew that if I joined them, I could not be independent and free. I would be part of a group and would be expected to believe what Moses David taught. I knew I did not want to do this. I enjoyed being enrolled in my own private school of God. I knew freedom was my most cherished value.

I watched their lips moving and hands flying in excitement as I thought to myself, *I couldn't leave America and Paulie and I really needed Dora and Ed in my life. How could I explain this to Sue and Jesse without hurting their feelings?* The sun gave me my excuse as it moved from the backyard. I said, "Hey, it was way cool to see you both, and this dude seems out of sight, but you know what, I think being born on the Fourth of July has actually imprinted me with a need for freedom; I just want God to teach me directly. And I like Cat Stevens' words, 'I am happy lately thinking about the good things to come,' so I'm gonna hold that dream for America. I agree our government sucks, but I love America,

I love the people, and I'm very proud to be a Bostonian. Maybe it's just time to throw the tea in the harbor again!" I laughed to keep it light. "Well, okay then, we'll be praying for you and Teresa, too." Sue said, as they followed me to the door and Jesse chimed in, "We'll send you a postcard." Off they went down my driveway laughing and hugging each other and I could see that they were truly blissed out on love and Jesus.

Alone again, I said to myself as I went into the kitchen, picked up the phone and called Dora and Ed. I told them I was off to work and that I would pick up Paulie in the morning. "No, Ed will drop him off on his way to the ten o'clock Mass," Dora said, sounding a bit weary. *Even better*, I thought, remembering how tired my feet can be after a Saturday night waitressing shift and a bike ride home. That day, I took the back roads to work on my bike, leaving a little early for my shift so I would have time to think. As I peddled past newly blossoming maple trees, I found myself singing "God Bless America" and praying, *God, please bless America, we are a mess that is for sure. We need grace, amazing grace,* and I burst into that song as I circled into the restaurant parking lot.

The next morning Ed brought Paulie home. I thought Ed looked tired and I noticed he had an unlit cigarette in his hand. "Are you and Dora okay?" Paulie ran by me into the kitchen where he began jumping up and down on Teresa's bed; he did that every time he came home. "Dora isn't sleeping well, she's up half the night listening to Larry Glick on the radio," Ed answered. I gave him a kiss on the cheek and reluctantly asked if they had heard from Paul. "No, that's the problem. Dora just goes over and over all the bad things that could be happening." I lowered my chin to my chest; "I try not to think about Paul, it hurts too much," and I squeezed Ed's hand. Ed turned away and got into his car; he didn't look me in the eyes, he didn't want me to see his pain.

Teresa's vacant bed had become Paulie's trampoline and he landed on his butt as I entered the kitchen. He bounced to his feet and sat at the table and started counting my tip money from the night before, which I had laid out on the kitchen table, all forty-eight dollars of it. "Let's count your loot, mummy," he said, happy to be home where his Superman cape and Big Wheels were. I picked him up in my arms and said, "First a big smack-a-roonie for your mother." I loved the feel of his small arms around my neck and his soft strawberry blonde hair tickling my cheek. I walked him over to the wall calendar. "Look, Paulie, it's a new month, it's April. Did I ever tell you that when I was seven years old I tried to change my name to April?" We stared at Norman Rockwell's painting of *The Rookie* while I continued. "Yup, I just casually wrote 'April Adams' on the top of my papers in school every day and the teacher didn't say anything for a whole week." Paulie flipped up the calendar page to look at the next picture and said, "Then what did your teacher do?" We sat down on Teresa's bed and I said, "She handed me a note and told me to give it to my father." "Did you give it to him?" Paulie asked pinching my cheeks. I Eskimo kissed him with my nose and said, "Yes, I gave it to him." As I spoke I could see the scene clearly, as if it happened yesterday—me at my dad's side, in my yellow seersucker pinafore. "My dad read the note and burst out laughing. "April Adams," he said, "you sound like a little black girl." "What's a little black girl?" Paulie asked; he was quickly losing his attention span. "Well, some people aren't white skinned like you and me, they have dark skin like chocolate and their names are often different from ours, too." "Where's my cape, ma?" Paulie asked, wiggling out of my arms, done talking with me.

Chapter Nineteen

Answered Prayer At Last

I TURNED ON WBCN AND HEADED TO THE BACKYARD with my coffee. "Oh, thank you for April sun," I said as I pushed open the screen door, and then Teresa's voice, like a blessing from the void, yelled, "Hey Renie, I'm back." The door slammed and hit my coffee cup, spilling half of it on the floor as I turned and saw my bedraggled sister walking towards me. I put the coffee cup down and ran into her arms. As we opened our hug to arm's length looking at each other, I saw her boyfriend, Charlie, watching us from the hall. I tensed up and Teresa reacted to the negative look on my face by pulling me in close again and whispering in my ear, "He's not staying, we're splitting up." I smoothed back Teresa's hair from around her face; noticing the puffiness in her cheeks. I said, "Damn you need a shower, you look like a stray cat." "Oh thanks, Rene, you still have such tact, I see," she teased as we sat down on her bed. Now that I knew Charlie was leaving I could be polite to him so I asked, "Hungry Charlie, want a tuna sandwich?" "I'm gonna go shower," Teresa said as she pushed past Charlie quickly. I began making tuna fish; Charlie flopped on the kitchen bed and immediately began to snore.

I left the tuna unfinished and looked out the front door for Paulie. He was sitting under the sycamore tree talking to

Irene Isobel Carver

ants; I yelled, "Hey, Paulie, Auntie Teresa is home!" "I know; I already saw her; she brought me an alligator pin." I went upstairs, sat on top of the toilet seat, and asked Teresa questions while she showered. "Well, let's see, the short story is, Charlie got us kicked out of the house where we were staying when he broke a bottle of Jack Daniels on the windshield of our housemate's car." "Charming; has he been drinking the whole time you were gone?" "Just about," she said, sounding defeated. I handed Teresa a large towel as she stepped out of the shower. It seemed odd that her face was puffy and her body was thin, too thin. "And how have you been doing with drugs, Tee?" I tried not to sound scared. "Not good, those damn Librium just won't let me go. They are so fucking addictive. I don't care what those bullshit doctors say, those things screw you up." She ranted as she towel-dried her long black hair. My chest tightened and I thought of Paul. *Those pills strangle you,* I thought and I batted tears from my eyes. "Well, you can't be too screwed up; you migrated back from Florida the same day as the birds." I said, pushing away my fear as I looked out the window, spotting my first robin of the season. I felt a sense of hope, like a light, drowning out the dark cloud that wanted to overtake my breathing. Fear would suffocate me if I let it, I knew.

I stared out the window as Teresa dressed and I said, "Tee, I was really worried when you were on the road; not knowing if you were okay sucked." She ran a thick comb through her hair and said, "Sorry, Renie, I promise I won't do that again." I tugged a piece of her hair as I walked out of the bathroom, "Better not," I said, adding, "I'm gonna go give Charlie bus fare and kick his ass out of here, I want my sistah all to myself," and that thought made me smile. "You do that, Bossy Gillis, and tell me when he's gone; I've seen enough of that asshole." Teresa said with a certainty I hadn't heard from her in a long time.

I woke Charlie up and asked him to leave. I gave him bus fare and watched him walk down my driveway; this time it was with a great good riddance. I went in the living room and put on Carol King's *Tapestry* album. I yelled up the stairs, "He's gone" and then turned the volume up high; it was celebration time. Teresa, all clean and pretty in my bellbottoms and purple paisley blouse, came in the kitchen. We lit a fat joint and spun around the kitchen singing …" So far away doesn't anybody stay in one place anymore." And just like that, Teresa's runaway chapter ended and my heart felt peaceful. I made us tuna sandwiches and Paulie ate his sitting on Teresa's lap. After lunch, Teresa took Paulie to bed and read him a book. When I peeked in an hour later they were both cuddled up asleep. I picked up the phone and called my mother.

"Ma, Teresa's home safe and sound."

"Renie, oh Renie, how does the prodigal daughter look?"

"Well, she looks glad to be back, and she's asleep with Paulie."

"Thank God for that. Why don't you three come up for dinner tonight?"

"I better talk to her when she wakes up and see how she is really doing before I say yes to that. Call you later, mum."

"Okay Renie, I'm going to go say the rosary. Thank you, Mother Mary, a prayer answered." mum exclaimed.

"Hell no, I'm not going to ma's for dinner," Teresa snapped. "The last time I was there I was hallucinating on Nyquil and you all put me in rehab; I'll pass thanks." I sensed a new strength in Teresa. She was harder; life on the run had changed her, and I wondered if this new Teresa could

Irene Isobel Carver

somehow go back to being my happy sister in her nurse's uniform with her little white cap held down with bobby pins. I called my mother and diplomatically lied about Teresa's feelings and got us off the hook for dinner. We decided instead to take the bus to Mount Auburn Cemetery to have a picnic. So with three backpacks full of baked chicken, French bread, cucumbers and toys, we headed to the bus stop to begin our new life together. I was happy.

My Chariot Arrives

About a week later the phone rang about 8:00 a.m. When I answered the phone in my bedroom, I heard my cousin Billy's voice rambling on about seeing me riding my bike late on Saturday night.

"Yeah, that was me, I ride my bike to work at Rosario's," I explained.

"Do you need a car or are you just riding a bike for exercise?" he asked.

"I'm not sure *need* is the right word," I answered. "But yes, by October when the weather starts to shift, I will need one, why do you ask?"

"Cause I have this Mustang at my garage and the owner wants to sell. It's a 1962, and it's in really good shape. When I saw you on your bike at 11:00 p.m. I just thought…" and he hesitated, "of you," and I could tell that he had heard from the family grapevine about Paul and our separation.

"How much does he want for it?"

"Only $250; it's a good price. I checked it over and she's got a few good years left in her."

"Well, I don't have the money right now, but I am interested. Let me see if I can pull together the dough and I'll call you by tomorrow, is that okay?"

"Sure tomorrow or the next day, I'll hold on to it for you, Renie. Take down my number and get back to me before I close at five o'clock on Wednesday."

"Alright, will do," I said as I hung up the phone, feeling my angels at work.

It wasn't a coincidence that Billy saw me in the dark riding my bike, I told myself. *This is my car; I just need to borrow the money from someone.* I immediately knew I should ask my dad. In the past two years, since being on my own, I had never asked my parents for a dime. I felt I could ask for help now and so I set a plan in motion. I dressed quickly on this last day of April and sat down next to Teresa on her kitchen bed. "Tee, wake up, something cool is happening and I need to share it with you." She put the pillow over her head and asked what time it was. "It's 9:20, where the heck is Paulie?" Teresa sat up at my startled voice. I opened the front door and saw Paulie standing next to his Big Wheels, polishing it with one of my kitchen dishtowels and he had his superman cape on. "Paulie, who tied your cape on you?" "No one, I did it myself," he answered and I saw he had made a knot. I knelt down next to him and began to open the knot so I could tie a bow. He pushed my hand away and said, "Stop it, I like knots, girls have bows. "Hmm, you are probably right. Why didn't you wake me up when you got up? I don't like you coming outside without me knowing it," I said, combing my fingers through his hair. "Stop it, mummy," he said and pushed my hand away. "Okay, okay," I stood up, "but come inside and I'll make us some French toast," I said, hoping that some part of superman still needed a mother.

Teresa was already up and the coffee was percolating when I went back into the kitchen. She said, "So what's the cool news?" "I've got a lead on a car and I'm going up to ma

Irene Isobel Carver

and dad's to see if I can borrow the money, will you watch Paulie?" "Sure, but ask dad, he's the generous one; ma's so … Scottish. You'll get the lecture about how she saved up all her own money to pay for her wedding; her parents didn't give her a cent." I smiled as I remembered hearing that lecture many a time but I knew I was going to ask them both together; I felt that would give me a better chance of an instant answer.

I picked up the phone and called my parents' house. My mother answered the phone in her customary singsong tone, like the eternal hummingbird, "Hellooo." "Hi ma, I was thinking of coming up to have lunch with you and dad at noon, is that alright?" "Sure. I hope you will bring Paulie and Teresa." "No actually, Teresa is going to watch Paulie because I have something I want to talk to you and dad about." "Okay. We will be having cheese, crackers, and fruit," she said. "Great, see you soon," I said, excited to get my plan in motion.

A car, oh my God, a car, I said to myself as I peddled up Larchmont Street, sensing a new door opening, and at the same time appreciating my strong thighs. Bike riding had been good for me I knew, and it definitely pushed away the anger or depression that could have overtaken me. I got off my bike and pushed it up my childhood street. As I walked through the arched maple trees, I remembered the Easter Sunday I walked down this street in my first pair of high-heeled shoes; I was thirteen.

By the time my parents and I were having desert of red rose tea and chocolate chip cookies, we had a financial plan worked out. They would loan me the $250 to buy the car and I would pay them back ten dollars a month for the next two years. My mother pulled out her typewriter and wrote up an agreement and we all signed it. I called my cousin Billy from my parent's house and we arranged for my dad and I to go over and test-drive the car. When my dad stopped at Larchmont Savings Bank to withdraw the money, he shut off the car and took my hand and said, "Renie, I'm glad I can help you, I'm proud of you holding up so well during these difficult times." Tears filled his eyes and we squeezed one another's hand. Clare and John informed my parents what had happened to my Toyota when they gave me the bike, and my parents were kind enough not to require me to talk about it. We were all suffering in our own silence as the emotional shrapnel of Vietnam continued to wound our lives.

All my mother said the first time I arrived at their house on my bike instead of my car was, "We're Scots, remember that, Renie, we will lay down and bleed awhile then get back in the battle again." One evening soon after making that comment, I smoked some weed and pondered, *is all of life a battle?* Abruptly, an anger that was strong enough to push its way through the peaceful medication of marijuana, surged through me and said, *life is a battle because we make it so,* and I thought of my Western Civilization class. The whole course seemed to be about people conquering other peoples and lands, and countries overtaking and enslaving other countries—always involving power and greed—and they called it "civilization." That class was sickening to me; I flunked it. My whole body hurt. Anger hurts, greed hurts, and war hurts. I began rolling back and forth on my spine on my brown shag rug, doing survival yoga while breathing and moaning, and releasing the pain of life. I yelled through the ethers to the souls of my ancestors, " Let's just stop believing life has to be a battle." With that thought I sat up straight, landed in a lotus position, and saw the face and gentle eyes of Yogananda. He said, "Choose the battle of character, of will, of dominion over the self." I began moaning again. One way or another, life is a battle, and Paul was losing his and there was nothing I could do to help him except pray. My whole body seemed to wretch. I gagged a bit as a volcano of pain erupted from my gut and I dry heaved. I twisted and writhed as old buried and ignored trauma came flooding out of me. As my pain ebbed, I curled into a fetal position. Is this the bleeding my mother spoke of? Is this how we bleed out pain, like an emotional bloodletting? My body finally relaxed and only relief remained; then I slept.

GOD IS MORE POWERFUL THAN DRUGS

The next weekend Teresa and I decided to celebrate having a car again by going to Boston to the dance club, The Groggery. It was a gorgeous spring evening as Teresa and I sped along Memorial Drive in my blue Mustang. I noticed the floodlights were on at Fenway Park and said to Teresa, "Ah, baseball, all is right with the world." Teresa looked over at me as she pulled her hair back into a knot to keep the wind from blowing it in all directions and said, "Well, you're easy to please." We laughed and I turned up the radio, which was playing Traffic's "Pearly Queen" and we sang in unison: "She has some gypsy blood flowing through her feet." I yelled, "Boy, am I ready to dance!"

The club was in a basement, which seemed to add to the ambiance of losing oneself in the wild world of music or of a different persona. We found a table in the corner and went to the bar to order a pitcher of beer. The band was already playing and the floor was packed with dancers. A guy came right over and asked Teresa to dance while I sat sipping beer, watching them. I was overcome with happiness as I realized I had survived the long winter. I lost a car and got another one. I lost Teresa and got her back. I drank half a glass of beer thinking, *I lost Paul but I haven't lost myself.* I looked up from my glass of beer and into the eyes of yet another hunk of a man who said, "Want to get up and dance, beautiful?" As I stood up, I thought being kissed would be a good thing, and I joyfully joined the bouncing bodies on the floor as the music of Creedence Clearwater Revival played. After my second dance with the cute guy, I noticed Teresa talking to a very handsome man at the bar. I leaned into my dance partner and kissed him on the cheek as I said, "I'll be over there with my sister, see ya."

As I got closer to Teresa, I thought I recognized the guy she was talking to but I couldn't quite place him. Teresa spotted me and yelled out over the music, "Renie, remember Carlo Genoa, Gwen's brother?" *Oh yeah, that's who he is,* I thought, and remembered Gwen telling me that her brother was a heroin addict. I faked a smile as Teresa introduced us and I noticed that Teresa's eyes were droopy; she looked a lot more stoned than a couple of beers would have made her. *Oh shit, there goes my night out,* I thought, *now I have to worry about Teresa.* But that thought was blown right away as Mr. Cute Guy with his bushy mustache put his arms around my waist, kissed my neck, and whispered, "Another dance?" I looked at the bartender and said, give me a shot of Cuervo Gold, please," and I put two dollars on the bar. *Damn, this is my night out to celebrate my new car and I will not let it be ruined.* I downed the shot and spun onto the dance floor with the guy. *I'll sober up before I need to drive home,* I assured my sane self.

I didn't see much of Teresa after that as we were on

Irene Isobel Carver

different planes; I was on the slightly psychedelic high of tequila and she was, apparently, on some kind of a downer. At 1:00 a.m. I asked the bartender for a cup of coffee and I began searching around for Teresa. When I finally located her outside the club, she and the handsome Italian Genoa guy were passed out shoulder- to-shoulder, sitting against the wall at the top of the club stairs. I sat down next to Teresa and nudged her awake telling her it was time to go home. She smiled at me and said, "Isn't he gorgeous?" I looked at him with his sharp Roman nose and long black ponytail; he was quite the handsome man but his passed out snore was a big red flag for me. "Yes, he is cute, Tee, but come on, take a sip of my coffee; we're gonna have to leave in about fifteen minutes." I held my coffee to her lips and as she moved her shoulder, Carlo woke up. "What time is it?" "Time to wake up," I said annoyed, and Teresa nudged me again and said, "Carlo, do you need a ride home?" "Tee, I've been drinking too, I don't want to drive him home." I groaned. "Carlo, can you just come and crash at our place, Renie doesn't want to drive around," Tee said trying to sound in control. With that, the two of them pushed themselves up against the wall in unison and leaning into one another for support, they began to walk down the street towards… *towards what*, I wondered. As I walked behind them I watched as their bodies formed a support wall for each other. Together they looked like one person with perfect balance. They didn't even stumble. The words from "Pearly Queen" flooded my mind … "and when the time was right, she would meet her destiny."

I barely remembered where I had parked, so I just followed them while drinking my coffee. I finally recognized the street and yelled, "Teresa, take a right at the corner, I'm right behind you." I stood there a moment, gazing at the stars wondering if I would lose Teresa again. But the tequila wouldn't let me be afraid. I just shrugged my shoulders and said to no one, "Seems they belong together." As I drove my new car home, chauffeur of the very stoned, WBCN blasted the Rolling Stones song, "You can't always get what you want." I rolled down my window and yelled into the night air, "But I got what I needed. I got a car with a radio; what more could a girl ask for?" *Someone to hold me*, my heart tried to say, but I wouldn't allow that thought to ruin the nice tequila/coffee high I was on. It was actually a good combination, I realized, drunk and awake—interesting.

SWINGING ON THE PENDULUM OF LIFE

It seemed as if I was energetically connected to Paul, because out of the blue I would begin to plunge from my happy feelings of new growth and moving forward in life, to a sudden flash of Paul's despair. One day while I was cooking dinner and listening to an album by Traffic, I flashed back to the time when Paul and I had fought over whose album this was. I suddenly slipped from my world of "Pearly Queen" into the song "No Time to Live." I felt as if I became Paul and I could absolutely feel him thinking the words, "Now there is no time to live." Hopelessness filled me as if Paul had walked right into my body and I had to create an elaborate fantasy to pull myself out of the hell of hopelessness. I stopped what I was doing and sat at my altar. I sat there breathing, asking for a vision to arise.

In my vision, Paul did not take the Toyota to sell, but instead drove to our spot in Franconia Notch, New Hampshire. He finds a cabin that is abandoned, an old fur trappers hut from the 1600's that angels lead him to. He has

Irene Isobel Carver

no food so he just drinks water while he detoxes his body from heroin and he begins to hallucinate as he struggles out of hell. His body writhes and sweats and all the visions of Vietnam and the Tet Offensive sweat out of his cells. He finds a pure spring to lie in and it becomes the river of life. Jesus meets him there and Paul becomes purified. I see his pale blue eyes coming alive again. I join him in the stream and we sit across from each other holding hands and I tell him that I love him and that the war is over and he can come home.

When I again felt peaceful, I drove down the broad back roads of Larchmont that were lined with homes of brick, and I ended up at Our Lady of Mercy Church where I once made all my sacraments, and where Paul and I were married. I knelt in front of the statue of Jesus and asked him to please make my vision real.

I didn't think anyone could tell how confused and crazy I felt most of the time. I kept up a strong image for Paulie, Dora, and Ed, and my parents—or so I thought. Then one day when I went to drop Paulie off at Dora and Ed's house, Ed called me into his office and gestured to me to sit down. He handed me an Exxon gas card. I just held the card in my hand, staring at it. I knew it was a symbol of something much deeper. My eyes strained; I felt as if I was looking into the depths of the ocean. Big tears ran down my cheeks and something in me collapsed. Ed's love and caring was like a sword through my façade of strength. My heart fluttered as huge sobs erupted from so very deep within me. This gesture of support said to me that he knew his son could no longer care for me and Paulie and that *he* would step up to the job. My heart broke open right there in his office. I could no longer live in my fanciful visions of Paul's recovery; it was time to face reality. Dora walked in and seeing me sobbing, she handed me the Kleenex she kept rolled up in her sleeve. "One of my friends at the registry of motor vehicles told me Paul sold the Toyota," Ed said as he lit a cigarette and choked back tears. "We are so sad, Irene; our hearts are broken and we feel the only thing we can do is help you and Paulie," Dora said as she blew her nose. When I finally looked up, it was as if even the walls were trying to absorb some of the sadness for us; it was just too heavy. I made myself stand up. I kissed both of them on the cheek and left the house without saying goodbye to Paulie. I needed to be alone. I could not speak.

Chapter Twenty

War, What Is It Good For?

A FEW DAYS LATER MY SADNESS HAD MORPHED INTO anger. In an effort to suppress the anger, I decided to take Paulie on a picnic to Mt. Auburn Cemetery, where we could climb the stone tower, which had a spiral staircase that stood in the center of acres of trees and burial plots.

First, I had to find the closest Exxon station so I could use my new gas card. It was liberating to know I no longer had to make sure I had a five-dollar bill in my purse for gas. When the station attendant walked up to my window and said, "How much?" I handed him the card, feeling like a different person, and said "Fill her up, please." A sense of peace came over me and I took a deep breath. I looked over at Paulie who was sitting in the seat next to me with his small backpack clutched close to his chest. "This is the way to live," I said to him and he answered with a huge grin, "Yeah, we should go on a picnic every day." *How nice to be oblivious of the adult money world*, I thought.

I parked in my usual spot in the cemetery, close to the tower and near a pond where we could spread out our blanket and picnic. Paulie heaved his backpack onto the blanket, holding it upside down, and dumped out his toys. I set down my pack of food and watched as his array of miniature army men landed on my woven Mexican blanket. I knelt down next to him and picked up one of the pieces. I stared at the intricate details in the green plastic. I was amazed that a one-inch figure could express so much. They were all poised in different positions such as kneeling, about to throw a tiny hand grenade, standing with a rifle in hand, or lying on their stomachs aiming a gun. I looked on the bottom of one of the figures and it said Mattel Corp. I watched Paulie line the men up on top of a nearby gravestone. He would push one off the stone, yelling "boom" and then he would mimic the soldier and roll down on the grass. I was appalled, and a dialogue went off in my head resurrecting the anger I had felt earlier. *Are we all unconscious, oblivious, or brainwashed? Here we are in the middle of a torturous war that is destroying our families and we are giving our children little war toys!* I got up and paced around the small pond, looking like an insane person muttering to myself. "We do this year after year, generation after generation, without realizing the deep subliminal message it is instilling in the children."

I watched Paulie from a distance. He was totally engrossed in his war game. Part of me wanted to scoop up all his men and throw them in the pond, but I knew that would cause a big scene. My anger at Mattel Corporation for getting rich while programming another generation of little boys to grow up and play war pushed me into a plan of revenge. I walked up to Paulie and asked, "Can I play with your army men, too?" "Sure, mummy, you can have this one, and this one," he said as he handed me two of his "guys," as he called them. When I looked into their tiny faces, I suddenly flashed on President Johnson's face when he came to Fort Bragg and announced that he needed the 82nd Airborne to go back to Vietnam for the Tet Offensive. I looked over at Paulie's sweet little face, recalling that I had been six months pregnant with him at that time. I suppressed my tears as I saw all these tiny action figures turning into Paul, jumping out of a helicopter into Hue, Vietnam. Below them were tiny dolls of mothers, wondering if they would live through the day. *Oh, Jesus, help me, I'm hallucinating,* I exhaled. *Just keep breathing,* my mind answered, and I began my game with Paulie.

"Paulie, I have an idea," I said excitedly. "Let's collect some big leaves from that hydrangea bush over there and make boats out of them for our men. "Yeah, we can push them out into the pond and then bomb them with rocks," Paulie said, happy to have a playmate. I started softly singing the song by Edwin Starr, "War, what is it good for, absolutely nothing" as we each collected a handful of leaves. *If corporations could wage subliminal warfare, so can I,* I thought. "War leads to the undertaker," I chanted on as we walked down the grassy slope to the pond. As we lay on our stomachs like our action figures and pushed off our first men, I chanted more words to Edwin's song, "War, it takes life away." When one of our leaf boats got caught in a lily pad Paulie jumped up and went hunting for rocks. He soon found a pebble pathway and stuffed his pockets with them. We sat next to each other, each holding a handful of pebbles.

"Let the battle begin," I yelled as I aimed at the stuck leaf.

"Aw, you got him," Paulie said, clapping as the two figures floated face down in the frog- filled pond. Paulie capsized the other leaf and quickly shoved off two more leaf boats with men on board. We did this until all our leaves were gone and then Paulie said, "How do we get them back, mummy?"

"We don't, Paulie, they are dead; war killed them. Now they can't come home to their families, ever." Paulie looked at me with a blank stare and said, "No, they can swim back and then get on a plane back home." I closed my eyes. Had my son been eleven years old, I may have been able to continue with the reality game, but his five-year-old look of wonder turned my heart around. I couldn't go on, not then and not there, not under the blooming dogwoods and Japanese maples on a beautiful spring day. "Okay," I answered, shifting myself into his game, "but we're going to have to help them swim. We'll each need a stick. Call in your Green Beret guys to help us, Paulie," I said, turning into a little boy myself. I had a vision of Teddy Reid at his finest, giving his life to be that guy when needed.

We spent the next hour rescuing our men by making waves in the pond with sticks and also strategically bombing the water around them until they floated into grabbing distance. It was actually fun and I could see why little boys like to play war. I was not so angry anymore but I was more confused than ever. We washed our muddy hands in the pond and dried them with our paper towels. We sat quietly on our blanket eating peanut butter and jelly sandwiches and drinking chocolate milk. We listened to the frogs make ribbit sounds while dragonflies, looking like mini-helicopters, appropriated the pond. "Okay, Paulie" I said and stood up, "let's go climb the tower and rescue Rapunzel." I felt renewed strength, like I had already rescued myself from some dark pit of pain.

When I fell asleep that night, emotionally exhausted, I knew I had somehow made an opening to start showing my little boy that when men go to war for real, they don't always get to come home.

Irene Isobel Carver

It's Always Darkest Before The Dawn, Or So I Have Heard

I saw less and less of Teresa after she met Carlo. She began to sleep at his apartment and would only slip in and out of our house to grab more clothes or to shower; just enough for her to pretend she wasn't living with him. When I asked her to tell me more about Carlo, she said he worked at his father's furniture shop and that they were good for each other. I knew by her tone that she didn't want me to start worrying about her or prying. But I had lost a level of trust in her and so decided to call Gwen and try to get more information about her brother. When Gwen answered the phone she exclaimed loudly, "Irene, this is so bizarre, Billy and I were just going to call you to see if you want to come to Charlie's Kitchen with us for a beer." "God, I'd love to," I said immediately, "but give me an hour. I need to get Paulie to his grandparents' so I'll just meet you there."

Within fifteen minutes, Ed was at my door where Paulie stood waiting with his backpack stuffed with clothes and toys that he insisted on packing himself. He was always excited to go to his grandparents' house where Ed taught him to play cards, and Dora served him butter cookies and milk on a TV tray. I kissed them both goodbye, and with wings of freedom I flew up the stairs and stood staring into my closet. "Let's see," I talked aloud to myself. "Harvard Square, Friday night, what color should I be?" "It's a red kind of night," I said as I turned to my dresser drawer and pulled out my red scooped-neck top. I held it up as I looked in the mirror. *Yes, this will look good with my black and red beaded earrings.* "Red makes me happy" I said as I kissed my image in the mirror, excited to be going out on the town.

When I walked into Charlie's Kitchen I spotted Gwen and Billy in the very back booth sitting with a guy I had never seen before. As I got closer I watched Gwen's face as she laughed and I realized how much I missed my friend. She looked up and gave me a wave. Billy kept laughing as he adjusted his eyeglasses and he and their friend watched me walk towards them. I looked at this new guy, sensing an animal-like quality I couldn't place until I sat down next to him. It was his hair; he had the most beautiful, thick mane of hair I had ever seen. It was a rich brown, and coupled with his jade green eyes, he was just good to look at. I wished he were sitting across from me because I was suddenly nervous to be sitting so close, bumping elbows and all. I looked at his drink and said, "What's that?"

"Rum and Coke, you want one?" he asked.

"Can I taste yours, first?" I said nervously.

"You mean you have never tasted a rum and Coke?" he answered as he gave me an odd look like I had just dropped in from another planet.

"Actually, I haven't. I've been more of a pot kinda girl, no open bars in my world." I defended myself. He pushed his drink in front of me and put his hand up to attract the waitress. I took a sip and closing my eyes, letting the lime hit my lips.

"Oh yeah, I had one of these in Saint Thomas, pretty groovy, I'll have one." I answered.

"Two Bacardi and Coke, tall," he said when the waitress arrived.

"Okay, Arty," she said, "don't you want a double this time?"

So that was his name, Arty. No one had properly introduced us at that point, but who needs names? He was the

Irene Isobel Carver

lion king to me already. Had Mr. Tropical breeze blown in after a long, cold winter?

Conversation and laughter easily flowed for hours and the rum eventually loosened me up. I ran my fingers through Arty's hair and said, "Your hair is so beautiful, it looks like a lion's mane." "Yeah," he casually answered, "that's what a lot of people say and what's more interesting is that I am a Leo and my symbol is the lion." *Far out*, I thought, *he knows astrology.* Then, all of a sudden, Arty stood up and said he needed to get going so he could catch the last Waverly bus. I told him I would be glad to give him a ride as I was going that way anyway. Just as quickly, Gwen and Billy said their goodbyes, and I wondered if this had been a planned fix up. As I hugged Gwen goodbye, I realized I never once thought to ask her about her brother Carlo.

As Arty and I cruised down Mt. Auburn Street he told me he was sleeping on the couch at his mother's for a month because he was moving to Seattle, Washington in June. Before I knew it, I was pulling a Teresa and inviting him to sleep on the bed in my kitchen. When we walked into my house together he went right to my record collection and started flipping through the stack. He turned and looked up at me, "What, no Motown?" I felt embarrassed, like I was failing some coolness test. It triggered the place in me that never felt cool enough for Paul either. It was like I had this straight gene in me, a puritanical streak or something, and nothing I did could hide it.

"I have Jimmy Hendrix in there," I said hoping that his blackness would somehow be okay.

"Jimmy's skin is black, but his music is rock," Arty said as he chose Sly and the Family Stone. But as soon as it started to play he turned to me and said, "No, it's too late for this music, what we need is something soft." Then he surprised me by holding both my hands and looking me directly in the eyes said, "If you're into staying up, I can take your car to my mother's house and get some Al Green."

"Well… yeah, I feel like staying up, how far is your mother's?"

"Just three blocks," he answered as he grabbed his jacket.

"Okay, but be careful, don't get pulled over, I don't need any more problems."

"Will do," he said and he leaned in and gave me my first kiss on the lips as he headed out the door. The magnetism of his kiss riveted my feet in place. I stood there analyzing the feeling. It was like the energy got sucked from the bottom of my feet up through my lips. It caused a body rush like I once felt on mescaline. It was the opposite of a cold shiver; it was a hot shiver, an energy shiver. For some reason, I wanted to classify or name his kiss.

I was still standing in the same spot when Arty walked in with an armful of albums. He put on Lou Rawls and began singing and acting out the words to "Try a Little Tenderness." Then he pulled off his sneakers and spun around on the rug as if he was on a stage. I watched, mesmerized. He was Elvis flinging off his cape dramatically and I, the assistant, picked up his sneakers and moved them to the hall. When the song ended I tried not to appear awestruck, so I casually began looking through the rest of his albums. There was Marvin Gaye, the Temptations, Al Green—about eleven albums—all soul. A whole new world was opening before my eyes and I was completely swept into it—well, not completely. About 4:00 a.m. I said, "Hey, I have to crash now; I'm fading fast and I have to work tonight." I took his hand in mine as I walked him to the kitchen. I pointed to the bed and said, "Anytime you're ready you can sleep there." I stepped into his arms for another magnetic kiss of his. I turned, this time leaving him glued to his spot. As I walked upstairs to my bedroom, part of me wished that he would follow me, but I was relieved when he didn't. I just wanted to live in his kisses for a while. Considering that it was the height of the "free love" days, it was pretty amazing that Arthur and I hung out together for a whole week, drinking and dancing, before we slept together. Marvin Gaye singing, "Let's Get it On" almost landed us in bed on the third night, but one of the lines in the song, "I won't push you, baby," spoke to us and we slowed the movement down, savoring the dance.

I became a big fan of rum and Coke. The Coke made drinking feel harmless and the lime gave the illusion that it could actually be healthy. By the end of the week I could perform all the words to Marvin's "What's Going On" while Arty played his bongos in the background. In between songs and days, Arty told me about his year in Vietnam. He had been in the Marines and ended up spending most of his time in the Brig because he was charged with being a ring-leader and spreading dissension in his platoon about the war. That night, as Arty stirred that impressive information into my drink, I put on Tracy Nelson's album and let her lull us into the kitchen bed together with her words, "I want to lay down beside you and hold your body next to mine." Arty, who heard every word in a song, immediately asked me if I was on birth control. I told him that I was on the pill and he said, "Good, I do know the name I want for a daughter, but this is not the time. I have to get to Seattle next month and I want to travel light." Arty's words of traveling light, without me, caused my heart to close a bit out of protection and I actually felt my heart fold inward like a flower closing at day's end. I was still able to sink into his kisses and allow the rest of my body to stay open to this man who knew the name of his future daughter. I knew this was a unique man I was wrapping myself around and I felt like a crab finding shelter under a rock, if only for the moment. So I snuggled in and said, "Now that you know we are safe, what is her name going to be?" "Leah," he said and that was the last word we spoke until morning.

Once Arty and I had made love, it was a natural flow from his mother's couch to my house. Actually, once his albums were moved in, he mostly fell asleep next to them, as if standing guard duty over his most precious possession. Besides his albums, all Arty owned was a backpack full of clothes and the book he was reading, *I Ain't Much, Baby, But I'm All I've Got* by Jesse Lair. Originally, Arty was going to start hitchhiking to Seattle by the end of June, but we were having so much fun together that he delayed his trip until July 23rd. He said he could leave no later than that as he wanted to be in Seattle for his birthday on July 31st and that was a plan he was not going to alter for any reason. He showed me the catalogue his friend mailed to him from Seattle for Central Community College. Arty had already sent in his registration for the fall semester, registering in the boatbuilding program. I didn't want to dampen Arty's excitement, but I sure was feeling left out, so I asked him how he could part with his albums. He looked at me, appalled that I would even consider such a thing. "Hell, I'd never part with these," he said hugging Al Green to his chest. "I'm going to mail them to my friend's house so they will be in Seattle when I arrive." "Oh," I said, surprised that he had a world of plans going on in his head that didn't include me. There was obviously a corner of my heart that hoped at any moment he would drop his plans and stay with me.

Some anger awakened in me and I said, "What the hell could be so wonderful in Seattle?" I paced about the kitchen. Arty looked startled as I continued. "The only thing I've ever heard about Seattle was the World's Fair in 1962 and they built a Space Needle, whoop de do," and I plunked myself on the bed's edge pouting. Arty pulled out his map and sat next to me. When he spread it out I saw that Seattle was in the furthest possible corner of the northwest so I frowned at him and said sarcastically, " Look at all those forests, they are probably still having Indian wars out there; I'm sure there won't be any concert tours." Arty put his arms around me and laughingly said, "Well maybe you can be my mail order girlfriend." I didn't laugh but instead looked closely at him wondering if there was any seriousness in what he had said. Then I looked away, not wanting him to see my face as I continued. "What does your mother think of you taking off across country, anyway?" I hoped to open him to a sense of family loyalty. "She thinks it's great; she only let me crash on her couch 'cause I was leaving soon." The world beyond Harvard Square barely existed for me and I didn't really feel I wanted to change that.

Having a small child kept me in a circle like Mr. Roger's neighborhood. In fact I loved watching that show with Paulie; it helped me to pretend the war was not still going on. Sure the U.S. had signed a Peace Treaty in Paris in January, but now we were bombing Cambodia. I guess the Peace Treaty ended conveniently at the border of Vietnam and now America was free to invade the next country. I was convinced our government was evil and my psychic defense was to join Paulie and Lady Elaine in the land of make believe and avoid the news at all costs. When I did let myself think of Paul, I figured that heroin was his Lady Elaine.

June faded into July. I celebrated my twenty-fifth birthday on the Fourth of July and I was grateful that I had a boyfriend for the big occasion of turning a quarter-century old. This year, as I watched my friends travel to the Newport Jazz Festival, I was content to stay home and play house with Arty. We invited any friends left in town to come to a barbeque. Arty strung lantern lights in the backyard and put one speaker in the kitchen window; we were happy. For a gift, Arty bought me the book *Buried My Heart at Wounded Knee*. As I opened it he said jokingly, "I just wanted to include you in the Indian wars I'm heading for." He held my hand and after he kissed my cheeks and hair, I leaned into his embrace and he began to tell me the story of when he was nine years old:

"I was lying on our front lawn, just watching the summer clouds drift by, when a huge puffy cloud turned into the face of an Indian; it was just like the Indian head on the nickel. The vision lasted quite a few minutes and ever since that day I always look for the Indian in the sky, but I have never seen him again; maybe I will in Seattle."

We held each other for a long time as the essence of the story transferred to my heart and I sensed that he had told this to very few people. It was a precious birthday gift.

As the humid July days blended into one another, Arty talked more and more about his Seattle plans. He would recount his conversations with his Seattle friend about the beauty of the sun setting behind the Olympic Mountains and tales of Chief Seattle and the mini Statue of Liberty on the banks of Puget Sound. One time when Arty sensed

Irene Isobel Carver

my sadness he said, "I'm pretty sure your breasts are more beautiful than those mountains, but I just gotta go find out." We both laughed and I realized Arty's humor was one of the reasons it was going to be so hard to let him go. My life had become way too serious with war and addiction, and I was afraid of how I would handle the change, the loss. Then on a Friday morning in July, the warm tropical breeze of love that May had blown into my life lifted, as Arty swung his pack onto his back and with a wink from those beautiful green eyes, he hopped into his friend's car in my driveway and headed to the entrance of I-90 where he would be dropped off to begin his solitary journey.

Chapter Twenty-One

The Web Of Life Weaves On

BEFORE ARTY LEFT ON HIS JOURNEY HE GAVE ME A very valuable present. He introduced me to Donna Fremont. Donna was the single parent of a two-year-old son and her sign was Cancer, like me. Our needs were pretty much the same. Arty sensed that Donna and I had a lot in common, so he invited Donna over to meet me on the Saturday afternoon before he left. Paulie, now five, was gentle with her son Michael, and shared his Lincoln Logs with him; it was a good sign. Three hours later, after we both hugged Donna good bye, Arty turned to me and said, "A match made in heaven, just as I thought." And he was right. Donna and I easily talked about how much we needed to live with another adult so we could give each other the freedom to go out occasionally, taking turns being the babysitter. "And companionship," Donna just about moaned, "to have someone to cook with and to watch *The Mary Tyler Moore Show* with," she continued as she threw her arms around my neck. I opened up and confessed how the isolation of living alone the past winter was a major contributor to my almost nervous breakdown. I knew that Donna understood completely.

Irene Isobel Carver

By the time I had the courage to wash Arty off my sheets, Donna and I began looking for a house big enough for the four of us. We saw an ad in the paper for a four-bedroom house on the Arlington/Lexington town line. When we went to look at it, the real estate agent told us it had been the first Jewish temple in Lexington. We both gasped at the same time—A TEMPLE! We looked at each other and mouthed the words "we'll take it." That night I called Clare to tell her about my new "Temple" and she quickly said, "Are you sure, Renie? It's not always easy to live with someone who isn't family, it's not like she's a sister that you can yell at." But all I really heard was the word "sure," as it stabbed through my heart. "How the hell can anyone be sure of anything? Who is ever sure? We can only hope to be sure," I snapped at her, trying to convince myself. I hung up the phone and the truth of what Clare said struck me. I missed Teresa so much. A sister can be dangerous with the capacity to break your heart. I was rapidly feeling *sure* that a roommate would be easier.

Later that night I began to re-read *The Drifters*, needing something familiar to comfort me. I was still annoyed at Clare for bursting my "temple" bubble. As I searched the book for a part I loved, the universe was kind to me; I landed on just what I needed to read. It was a quote by Disraeli: "The blunders of youth are preferable to the successes of old age." I read the quote a few times and then lay back with the book on my chest chanting "thank you, thank you" over and over, as the weight of the word *sure* lifted off my chest.

THE TEMPLE OF LIFE

September first was to be our move-in day. August sped by as the packing began and I barely had time to miss Arty.

When he called, I told him about our new place. He said he wanted full credit and thought we should get a lion statue for the front steps. What a joke that was, since we barely squeaked together the money for a deposit.

Donna and I each gathered up a crew of friends to help us move, and of course we set the stereo up first. The sound track to our new lives began with Carly Simon and we all sang along to "Anticipation" as we carried in boxes, chairs, and beds. "You find out who your true friends are on moving day," I whispered in Donna's ear and we realized we both had many. Donna and I split the cost of pizza and beer for everyone. We both planned well by leaving our sons at their grandparents' houses overnight so we could kick off "temple life" with a party.

By nine o'clock that night, Tina Turner ruled, and Donna and I set out to see who could dance the longest and wildest to "Proud Mary." It turned out we were an equal match and the hardwood floors in the living room made a great dance floor. When the beds were all assembled and the beer all drunk, our helpers straggled out one-by-one, flashing the peace sign with big satisfied smiles. The "Temple" had been baptized properly. But when I was alone, putting the clean sheets on my bed, a terrible longing filled me. I wondered if I was longing for Arty, for Paul, or for a man. I started to get teary, but Donna's voice drew me from my thoughts as she yelled from her room, "Do you think there are Jewish ghosts here?" I burst out laughing with a memory of scaring Teresa and Brigette with ghost stories when we were small. I quickly slid between my sheets and yelled back, "We'll find out." I rolled onto my stomach hoping for dreams.

In the morning Donna and I strolled into the kitchen ready to set the routines that would order our new lives.

Irene Isobel Carver

Donna placed her most important box on the kitchen table, pulling out her bottle of Kahlua with one hand and her can of Nestle's Quik with the other. She gave each of them a kiss saying, "I'm not sure which one I love the most" and we laughed. She opened the refrigerator and pulled out her milk, the only item actually in the refrigerator. "I always have milk," she said with glee as she stirred in the Quik, "do you want one, too?" "Sure, it looks delicious actually and aren't you organized to have milk on moving day?" We clicked our glasses together as we gulped down our drinks. "It's not organization; it's survival," she said. "I have to have either Nestle's Quik and milk or Kahlua and milk every night in order to go to sleep; so never, ever, drink the last of the milk in this house or you'll see a side of me you won't like." Having been raised with four sisters brought forth my peacekeeping skills and I suggested that we each buy our own milk and label them. "Groovy," Donna said and we clinked our glasses again. Then we each opened a kitchen cabinet and began to put our food away. I filled my cabinet with tea and tequila and stood back and said, "Cool, now we both have our important libations, and if you get to the worm, don't drink it." I felt the fun of friendship begin to bloom.

Donna and I felt like two goddesses; Donna cruised around in her 1964 white T-Bird and I in my 1962 blue Mustang. We were cool. Donna had been raised on the rich side of the Larchmont tracks and could have asked her parents for money at any time and gotten it, but she preferred to work three jobs to come up with the money she needed. She didn't like her parents' conservative politics and wanted to have little to do with them. They were members of that martini- drinking establishment that voted in Richard

Nixon, after all. She didn't even allow talking about them in our temple, saying she didn't want to pollute our air. Instead, Donna would get up at 4:00 a.m. to deliver the daily paper door-to-door in her T-Bird. She then worked the lunch shift waitressing at Jimmy's Restaurant just down the hill from us and in the evenings she would type addresses on envelopes. She said this was her party money, after the bills were paid. She also got child support from her son's father, so she always managed to afford her Nestle's and Kahlua. I had waitressing shifts four nights a week and would pay Donna to watch Paulie on two of those nights, so I wouldn't have to cart him over to Dora and Ed's house and pick him up late when he had kindergarten in the morning. It was well worth it; between tips, public assistance and Ed's gas card, I always had the money I needed.

In the fall of 1973, it seemed that everyone I ran into was talking about the book *Living the Good Life* by Scott and Helen Nearing. I wanted to join the crowd, so I used this as an excuse one lovely fall day, to ride my bike around my new town and get a library card. The book was not in when I got there, so I found a bookstore in the town square and purchased a copy. That evening I curled up on the couch with tea and entered the world of a commune in Vermont. The Nearings were twentieth-century pioneers, living off the land, a "scientific experiment on common sense." Hundreds of city people would drop in on their farm, stay awhile, learn, find some serenity, and then leave. The Nearings were teaching by example how to move back to nature, how to live communally and make it work. Two weeks later, I put the book down, thinking that if every person always remembered to put every single item back in its proper place, a commune might actually work. I obviously wasn't the commune type because I found it difficult enough to share the kitchen with one other woman, let alone five or six people. When I read a paragraph to Donna, thinking I'd make us laugh, she said very seriously, "I could have my own cow and I'd never run out of milk." I still wanted to laugh, so I said, "Yeah, and you could learn to make your own Kahlua and you'd be the farm queen. Everyone would love you and you would never get bathroom detail."

"Can I read that after you?" Donna asked as she walked to the bathroom to fill the tub with water. "Yes, of course, but I'll tell you right now that on a commune you would never be allowed to fill the tub with scalding hot water and then let it sit for a half hour until it's cooled enough for you to sit in, queenie." "Do you have any pot?" She ignored my comment completely. "You know I have pot Donna. I've told you that it is a sin to run out of pot. Not a mortal sin but definitely a venial sin." She looked at me calmly and asked, "What language are you speaking?" "Catholic," I answered. "I'm just playing; I'll go get you some," and I walked away. I went to the stash box in my closet and as I rolled a joint, I thought how grateful I was for my friends Tim and Danny who always brought me pot. I think they felt sorry for me; they watched as I battled Paul and heroin and lost. They probably didn't want to lose me too. I held up the joint and smiled; it was a work of art. *I've come a long way*, I thought as I walked to the bathroom and held forth my creation to Donna. Both our boys were asleep so I sat on the toilet seat while Donna soaked in the tub and we passed the joint back and forth and began to imagine our futures. Somehow we both knew that we were just in a holding pattern, living in a "temple" between men.

The "back to the land" vibration was in the air and for

those who weren't moving to the country, the choice was to bring nature into our city apartments and homes in the forms of houseplants; it was all the rage. Every window was decorated with rows of shelves to hold tiny succulents that would burst into unexpected color, allowing the illusion of a desert in a sunny New England living room. I had just bought a wandering jew and a purple passion that morning to add a touch of velvety class to my bedroom windows. As I hung the purple passion in a macramé hanger I had made, the phone rang and it was Gwen. She began talking at full speed, she had just decided on a huge career move. "I've decided how to use my inheritance from my dad," she said, stopping to breathe. "Billy and I have been talking for weeks of opening a plant store and I will finally get to quit nursing." I didn't respond; I knew there was more coming from the exuberance I heard in her voice.

"Do you want a job?"

"Well, of course, I do."

"I'm going to start looking for storefronts in the Brookline area so maybe within a month I'll need your help."

"Perfect; that will give me time to arrange my schedule at Rosario's and get daycare for Paulie."

"I'm thinking I'll need you Monday thru Friday 10-4."

"Wow, I love this idea. I'll have time to get Paulie off to school and I can still work Saturday nights at Rosario's."

By the time I hung up the phone I was as wildly excited as Gwen was. Two weeks later when Gwen called to tell me she had found her storefront, I got out my astrology book. I had been waiting to read it to her at just the right moment. "Gwen, listen to this: *Libra's approach to life is through beauty, they are most productive when they create surroundings of tranquility that are aesthetically pleasing.*' This sounds just

Irene Isobel Carver

like you. Gwen, this is so cool; I think you have found your true path. Have you thought of a name for the store?"

"Oh my God, Irene, that is so right on, and yes I am going to name it PLANT HAVEN. I've rented the space starting November first. Billy and I will spend November setting it up. Billy is going to build all the shelves and we'll open on December first, just in time for the Christmas business."

"When do you want me to start work?" I was hoping she would say November first; I wanted in on all the action.

"I won't need you until just after Thanksgiving when I can train you to be ready to handle the front counter sales. Also, I've got a book I want you to read so you'll know how to help the customers."

"That's great, can I get the book, like now? I'm so ready to do this with you, and I'm excited to start making those little greenhouses."

"Yeah, me too. They are called terrariums, and I have a book just on those, we're gonna have a blast, Irene."

Paulie was sitting on the floor next to me playing with his Lego's while I talked to Gwen. "I found out that public assistance will pay for Paulie to go to afternoon daycare after his morning kindergarten, and they will pay for him to take a cab from school to daycare so I can work." Paulie looked up at me when he heard his name and I smiled at him when he purposely stuck out his bottom lip so I would know he felt sad. "Wow, Paulie in a cab, how weird." I felt Gwen's motherly concern.

I hung up the phone and tucked away some of my excitement as I knelt on the floor next to Paulie. "So what's the big lip about?" I asked as I snapped together a couple of Lego's.

Paulie threw a Lego into the little Lego barn he had built and said, "I don't like my new school, and I don't like our new house; I want to go back to our old house." I tried to stay calm, putting my hand on his back hoping he'd calm down but he didn't. He stood up and kicked the Lego's, "And I don't want to take a cab either." He ran to his room and slammed the door. My happy little temple world screeched to a halt. I remained kneeling on the floor wondering what to do next.

Could it be that what was good for me was not good for Paulie? I had not thought to question this before I leapt at the chance to have a roommate. *Had I even sat at my altar and asked for guidance before I made this move?* Clare questioned me about this decision and I had immediately dismissed her comments. I recalled how I desperately did not want to spend another winter alone. It was that desperation that moved me out of the safe world Paulie had been thriving in and I was shriveling in. *Oh, God, help me*, I thought as I stood up to go to Paulie and console him.

He was lying face down on his bed when I walked into his room. "Go away, you're mean," he mumbled into his bed and then turned his head sideways into his folded arms. "Please let me stay, Paulie, I want to tell you why we moved." I didn't wait for an answer; I just sat down on the bed next to him and began rubbing his little back. "I moved us to this new house because I needed to live with another adult; I was too lonely last winter. I was afraid to be that lonely again, and I thought you would like having another kid in the house to play with. I'm sorry you don't like your new school, but I think with a little more time you will make friends and start to like it."

Irene Isobel Carver

Paulie rolled over and said, "So we are both sad; let's go watch TV."

"Okay. TV it is. How about a hamburger for dinner?"

"Can I eat it on a TV tray?" even his eyes pleaded.

"Sure, if you promise to eat all your carrots, too."

"Alright, just don't ever, ever give me tomatoes again," Paulie bargained as he jumped off the bed. "It's a deal," I said, tickling him as we both ran to the living room laughing.

PAUL

Paul managed to stretch the $1,000 from the sale of the Toyota until early November. He kept himself in heroin by buying a gram and then selling dime bags, doubling his money while maintaining his own habit. But eventually his habit got more aggressive and he was too addicted to be a competent pusher. He ran out of everything—money, energy and hope. He hit a dead end on November ninth. With twenty dollars left in his pocket, he asked his friend Drew if he would drive him to the methadone clinic. As they drove to the clinic, silence filled the car. It was like a time warp—a déjà vu of sorts—of the day six months earlier when Paul returned from the Virgin Islands and Drew picked him up at the airport; he had offered Paul some smack and that was the road Paul went down. It led to this moment when Paul had no car, no money, and no Irene.

Drew pulled up next to the door of the clinic and without putting the car in park, he reached over and punched Paul lightly on the bicep saying, "Righteous, man." "Stay cool," Paul said, which was the opposite of how he felt. Fear set into his gut and he wondered if the counselors would let him back on the methadone program. Paul knew the routine so he got in line to sign in as a returning patient to the clinic. Suddenly he felt sick, as if could throw up, so he left his place in line and went to the men's room. He dry heaved a few times, took some Kleenex and shoved it in his pocket. He walked back to the counter, relieved to see there was no longer a line. The male receptionist looked up at Paul. They did not recognize each other, so Paul told him to look up his case, and just get him into the counselor's office as quickly as he could. The young man was used to the desperate voices of veterans. He rang a small silver bell and a familiar counselor stuck his head around the corner. "Holy shit, Paul, man, get in here, you look like hell." Paul smiled, relieved to be in the care of this particular man who was a veteran himself and seemed to care about the junkies that came into the clinic. As soon as the counselor closed his office door he said to Paul, "Let me see your arms." Paul pulled up his sleeves, exposing weary track marks. "Let me see your ankles," the counselor demanded. Paul rolled down his sleeves and then exposed his ankles. The counselor dropped his head and shook it back and forth. "Fuck man, you're a mess." He leaned back in his swiveling office chair and continued, "I'm surprised you made it back, Paul. You know what? A lot of guys don't. There is some strong shit on the streets. This is no game, Paul." His voice was harsh and discouraged at the same time. "I know," Paul said and in all seriousness he added, "I should have just shot myself in the head when I had the chance."

The counselor stuck his head out the door and called for a co-worker to join him. The two men stood outside the

Irene Isobel Carver

door and talked a few minutes. Paul could see them both. He knew the co-worker was more of a hard ass and Paul began to fear that they wouldn't help him. Then the first counselor walked back into the room and said, "Okay, Paul we're gonna give you one more chance on this program. But you are going to have to come to group counseling every week or we are going to drop you and suggest that you go into the VA hospital." Paul was beginning to shake from detoxing so he said, "Fine, I'll make it this time, but you are going to have to up my dose from last year; I'm really hurting here." The counselor looked at Paul's records and then passed a paper to Paul ordering him a dose of 60 milligrams of methadone. Paul looked at the slip and said, "I don't think this is enough." "Well, let's start there; if it isn't working and you start cramping then we'll raise it a bit." Paul stood, shook the counselors hand, and got in line to receive his cup of liquid relief. After Paul drank the methadone, he looked over at the calendar on the clinic wall; he felt like he could actually think now. November, he said to himself. It's fall, Paulie is five, I think. The methadone was already helping him get a grip on reality. Irene, he thought, and her face flashed by; my parents, I need to go see them, and he walked out the door saying to no one, "See you tomorrow."

Once Paul had put heroin in his arm, he didn't allow himself to think of his other life, it hurt too much. But now he forced himself to allow memories to wake him up. He touched the twenty- dollar bill in his pocket and decided he'd get the bus to Larchmont and go visit his son. He forgot which stop it was and got off the bus at Cushing Square, realizing he had to walk about ten blocks to Irene's. *It is nice enough out,* he thought; *this will give me time to decide what to say to Irene before she has a chance to get all weird on me.* Then, suddenly, Paul felt like a noose was thrown around his neck and reality screeched to a stop. He looked up and saw he was standing right in front of Stanton Funeral Home. It was a big white house with wrought iron railings around a large front porch. He remembered that this was where Teddy's wake was held. Paul thought he would vomit; he put his head between his hands. He lost connection to time and his body jolted sharply as he ran across the street. He had to get away from that place; it was poison. Once across the street Paul looked back and an oozing puss was chasing him. His eyes searched the terrain in front of him. He began to run, his legs becoming those of the tiger in the jungle in Nam. He ran, springing down the street, searching for his rifle. He spotted a park and dove under a row of bushes crawling inward, expecting a grenade to go off. He lay there panting, then, he rolled into a fetal position. He squeezed his eyes shut, pushing back the vision of Teddy's body lying in a casket draped in an American flag, a tiny bullet hole through his forehead. Then mercifully, the picture in his mind switched to seeing Teddy on the day they had joined the Army together. Teddy's enthusiasm had been so catchy. Paul let go of his knees as his mind slipped back into that Fall day when he and Teddy left their college classes on a dare to join the Army.

Paul's muscles began to relax. He rolled onto his stomach and slid out from under the bushes, looking around to see if anyone was watching him; he was safe. He stood,

Irene Isobel Carver

brushed himself off, and sat on a nearby bench and lit a cigarette. He was still partly altered because he heard Teddy ask the recruiting officer how he could become a paratrooper. Paul sat smoking the cigarette down to the filter and then stepped on it, slowly remembering he was on his way to Irene's house. He stood and walked as fast as he could to Irene's street. When he walked into the front entrance porch to her door he ran his fingers through his matted hair and knocked with some force on the wooden door.

An older woman answered and stepped back when she saw Paul and said, "Can I help you?"

"I'm looking for Irene and my son, are they here?"

"I just moved in last month, so I'm guessing that's the gal that moved out. The landlord's daughter lives next door, maybe she knows something," she added with a bit of kindness and then shut her door and turned the lock. Paul looked around the yard expecting to see Paulie's Big Wheels, not wanting to believe that they were really gone; but there was nothing in sight to connect him to his son; he turned and walked up the alley headed for his parents' house.

Paul chain-smoked as he walked, feeling unprepared to see his mother. His father he could handle, but his mother's nervousness had always made him anxious, even before the war. Paul rang the doorbell anyway. He would need a place to sleep and he thought he could fake acting normal around his parents. His seven-year-old niece, Annie, answered the door and said excitedly, "Oh good, Uncle Paul, I need someone to help me with my puzzle, it's hard." She grabbed his hand and dragged him into the living room. Paul could hear his sister and mother talking and cooking in the kitchen and he was glad he had a place to hide. Paul took a seat at the card table where the puzzle pieces were laid out that would eventually be a scene from Disneyland with Mickey Mouse at its center. Paul looked at Annie and said, "Go tell your grandmother I'm here." Annie went running to the kitchen yelling, "Grammy, mum, Uncle Paul is here to help me with the puzzle." And then she ran back to her seat next to Paul.

When Dora heard her son's name she collapsed onto the kitchen chair and clutched her heart. Her daughter Charlotte, who was molding cookie batter, angrily put down her spoon and stomped into the living room. Paul kept his gaze downward, staring intently at the puzzle pieces, hiding. Charlotte softened her tone of voice because of the presence of her child and said, "Paul, did you think after months of torturing mum and dad, you could just walk in and sit down like nothing is wrong?" Paul placed a puzzle piece of Goofy's ear into its spot and looked up at his sister. He stared at her like there was a wall of worlds between them and said, "Is dad home from work yet?" Charlotte took Annie's hand and said, "Come with me, Annie; I want you to help me in the kitchen for a minute." When they left the room, Paul looked over at the windowsill that was lined with family photos and thought, I'd like to cut them all up and make a puzzle out of all of us, mixing and matching heads and hearts. I'd like to give my sister my brain just for one day and then see what she has to say. Paul resisted the idea of picking up his high school photo and smashing it. Instead *he walked quietly up the stairs to his old bedroom. First he went into the bathroom. In the medicine cabinet, he saw his mother's Valium prescription. He took out four pills and downed them with water.*

Paul slept deeply until he woke up in the middle of the night to the sound of his mother listening to Larry Glick on the radio. He suddenly felt sorry for her. He knew she had trouble sleeping most nights and lay in bed listening to the all night talk show where people, who also couldn't sleep, would call in with questions. Needing to use the bathroom, Paul finally got up and peeked into his mother's bedroom. Seeing her lying there with big soft bags under her closed eyes he said, "Hi mum, sorry I never called." Dora opened her eyes and smiled weakly at her son. He smiled back and closed the door.

In the morning when Paul woke, he realized that he had slept deeply and without nightmares. He pulled on his jeans and long sleeved shirt and went to the bathroom to find a toothbrush to brush his teeth. His dad was in the bathroom shaving. He told Paul there was coffee ready in the kitchen. "No thanks, dad," Paul said, noticing the apple-shaped clock that still hung on the wall as it had throughout his childhood, "I've got to get downtown to the clinic for my methadone by ten o'clock, I'll see you and mum tonight." Paul put his hand on his dad's shoulder. Ed reached up with his free hand and laid it over Paul's saying, "See you tonight then, son."

"Dad, do you know where Irene and Paulie moved to?"

"She and another girl with a child got a house together in Arlington. We miss having Paulie right down the street."

"Does Paulie come over here to sleep still?" Paul poured a cup coffee after all.

"Yes, every Saturday, when Irene works."

"Oh cool, if it's okay with you and mum I'd like to crash here for awhile and then I can see Paulie, too."

"Yes, of course Paul, we would love to have you but we are going to have to make some rules for your mother's sake. This is all very hard on her nerves."

"Sure dad, see you later then."

JOURNEY OF THE SELF TOWARDS THE SELF

"This is worse than going on a date," I said to my closet as I searched for just the right outfit for my first day of work at Gwen's shop. "Let's see—comfy, warm, or stylin'? I finally settled on jeans, leather belt, green ribbed turtleneck and boots. "That's it." I smiled at myself feeling cute when I was all assembled. I practiced in the mirror as I put on my beaded green and black earrings: "Hi, welcome to Plant Haven, can I help you find something?" Paulie came running into my room asking, "Who are you talking to Mummy?" "Myself and my clothes; now let's go talk to your clothes and see which ones want to be worn." I took his hand and guided him towards his room. "Today is a big day, Paulie, you'll be going to your new daycare in a cab after kindergarten, so let's pick out something cool for you to wear." I could see by the look on Paulie's face that he was more afraid than excited so I crouched down to his level and said, "When I come to pick you up at 5:30, we are going right to the sub shop and order you a meat ball sub for dinner!"

"Can I have a Coke with it?"

"Oh, no, Paulie, no Coke for dinner but I will buy you a bag of potato chips to go with it, just 'cause I love you." I kissed his cheek.

"Oh alright, I guess, but you have to let me wear my cowboy shirt, too."

"Well then I guess you will just have to wear your cowboy boots with it."

I walked Paulie into his kindergarten classroom as usual and reminded the teacher that Paulie would be going by cab that day to his new daycare, and that her aide was supposed to walk him to the cab, which would be waiting out front of school at noon. I was relieved when Paulie dropped my hand and ran over to a boy and began to play, but my stomach fluttered anyway as I walked briskly to my car. I looked back at the school and then up to the sky. I pictured a guardian angel hovering close over Paulie, like the picture I had of the angel watching over the children as they crossed a bridge. I inhaled the cold November air and then settled into the blue vinyl bucket seat of my beloved Mustang. I took the Storrow Drive route to work just so I could cruise along the Charles River and let the flow of the water carry me into my new life. The fluttering in my stomach changed to excitement as I turned up the car radio. WBCN and Art Garfunkel accompanied me as my new journey began.

Chapter Twenty-Two

Linger On Those Pale Blue Eyes

—Lou Reed

IT FELT LIKE A FORGOTTEN DREAM WHEN PAUL called me the next week. He said he was staying at his parents' house and he wanted to come visit Paulie, and I began to feel the old familiar threads that had once woven our hearts together. I found myself saying, "Oh sure, I can work an extra Friday night waitressing shift and you can come to our new house and be with Paulie."

"If it's on the bus line, I can, I don't have the car anymore." I could feel shame through his tone.

"Yes, it's on the bus line," I answered, not pausing to let that painful memory of the car register. "And I have a futon in the living room you can crash on because I don't get home from work 'till after the buses stop." I wondered why I was inviting him into my world so casually.

"Thanks, Irene," Paul said even more softly, like it hurt him to speak. I heard him suck in cigarette smoke. "What time should I show up?"

"How about four o'clock? Have your dad tell you how to find us. Okay, I've got to get going, see you Friday." I suddenly needed to disconnect.

As soon as I hung up the phone I realized I was frightened at what I had done. The memory of Paul pushing me up against the wall and taking the title to the car flooded in. I remembered how I had screamed at God. *Is it safe to leave Paulie with his dad*, I wondered and I felt the blood drain from my face. *What if Paul flips out again when I'm not even there? What if he is stoned and nods out and Paulie chokes or something?* I started to panic, and then a solution came to me. *I'll ask Donna if she will stay home that night and keep a back-up eye on Paulie. I'll buy her a bottle of Kahlua and Nestle's*; for that I knew she would do it.

I was completely unprepared for what I felt when I opened the front door on Friday afternoon and there stood my best friend. Paul's strawberry blonde hair still looked like it was made partly of the sun and his pale blue eyes still had the power to disarm me. My shock must have frozen me in place because Paul finally asked, "Are you going to invite me in?" The look on Paulie's face when he saw his dad must have been a reflection of my own as he edged warily up to my thigh and held on to me. "Paulie, I told you your dad was coming tonight to take care of you while I go to work; well, here he is. Why don't we show daddy around our new house," I rambled on as I walked backwards into the living room dragging Paulie with me. Donna walked in from her bedroom right on cue, greeting Paul with a big smile.

Paul took off his winter coat, which I recognized from many winters past, and threw it across the chair by the door. "Oh, Paulie, wait as minute; look what I found in my pocket." Paul pulled out a small toy man and threw it up in the air. A tiny parachute opened and the plastic man floated to the ground; Paulie let go of my leg and ran to catch it. "Wow, cool!" Paulie yelled. He walked closer to his dad. I took this as my cue to exit, but uneasiness swept over me. "Paulie, I've got to get to work, show your dad your cool bedroom and I'll see you in the morning." Paulie looked like he wanted to protest so I held my finger to his lips and knelt close to his face and said slowly and with assurance, "Paulie, have dad read you your *Flying Machine* book at bedtime and I'll let you count my tips when we wake up." I grabbed my coat and keys and pointed to the futon saying, "Paul, that mattress is actually pretty comfortable, see you both in the morning." I guess I gave myself the bums rush out the door because being around Paul was freaking me out big time. I blasted the radio and the heat in the car, trying to drown out the terror that was clenching my chest. "I can't love Paul," I yelled, "I hate him, I fucking hate him. He left me for Natalie, he left me for Rachael, he left me for heroin. He left me carless!" I pounded on the steering wheel with both hands and wept all the way to work.

At 7:00 a.m. the next morning, Paulie jumped on my bed and woke me up saying, "Okay, time to count the loot." Normally, I would have told him to go watch cartoons for a couple of hours and let me sleep but even in my morning fog I recalled that Paul was asleep in the living room. I sat up and looked around the room for my money belt. I pointed to a pile of clothes on the floor and Paulie ran to it flinging my skirt, blouse, nylons, and shoes out of the way until he located the pouch. He jumped up on the bed and dumped it on my lap. He gave me a big smile as he unzipped it. Dollar bills bulged out and Paulie turned it upside down and shook it to get the quarters out, also. I heard Joe Cocker in the background singing "With a Little Help From My Friends." I asked Paulie to shut my bedroom door and I sat up and ran my fingers through my hair. It felt so odd to have a man in the house in the morning. My routine was upset and I didn't know how to deal with that. Paulie closed my door and sat back on the bed, eager to count the cash, which he loved doing. He stacked all the ones in a pile, then the fives, and the tens. Then he started on the change.

There was a soft knock on my bedroom door. Paulie gave me a questioning look as I answered, "Yeah?" Paul stuck his head in the door and said, "Hey, I've got to get going, I have to be at the clinic by ten o'clock." I upset all Paulie's stacks of change when I got out of bed, pulling on my socks and slippers. I followed Paul to the front door, noticing how his brown tweed coat made his hair look like it was also woven. Paul grabbed the door handle but before he opened it he looked me right in the eyes said, "I'm glad I saw you again." I wanted to reach out and touch him but instead I just met his gaze and said, "Me too. Um, did you and Paulie have fun last night?" I forced myself to speak, afraid we might hug if we just stood there. "I think he was afraid of me, he cried after you left and it took me awhile to get him to remember me." "Oh, I'm sorry Paul, that was my fault, I shouldn't have left so fast...but . . ." Paul cut me off, "No, it was alright, I brought a deck of cards with me and as soon as he saw I knew how to play gin rummy like Ed, he stopped crying and we had fun." The air felt thick between us. Paul abruptly opened the door and the cold November wind slapped us, causing us to move in different directions without saying a word of goodbye. Paul headed down the hill to the bus stop while I went to the window and watched him walk away.

I felt dizzy as I fought back the memories that flooded my mind. There we were, eternally at the senior prom, me in my long blue taffeta dress, and Paul in a tux. We were waltzing to "Moon River," and Teddy and Beth were next to us making out on the dance floor. Visualizing Teddy so alive scared me and I turned from the window and dove back into my bed, once again disrupting Paulie's counting.

"Ma you keep messing me up."

"Let's go make cocoa," I said, ignoring the money. As we headed to the kitchen my eyes stopped on the partly built Lego house.

"Did you and dad make that?"

"Yeah, daddy said you and I should finish it, he was too tired." Paulie sounded disappointed. I looked at the roof-less Lego house and thought, *actually I do need to build something,* and felt my own yearning.

Donna and her son were at the kitchen table eating scrambled eggs and cocoa when we walked in.

"Morning, how'd it go with P-A-U-L?"

"T-E-N-S-E," I answered.

"Paulie, go put cartoons on and I'll bring you your breakfast on a TV tray." I needed a moment's space. Paulie ran from the room and I turned to Donna.

"God, I sure hope I hear from Arty soon. "Seeing Paul just fucked my head up." I organized the cinnamon toast and cocoa on a TV tray and carried it into the living room. I noticed that Paul had folded the futon up and placed the folded blanket on top of it. I sat on the futon drinking my cocoa. I loved Saturday morning cartoons as much as Paulie did. I tried to roll the tension out of my neck as I watched TV and for just a little while I let myself forget the adult world as I hung out with Paulie and the Flintstones.

PAUL

Paul convinced the clinic to up his dose of methadone to seventy milligrams; not because he was having stomach

Irene Isobel Carver

cramps, the dose seemed to be enough for his body, but it wasn't helping his mind. Even at seventy mills, he still woke up the next morning at his parent's house slamming his head against his pillow. "Something has to break, something has to crack open," he muffled his chant into the foam pillow. He remembered there was Valium in the bathroom cabinet. Paul felt like a frightened animal as he sprung out of bed and darted across the hall, closing and locking the bathroom door. When he opened the cabinet his eyes lit upon his father's razor blades individually wrapped in waxed paper sheaths. He longed to make a quick slice across each wrist. He pictured himself bleeding onto the floor, his misery gone. He fell to his knees; he couldn't let his parents open the door to that scene. He didn't want to live, to think, to breathe, but he was afraid of the act of dying. There was a knock at the door distracting him from his pain. Paul splashed water on his face, grabbed a towel, and opened the door. Paul looked at his father's furrowed brow.

"Hi, Paul, you doing okay? Your mother and I were thinking it must have been hard for you to see Irene and Paulie yesterday."

"Yeah, I'm okay, it was a bit strange seeing Paulie; he barely remembered me, but it was alright."

"You know, a friend of mine at the registry told me he has a son who has been going to AA meetings and it is really helping him move past the war and make new friends."

"Yeah, at the clinic counseling they mentioned AA meetings; maybe I'll get a schedule next time I'm there." Paul was trying to be the person who was this kind man's son. Ed placed his hand on Paul's shoulder for a moment and went downstairs.

Paul walked back to his bedroom and shut the door. He felt like such a fake and a liar, a shell of a man. He knelt next to his bed like he had done as a child. He folded his hands and leaned his head forward onto the mattress as if to pray. *Fuck, there can't really be a God; what the fuck am I doing?* Then Paul heard his mother call up the stairs to him, "Paul, Danny is on the phone." Paul smiled. *Well, if there is a God, he is sending me some pot so I won't combust.* Paul could sense his parents' fear as he talked to Danny on the phone, so he played his role, telling them what they wanted to hear when he hung up; that he and Danny were just gonna go out for a couple of hours to the Rack and Cue and shoot a little pool. He hoped they couldn't see that he was a rocket of rage about to explode and that he was just trying to cause the least harm to all of them.

Danny pulled up in front Ed and Dora's house an hour later blasting Blind Faith on his eight track. As Paul rushed into the front seat, Danny sang along, "I'm near the end and I just ain't got the time..." Paul chimed in with his own words, "Well, I hope you came to get me wasted and I don't care if I find my way home," and they laughed.

"Charlie's Kitchen?" Danny said as he handed Paul and already lit joint.

"Oh, shit no, not Charlie's, I don't want to talk to anyone; how about we just go listen to music at your pad."

"Well, okay, man but you're gonna have to crash there then, 'cause I'm not gonna get fucked up and drive you all the way back here."

"Remind me to call my parents and tell them, will you?"

Paul felt relief as his consciousness became altered from the pot. He threw his arms back over the seat, exhaling and coughing, and screamed, "Kill-o, kill-o, kill kill."

Danny gave Paul a questioning glance, "You gonna be alright, man?"

"Yeah, I'm cool, just decompressing; all this fucked up shit is just stuck in my head, but pot is a good release valve."

Paul forgot to call his parents and when he arrived home the next afternoon he was greeted by his sister and his brother-in-law who were sitting on the living room couch with Ed. Charlotte was angry. "Paul, you can't just stay gone like that without calling, it's not okay. You're gonna give mum a heart attack. She called me at 3:00 a.m. and woke everyone in the house. We're a wreck Paul, this has to stop." Ed leaned forward to light a cigarette, but instead he put his head in his hands and wept. Charlotte stood, "You see, Paul, dad can't take anymore of this either, this has to stop." She knelt and took Ed's hand in hers. Paul collapsed into the chair next to the couch envying his father's tears. He looked at his sister. He had no idea who she was. Long-buried rage erupted in a strangely calm way as Paul clenched his fists, contained his tone and said, "You think you know everything, right, but you don't, all you know is how to worry just like mum, worry, worry, nag and worry. If the two of you could stop for one fucking minute in this lifetime and let dad and I go from your terror grip then maybe, just maybe, we could breathe." Charlotte and Brian stood up in unison. Charlotte looked at her father with determined eyes and said, "He's all yours dad, we've got to go home to the kids."

Paul and Ed both lit a cigarette as soon as they were gone. Paul said, "Where's mom?" He sat on the couch next to his dad. With tear filled eyes Ed looked at Paul and said, "She's lying down Paul; we didn't sleep all night waiting for you." "I'm sorry, dad, I meant to call, but I forgot. But Charlotte is right dad, I shouldn't stay here, I'll ask Danny if I can rent a room at his place." Ed reached over and took Paul's hand. "Try to get a list of those AA meetings when you can Paul, I, we, love you Paul and we want you to get some help; we know there is nothing we can do." Ed crushed out his cigarette and lit another one. "I know dad, I will, I'll try," Paul said and he walked upstairs and sat down wearily on his bed.

Paul stared out the window at the almost-bare branches of the maple tree. Winter was closing in like a prison. He took off his shoes and socks and looked at the scars the jungle rot had left between his toes and he could feel the humidity of the jungle of Nam and its beauty. It should have been me that died that day when I was point man The scene came into focus. He had seen the helmet of a Vietnamese soldier only a few yards ahead of him. Paul had shot at him as he dove into the brush. He must have missed as a spray of bullets shot over him and one blasted through the chest of the soldier behind him—a kid from South Carolina named Roscoe. Paul had liked him, he was always whistling, "Dixie." Paul had seen Roscoe fall. He slithered on his belly into the brush getting caught up in a vicious firefight that took ten men from his platoon that day. What if I hadn't dodged that first bullet? What if I had taken it like a point man should have? When Paul came back to the present, his

Irene Isobel Carver

jaw ached from clenching and he was sweating viciously.
I should have died that day, Paul thought, as he closed
the curtains, lying down on his back, exhausted. How
pointless to have my body survive war, but not my mind.

It seemed like a long time since Arty had called me, probably because I let myself get emotionally sucked into the past. It had really only been about ten days when the phone rang and there was Arty's cheerful voice.

"So who won the game?'

"Bridgetown kicked Larchmont's ass 49 to 7 and it was freezing," I answered so relieved to hear his voice.

"Well, shit, guess it was just as well I wasn't there. I hate games when one team gets squashed, especially mine."

"Yeah, me too, there's no tension; it gets boring. How did you spend Thanksgiving?"

"It is really sad, Irene. Seattle is full of Indians who hang out in Pioneer Square, drunk. So Del, Terry, and I decided to make a big pot of chowder and we took it down to the center of the Square where the Indians all gather and we set up our own soup kitchen. It was a blast. We went to Goodwill and got a huge pot for a buck, and a bunch of paper bowls and plastic spoons."

"Is Terry a guy?" I was feeling left out and a bit jealous.

"No, she's a chick, just another east coast transplant hanging out with us."

"Is she going out with Del?"

"No, not really. We all hang out, we just need each other out here, it's lonely sometimes being so far away from home." That made me think maybe if he stays lonely he'd come home, but I didn't want to act needy so I didn't say anything.

"Tell me some more about Seattle." I said.

"Well, the most unusual thing I've seen is a billboard that says, "Last one out turn off the lights.""

"What the heck does that mean?" I stretched the phone cord to reach to the stove so I could flip the French toast I was making for me and Paulie.

"Apparently, with the Vietnam War coming to an end, the government isn't ordering any more airplanes from Boeing, so Boeing has been laying off hundreds of workers."

"Hey, I've got some French toast ready, you want some?" I was trying to play with him.

"It feels like the whole city was run by this one company and now lots of people are going bankrupt and fleeing the city." Arty ignored my playfulness. I began eating, not calling Paulie, so I could talk to Arty alone.

"People with college degrees are pumping gas, so newcomers like me are selling blood for five bucks a pint and collecting food stamps."

"Damn, that sounds awful Arty; sure you don't want to flee back to my cozy temple and warm bed?"

"Well, as nice as that sounds, I actually like school a lot and I love this broke city, it is so rich in mountains and water; it's the adventure I came here for."

"Well, if you ever run out of blood to sell you know where I am," I said feeling a bit hurt.

Arty started singing Carol King's, "So Far Away" so I sang back, "it would be so fine to see your face at my door." I was feeling a bit fragile and dejected so I said, "You know what, I've got to get going. It's Saturday, my waitressing night, call me again when you can." He made a kissing sound into the phone and said, "Dream on, Renie, dream until your dreams come true," quoting Aerosmith as he hung up the phone.

Holi-Daze

Christmas at Plant Haven was a blast. Gwen ordered a stag-horn fern, which was the most exotic plant we had. It had two big antler-like leaves growing out of a bed of moss set in a wood frame. We dressed it up like our pet reindeer with bells around a neck made from moss. My very favorite plant was the corkscrew plant, also called hoya. It was waxy and thick and actually twisted and hung like ringlets in a girl's hair. I laced mistletoe through one of the ringlets and hung it in the front window. I named her Missy; she was not for sale. Some days it was a bit of a struggle to stay cheerful; I missed Arty's laughter and I was afraid for Paul. It was heavy.

One day, while assembling a terrarium, I looked deeply into the tiny world I was creating and decided, as I added tiny blue stones under a minute bridge, that I was absolutely not going to let myself be sad over Christmas. Every time I passed a thrift store I went in and bought myself yet another red top. I started each work day choosing some flavor of red to wear with my jeans and I would pep talk myself in the mirror saying, *Cheer up, Renie, and decide how you want to bring in the New Year.*

1974—Endings and Beginnings

New Year's Eve was the best money night of the year, so of course I would work that night and there would be plenty of time to party afterwards. I began to call around to see where the action was. Rickey O. was having a bash in Bridgetown, and Karen Swanson was having an overnighter at her cottage in New Hampshire. I couldn't go to either. Paul could possibly be at Rickey O's and there was no leaving town with my late night work shift. Rosario's stopped serving food at 10:00 p.m. because it was a white table cloth dinner place, not a 2:00 a.m. close- the-bar joint, but still, driving after work did not sound safe or fun. I decided to call my friend from my Boston State days, and it was a good move because she had the perfect invitation—party at a mansion in Jamaica Plain! She gave me directions and told me to bring anyone I would like. *Far out,* I thought, *there's no chance of running into Paul and I could meet new people.* I knew immediately I would wear the bellbottoms I had embroidered with butterflies on each back pocket. When I wore those jeans I always got lots of attention. The chicks would give me compliments on the French knots that I used to make the butterfly eyes, and the dudes just loved the opportunity to look at a girl's butt and couldn't help but comment.

With my New Year's plan set, I relaxed for a moment. Then I remembered Christmas was in two weeks and I hadn't bought Paulie his Santa Claus gifts yet. I had to buffer myself from the sadness I felt each time I thought about Paul. I knew I was really on edge when the phone rang and I would tense up, hoping it wasn't Paul calling, so I made a plan—if Paul calls I will tell him that if he wants to see Paulie, we will meet at his parents' house and he can visit him there. I made my voice sound strong as I practiced saying this out loud. Then I tried to force myself to think about gifts, but I needed inspiration. I lit a joint and stared out the window at the winter sky. Aha! I immediately visualized a pair of black ice skates from Santa, red superman pajamas from me, and a red cowboy hat. I needed someone to share this vision with, so I called Dora and she told me that they were going to wrap a present to Paulie from his dad—a magnetic drawing toy called a Mega Doodle, and clothes from them. Suddenly Christmas felt settled and I tried to relax.

As the days passed, Ed, Dora, and I went out of our way not to bring up Paul's name because none of us knew what we would say to Paulie; we hadn't heard from Paul since Thanksgiving, and it was just too painful. It was as if on some level we were all holding our breath. Then, a few days before Christmas, Dora called me and said she and Ed were really worried about Paul; he had come to their house and asked for money but never asked about Paulie. She said he sounded so desperate they were afraid not to give him the money. Dora started to cry, and then anger rose up in her voice as she ranted into the phone that the government should be helping her son; he was a war veteran and needed help. Ed took the phone from her and said, "Don't worry, Irene, I'm going to call the Veterans Administration in the morning and see what help they can offer."

"Thank you, Ed; I think that's a good idea," I answered, shocked at this new information. "I'm afraid for Paul, too; let me know if there is anything you want me to do." I hung up the phone, feeling like there was a brick on my chest.

After I read Paulie to sleep that night, I went straight to the kitchen and poured a shot of tequila into my favorite glass. I slugged it back and collapsed into the comfortable parlor chair we kept in the corner of the kitchen. I closed my eyes and allowed the tequila to do its hallucinatory work as I flashed back to the Christmas when I gave Paul the black leather vest he had loved so much. He had worn it just about every day since I gave it to him. He often commented on the tiny pocket that was just big enough to hold a joint. He called it the "magic pocket" whenever he pulled out a perfectly rolled joint, as if the pocket itself had produced it.

I jolted upright in my seat; it hurt way too much to think of the Paul of the past. Tequila had been a bad choice; I wanted something to knock me out, not flash me back. Just then Donna walked into the kitchen and I burst out crying.

"What the fuck? I take it visions of sugarplums are not dancing in your head," she joked.

"It's actually not funny Donna, I'm having Paul flash-backs. Help me, remind me who I am, will you?"

"Okay, let's see. You are twenty five, you have two jobs and a very handsome boy friend who lives far away." She began to heat up milk to make her evening drink. I cried harder at the memory of Arty and the distance between us. I went into the living room and put Marvin Gaye on the record player and began dancing, pretending Arty was in my arms.

"How sweet it is to be loved by you," I sang to myself and Donna joined me with her hot drink in hand. Then she sat down on our couch and motioned for me to join her.

"I guess this is as good a time as any to tell you what I've been thinking," she said as she settled in. I turned down the volume on the stereo and sat next to her.

"Bobby and I have been talking about moving in together, getting our own place, in the spring, when our lease is up."

"Well, I'm not really surprised," I said, "I guess we both know we would rather be living with our men."

"Yeah, I want to have more children, don't you?" It seemed like she wanted to get some things off her mind.

"Yeah, eventually I do, but first I have to figure out if Arty is gonna come back here to Boston."

"Have you thought of moving out to Seattle?"

"Well, I hadn't even thought of that," I answered surprised at how casually she introduced such an enormous idea. "But now that you mention it, I don't think Arty has any plans of coming back here, and actually for me to hang around Boston and watch Paul kill himself on smack seems like a really sad idea."

I stood up thinking what a heavy damn night this was. The tequila was wearing off and Donna's reality bite was like a sobering slap. She wanted to move in with her man, what was I going to do? As if Donna read my mind she said, "Well, you could get another roommate here and maybe Arty will come back." But her words felt all wrong. It was as if her idea of me going to Seattle had been prophetic, and could not be taken back or ignored.

Chapter Twenty-Three

God—The Space Between Everything

THE HOLIDAYS CAN EITHER BE HEAVEN OR HELL depending on what's going on in your life. Heaven is the Christmas when you're in love and magic fills everything you do. Hell is the Christmas to make it through, to bear with the broken heart. That being said, this was my Christmas in limbo?

The Saturday evening before Christmas, Paul and a couple of his friends came into Rosario's looking like the scraggliest, drugged-out hippies in town. They sat down in the plush lobby on red velvet chairs and lit up cigarettes. When the maitre d' asked if he could help them, Paul stood up and said he'd like to see his wife, Irene! It was 5:00 p.m.; I had just come on the floor when I was called to the lobby. I was totally shocked seeing Paul sitting there. These two worlds of mine did not make sense colliding in the same space. I stared blankly at Paul. The maitre d' watched us, scared that he would be required to do something, when Paul calmly asked, "Hey Irene, got some money I can have?" I checked my apron pocket; I had a five-dollar bill and four ones, so I just gave it all to Paul. He counted it, turned and walked out with his friends without saying a word. I was too embarrassed to say anything; I just walked back to my station, hoping I was not about to get fired, and for just a moment I thought I might faint. Then another waitress came up next to me and nudged me. She handed me a glass of water. I made it through my shift that night, performing my tasks, writing down orders, and delivering cocktails to elegantly dressed couples, but the whole time I felt somewhat dazed, like my world was out of balance.

Then there was the evening that Dora, who had never said an unkind word to me in our lives, called me after having a few drinks and told me more or less that I should go back with Paul. She said I was still married to him and it was my obligation as his wife to help him. She ranted on about how I had chased Paul all through high school and now he needed me. I couldn't say a word in response since all I could feel was how broken her heart was and how desperate she was as she watched her son suffer. I listened to her and began to quiver internally at the thought of me being the one strong enough to help Paul. Finally, I said, "I have to hang up, Dora, Paulie needs me," and I gently placed the phone on its hook. I walked into my bedroom feeling dazed, and looked into the mirror. I kindly said to myself, "Irene, you are twenty five, you have a five year old son and that is all you can hold together; that is your obligation."

I think that was the first time I had a sense of my *higher self*. I didn't cry. The internal shaking stopped and I was filled with compassion for Dora and the horrific suffering that allowed her to lash out at me. I stood still, witnessing our world of pain. Then, as if the universe knew I needed something of beauty to survive, my parents gave me the most precious Christmas gift I could have imagined; a woolen poncho that was imported from Peru. It was lush and expensive looking. I was so amazed that I asked my mother where she had gotten something so exquisite and she said that she had given Clare money and asked her to pick me out something really special. I held its soft chocolate brown alpaca wool next to my face and breathed in my parents' caring concern for me.

Clare later told me that Mum had given her a hundred dollar bill and told her to find me something special. Clare said she had found the poncho in a small import store next to the Algiers coffee house in Harvard Square. I had never received such a special gift, and it may just have saved my sanity that winter. Each time I threw it over my head and let it drape my body I felt as if I entered a beautiful world of mountains, and pure air; it felt magic.

New Year's Eve 1974

I made seventy-eight dollars in tips on New Year's Eve and my feet were killing me when I finally got to sit down and pull off my panty hose at 11:00 p.m. A dozen waitresses were jammed into our locker room excitedly preparing to get to our New Year's destinations before midnight. Some of the women were opening champagne bottles as we changed, but I knew I had to get across the city to Jamaica Plain so I passed on any offerings. I unfolded the two steaming hot lobster towels that I had taken from the kitchen and washed the sweat from my face before I applied my black eye liner and burgundy lipstick. I pulled on my butterfly jeans and a sexy French-cut white velour top. I put a couple of drops of rose essential oil on my hair brush then bent over flinging my long hair forward brushing vigorously to fluff it up. I zipped up my brown leather boots, threw on my magic poncho, and charged to the parking lot where my faithful

Mustang awaited me.

Just before midnight, I drove through the wrought iron gate that took me around a circular driveway, which led to a front door that looked like something right out of a Hitchcock movie. It had two iron knockers on double wooden doors. Without using the knockers, I walked into the cathedral-like entrance hall. Pink Floyd's *Dark side of the Moon* album was blasting from speakers that were set into the walls on shelves. I walked through an arched entrance to the living room and I saw a bay window framed with luxurious purple velvet curtains. Two arms reached around me from behind. The hands were closed in fists in front of my chest and a male voice spoke into my ear, "Pick a hand." "Hmm…" I said as I tapped the left hand. I felt a bit frightened as I had no idea who this was and his arms felt slightly controlling. He opened his left palm, which held a tiny slip of blotter acid. I turned around to see Mikey Cleaver, the guy who had sat behind me in Western Civilization class.

"So do you want to get lost, little girl?" he asked in a very seductive Jim Morrison kinda way. I knew immediately that I was more interested in getting found than to take a New Year's detour into Neverland. "You know what, Mikey," I said and trying to sound playful and not straight, "Life has changed a lot since Western Civ. class. I have a five year old son and I need to be able to drive home tonight, so I'm gonna have to pass. But I'd love to see the rest of this place." Mikey grabbed my hand and we headed into the scene, and what a scene it was! There appeared to be around 200 people spread out through twenty or more rooms and judging by the way everyone was undulating to the music, it seemed like most of them were getting off on the blotter acid.

Suddenly the music stopped and a Tibetan gong reverberated throughout the vaulted ceilings. In unison people began to chant "OM" over and over, then the gong was struck again. I didn't know where the sound was coming from until a woman in a long white satin dress walked into the room holding the gong from a rope announcing the midnight hour. I closed my eyes and felt the whole room vibrate. *Who needs acid*, I thought, as I dropped Mikey's hand and flowed with the sound into the next room. Everyone yelled "Happy New Year" and the music started up again, blasting Boston's own boys, Aerosmith, singing "Dream On." At that moment memories of Arty fluttered through my heart. *Wow, these people are rich*! I thought, as I danced my way around plush couches and chairs. I drifted over to a circle of people I saw passing a joint. I took a couple of hits and smiled at the woman who handed it to me and said, "Happy New Year," and we hugged.

I looked across the room and spotted my friend Maryanne, who had invited me to the party. She saw me walking towards her and we yelled "Happy New Year" and fell into a deep hug. She held up her glass of wine to toast and saw that I had nothing to toast with so she said, "Come, I'll show you the kitchen, it's big enough to roller skate in." She was right. In my stoned mind I saw myself as a housewife roller skating from stove to refrigerator, and into the pantry, doing a spin. "Wow!" I said as Maryanne poured me a glass of white wine in a beautiful goblet. Then we toasted, "Cheers," and I took a big swig. "Follow me," she said and we headed upstairs to a bedroom that had a huge stone fireplace, with a perfect fire raging in it.

We settled onto a comfy couch in front of the fire with our wine and I felt something shift within me. *Had I really been waitressing just a couple of hours ago*? I looked around the room and saw an armoire of blonde maple wood with 1920's art deco surrounding it. The room was steeped in luxury. There was a bearskin rug on the floor and fifteen foot tall windows draped with gold brocade drapes. I felt like I was in a movie scene. "I wonder who shot the bear," Maryanne said, when she noticed me staring at it. I ignored the question and we began to talk.

"So how the heck are you my friend?" I asked.

"Well, I got a job teaching first grade, and thank God, the kids are still easy and fun. My boyfriend teaches fifth grade and those kids are mean and the parents are worse."

"How about you, what have I missed?" she asked.

"I think I'm moving to Seattle, Washington this year," I heard myself say. Maryanne's boyfriend walked up with a bottle of wine and refilled both our glasses. *I am surely in heaven*, I thought, and added, "I can't believe I just said that."

"Why," Maryanne said, "is it a secret?"

"No, it's not a secret, it's just an idea that I haven't really thought through entirely. It's like it just dropped out of the ethers," I said feeling a little frightened as I gave the idea reality.

"Did you take that blotter acid Mickey has?" Maryanne asked.

"No way in hell would I be taking acid these days, Maryanne. I have a new boyfriend who just moved to Seattle and I just feel like…well, running away," I admitted.

"Tell me more about him," she asked.

"Well," I said as I sipped my wine, "we spent a couple of amazing months together and then he moved to Seattle to go to boat building school."

"Boat building—he sounds cool."

"Yeah, but up until this minute, I kept hoping he'd just come back here; not me move there."

"Isn't Seattle up by Alaska?"

"Yeah, it's far but it has been depressing here watching what Paul has been going through since Nam. It may be a good idea for me and Paulie to move away and not have to watch Paul slowly dying."

"Dying, is it really that serious?" Maryanne's face totally changed.

"He's not able to stay away from heroin, it seems to be his only relief from the trauma he experienced when he was sent back to Nam into the Tet Offensive." I realized that I needed to change the subject before it completely ruined my New Year's night. Maryanne felt the same vibe and called to her man who was across the room.

"Hey, Roy, can you get us a joint? We need to change our head space."

"At your service, madam," he said, pulling a joint from behind his ear. He lit the joint and Maryanne took a hit and slid off the couch onto the bearskin rug.

"Isn't Seattle where the Space Needle is?" She handed me the joint.

"Yeah, it was built for the World's Fair 1962, I think."

"Arty, that's my guy, says the mountains are incredible and the sunsets are worth staying there for."

Maryanne and Roy began making out and I suddenly wanted to call Arty and share my thoughts with him. I missed him and I wanted someone to kiss on New Year's. I hugged Maryanne from behind and said, "Hey I think I'm gonna head out of here, we'll talk later." Without waiting for a response, I floated downstairs to the kitchen. The clock on the wall said 2:40 a.m. and I suddenly felt exhausted.

I saw a teapot steaming on the stove so I grabbed a tea bag from a box on the counter, filled a large cup with steaming water, and found my way to the front door. *These rich folks won't miss a cup*, I assured myself as I traipsed past all the stoned and happy people. I walked into the cold morning of 1974 and as I looked up at the stars, I felt unusually connected. My future seemed to be falling from the sky, and as I sat in my car waiting for the engine to warm up, sipping jasmine tea, I knew I was ready to catch it.

COULD IT BE REAL?

Driving home along the familiar Charles River, I began to feel the power that verbalizing a thought really had. My stomach felt a bit jittery and I understood that I had frightened myself. I felt I had put something in motion that I just might not have control over. The top one hundred tunes of the year were playing on the radio, but my mind could not be distracted by the music. *Who is that girl anyway, that said so casually, I'm moving to Seattle.* My thoughts ran on, bumpy and jumbled, more in tune with the potholes in the pavement than with the slow and tranquil river moving along next to me.

When I got home it was 4:30 a.m. I flung my poncho on the couch, turned up the heat, went to my bedroom and put on my flannel pajamas. The phone rang. *Holy shit*, I thought, fear rushing in. Then I remembered that it would only be 1:30 a.m. in Seattle; it had to be Arty.

"About time you picked up," Arty said after I said hello. "I've called you about four times; it must have been a good party." He sounded jealous.

"Yeah, it was a very cool party at a mansion in Jamaica Plain and I'm exhausted," I said as I lit a candle.

"Did you dance much?" That was Arty's sneaky way of finding out if I had been with a man.

"No, not really. I mostly sat by a fire and talked to a girlfriend from college. When I told my friend that I had a new boyfriend who just moved to Seattle, she asked me if I was going to move there too." I did not really feel ready to talk about this with Arty, but the wine and pot were pulling it out of me.

"What did you tell her?"

"I told her I was hoping you would come back here," I answered truthfully. There was silence.

"Give me a second; I need to light a joint," he said. I heard him take a couple of deep breaths as I pulled the afghan around me and settled back on the couch and stared at the Christmas tree, waiting. Arty coughed and then cleared his throat.

"Irene I have no intention of leaving Seattle, I love it here." Now it was my turn for silence.

"Well, I guess I could think about moving to Seattle. I have to admit I could use a change." I started to get more comfortable with my honest feelings.

"I do miss you, Irene; do you think you would actually come out here or are you just very stoned?"

"As long as there are good schools for Paulie out there, I think I could figure out how to pull it off."

"You know, it feels too late to talk about this, Irene; I'm starting to fade, but I will say that the money trip is starting to get better here. I actually got a job painting a lady's kitchen," Arty said with a big yawn into the phone.

"You're right, it's too late, I can hardly think, I've got to crash. But here's a New Year's kiss first," I said as I made a big smack into the phone. Arty made a kissing sound back and said his usual, "Dream on beautiful, I'll call you soon." I hung up the phone with a shiver, unplugged the Christmas tree and collapsed under my thick comforter, calling it a year!

After New Year's Eve, I felt like I was suspended in time, living in a gigantic void that I had no words for. I didn't dare say anything about my Seattle plans as I wasn't entirely sure that New Year's Eve had been real. Maybe I had picked up a contact LSD high at the party and hallucinated my conversations with Maryanne and Arty. I had no phone number to reach Arty in Seattle so I called Maryanne and asked her if I had in fact told her I was moving to Seattle. She confirmed our conversation and she assured me that I was not that stoned when I left the party.

Mercifully, Arty called me on January 6th. Hearing his voice was like a grounding rod. I loved the way he dramatized things and made life fun, like theatre. He opened the conversation by saying, "The Mountains are so incredibly beautiful the way they surround the entire city and it makes me feel freer than I have ever been in my life." FREE was the word that struck me. I wanted more than anything to feel that way, too.

"Hold on a second, Arty, I've got to play you a song," I said as I put the receiver down and put on a Moody Blues album. Before I put the needle down on the cut "Your Wildest Dream" I said "Are you there?"

"Yeah, I'm here, I even had time to make a rum and Coke.".

"Okay then, listen I'm going to sing you the words," and I began: "Once upon a time, once when you were mine … I wonder if you think about me," I turned the music down and stopped singing, and Arty picked up where I had left off and sang, "In your wildest dreams." *Oh my God, he knows the words!* Every inch of me was smiling and I knew I was going to move to Seattle.

Arty called me every week in January and we began to make serious plans as to how we could actually make my moving to Seattle happen. Arty said he heard of a few people who had taken the Montreal Express train from Montreal to Vancouver, B.C. and that it was a far out trip for three days, and it was cheaper than flying. When we hung up I tried to picture Paulie and me on a train, just the two of us speeding into the unknown, and I became overwhelmed with emotion. I went to my hall mirror and looked into my eyes, trying to steady myself. First I noticed what Arty had pointed out, that my eyes looked like the rings of a tree. Something in that gave me confidence. I began to brush my hair and with each full, strong brush I felt as if I was brushing away my fears. My internal dialogue kicked in. *Damn, Renie, what do you think you're going to do, wiggle your nose and you'll be gone. What if you get out there and you don't like it?* I tried to brush that thought away. *How are you going to tell Dora and Ed?* I brushed harder. *What if they won't let you take Paulie away?* I collapsed to my knees with that thought and wept. *And what about Paul? Where the hell is he? Oh God, and then there's my parents.* I felt so downhearted, I couldn't get up. I crept into the living room and buried myself in a stack of pillows.

Paulie came running in the front door and seeing me on the floor, he jumped on top of me yelling "pig pile," which snapped me out of the terror that was gripping me. I let him tickle me as we rolled around our brown shag rug and I brushed away my tears with the sleeve of my sweater.

"I need a peanut butter and jelly sandwich, ma" Paulie said in between giggles.

Irene Isobel Carver

"Oh good, I need some tea," I told him and we stood up. *Saved again*, I thought as I grabbed for Paulie's hand.

"You're my little sidekick, aren't you, Paulie?" I put on the kettle for tea. He got the peanut butter and jelly out of the fridge and, standing up on his stool at the counter, began to make his own sandwich.

"Yep, I'm the sidekick," he answered as he licked the knife of the excess peanut butter.

My eyes filled with tears again as I realized I would have to explain all of this to Paulie, as well. I poured myself chamomile tea, hoping to calm my nerves, and I pulled out a pad of paper and sat at the kitchen table while Paulie ate.

"I need milk, ma," Paulie mumbled with his mouth full.

"Milk, of course, my little Rothschild," I said as I filled his favorite glass. *And what do I need? I need a plan*, I told myself.

My thoughts were jumping all over the place as I tried to decide how I would explain myself to everyone. I wrote the words SEATTLE PLAN in big letters and then pushed the pad away. *Just breathe*, I told myself, noticing that I was holding my breath. Paulie wiped his milk moustache on his sleeve and ran to the front door.

"I'll be out front, ma," he yelled to me.

"Come here, Paulie, let me zip your coat, it's cold." But instead I went to him, needing to stretch, avoiding "THE PLAN." When I came back to the kitchen table, I watched as a large hawk landed on a top branch of the maple tree outside my window. He began screeching repeatedly so I looked at him and screeched back, "What?" I felt like he was prodding me, taunting me. "Okay, okay, my plan," I said as I pulled the pad of paper close and began.

1) Let Donna know right away so she and Bobby can make their plans.

2) Tell Gwen, so she can hire someone to take my place at Plant Haven.

3) Find out how much the Montreal Express costs and figure out how much money I will need.

4) Moving sale: What big items do I have to sell? How much? Car, shag rug, stereo, beds, dressers, kitchen table etc.

That's enough for now, I told myself as I stood up and started looking at my brand new 1974 calendar. I stared at the large white oleander flower that Georgia O'Keefe painted for the month of January. I already was nostalgic for the 1973 Norman Rockwell pictures. Norman felt like family, and Georgia made me feel lost and vague; it wasn't a comfortable feeling.

Why did I buy this calendar? I felt disappointed. I flipped through the months of flowers and stopped at June, the California poppy. I felt better. *I'll leave in mid June,* I decided. *School will be out here and we'll have all summer to adjust to our new world before Paulie starts first grade.* I looked at the maple tree, the hawk was gone. I looked at February's sparse blue iris and wondered who I should tell first, my parents, or Dora and Ed? *My parents are stronger,* I thought as I looked at an audience of blank months before me. *I'll try out my explanation on them first.* The white oleander suddenly reminded me of Paul, and sadness washed over me. *Would he even care if we left or would it be a relief, a burden lifted?*

THE BEST LAID PLANS OF MICE AND ME

I picked the second of February, Saint Brigit's Day, to tell Donna that I was definitely going to move to Seattle in mid June. I wanted it to be a holy parting. So after we put our sons to bed, I fixed us each a Kahlua and milk and I announced, "I've got a plan, are you ready?" After I shared my basic ideas, Donna clicked my glass excitedly and said, "That's a fabulous idea Irene, and no offense, but I would much prefer to live with Bobby." "No offense taken. Arty brought us together, now Arty can pull us apart." I joked.

As we sat curled up on our couch planning our futures I recalled a scene that captured the true essence of Donna. It was a night when she was going out to pick up her boyfriend, Bobby, at work. As she slinked past me in the hall draped in her black fur coat with her long black hair blending into the shiny fur, I remembered thinking how she had the feel of an otter. She said ever so quietly, "I have nothing on under this, not a stitch!" I walked to the window and watched her slide into her white T-Bird, looking just like a movie star as she pulled on her black leather gloves. She had an aliveness that caught my breath and that feeling flooded back over me now as we were about to set our lives in different directions. I could feel myself tucking this memory in a tiny treasure chest in the place songs call "The bottom of your heart." I knew then that it was a real place and that no amount of time or distance could take that memory from me, it was part of me.

Next I had to tell Gwen my plans so that she wouldn't hear it through the grapevine. Gwen would need to hire someone to take my place. On Monday morning when I went to work, I began my usual routine of filling watering cans and letting them settle in the back room sink. As usual, Gwen had already been there for a couple of hours and was sitting at her desk doing paper work and preparing to make orders. I walked up behind her and rested my hands on her shoulders.

"Gwen, I have some great news. I am moving to Seattle

in June." She swiveled her chair around and stood up.

"I thought maybe that would happen," she calmly said as we hugged each other. "But damn, Irene, Seattle is awfully far away, what if you don't like it?"

"Well, I'll stay for a year and then come back, can ya hold my job?" I said laughingly, not wanting her to get too serious.

"It's nine o'clock, I better go unlock the door," I said as I walked to the front of the store, avoiding more conversation. I returned, bringing a Swedish ivy with me, and placed it in the sink. I began to trim off the long stems to use as cuttings to start another plant. Gwen stood next to me taking each cutting as I handed them to her and she asked, "Did you tell your parents, yet?"

"Not yet, I'm trying to get up the courage to confront all my mother's Catholic logic about sin." We laughed even though we knew it wouldn't be at all funny to face my mother's interrogation.

"What are you going to do with all your furniture?"

"I'll have a moving sale in May."

"Well, if you're serious, I want your shag rug," Gwen said, nudging me with her hip.

We both carried watering cans to the front room where I stopped and looked over at my friend the Libra, standing among all things beautiful she had created. The morning sun shone through the windows giving Gwen a halo of begonias, wandering jews and philodendrons. She wore a white tailored shirt with the sleeves rolled up. I watched her as she lovingly checked each tiny plant and, like I had done with Donna, I captured her essence and placed it forever in my heart.

A customer opened the door and Gwen headed to

the back room to continue her work. I smiled at the older woman and said, "Hi, welcome to Plant Haven, have a look around and let me know if I can answer any questions." I got teary as I realized that letting go of my world, my friends, and my sisters was going to be a pretty difficult job. *I hope he's worth it,* I said to myself as I grabbed the broom and began to sweep the aisles.

As I drove home from work that day, I was both disappointed and relieved. For some reason I thought Gwen would say, "No, no don't go, it won't be the same here without you." In that regard, I felt a bit hurt. But on the other hand, I was relieved because I didn't have to defend my position. *Was I just going to be allowed to let my life change?* I smiled at that thought. By the time I pulled into my driveway I felt some relief. I had tested the waters, and I was preparing for a far more difficult next step—my mother.

February brought in another nor'easter, and it gave me an idea. I called my mother and offered to come over and shovel their front walk in exchange for lunch.

"That's a great deal, will tuna sandwiches be okay for you and Paulie?"

"I'm gonna leave Paulie at Dora and Ed's house 'cause I want to talk to you about something and I don't want him to hear."

"Is it Paul? Has something happened?" her voice tensed up.

"No, it's not Paul; I just want privacy."

"If you don't want Dad to hear then lunch will be at one o'clock."

"Ya, let's make it one o'clock, but I'll come at noon and shovel snow while you two eat."

"Good thinking, Renie, see ya then."

The next morning I had to shovel my car out before I could leave, which was exhausting. Eight inches of snow covered everything and the plows left a bank of snow at my driveway that I had to make a path through. Paulie was too little to help so he just sat on top of the snow bank and licked the snow off his mittens in sheer bliss. Meanwhile, my car was running so that when the drive was clear she would be all warmed up.

When I was done we got into the car. I inched our way down our steep hill to Massachusetts Avenue, which was all clear and sanded. My heart and mind were racing as we drove past Wilson's farm. Their fields looked glorious covered in sparkling new snow. Visions of August's cornfields floated in the ethers above the snow and I thought, *I won't be here to see these fields next August,* and a twinge of sadness hit me. I've never known August without Wilson's farm stands. *Oh, don't be so nostalgic, Renie,* I told myself, while looking in the rear-view mirror, *Seattle will have its own fields of something to fall in love with, won't it?* I pulled up in front of Dora and Ed's house and beeped the horn as we had arranged. They opened the front door and Paulie leapt from my car and ran up his grandparents' shoveled steps. I made a U-turn and headed to my parents' house.

My Mom left the shovel stabbed into the snow next to the front porch and once again I heaved shovel full after shovel full of snow up onto the lawn until I finished the job and was happily at the red front door. I pulled my boots off after I entered and breathed in the warm Toll House cookie-drenched air. I almost burst into tears as I realized that this would be another of my life's treasured moments I would be moving away from. My mother came out from the kitchen and wiped her hands on her apron. "Here, give

Irene Isobel Carver

me your cold hands," she said, and as I did, she placed them under her arms—her wings—like she did when we were little kids. I naturally leaned into her and she kissed my cheek. I sensed, from her deep nurturing, that she felt I was about to tell her something important.

I sat down at the kitchen table where a tuna sandwich sat cut in half on my plate. My mother poured us each a cup of red rose tea and we each added milk to our cup. Mum sat down across from me and said, "Okay, tell me what's going on, is it happy or sad?"

"Let me eat half this sandwich first, I'm ravenous," I said.

"Okay, I'll tell you about dad and the foot doctor while you eat," my mother complied. As she rambled on about the gout in dad's big toe I looked around the kitchen. My eyes rested on the small statue of The Blessed Mother that sat on the window shelf where it had been every day of my life, and my eyes welled with tears again. I didn't think I could take this severing torture much longer so I blurted out, "Remember that guy Arthur I brought up here last summer for a cookout?"

"Yes, he moved away didn't he?"

"Yeah, he moved to Seattle and he loves it there and he wants me and Paulie to move there with him." I picked up the other half of my sandwich and nervously continued eating.

"Well, this is more shocking than I thought, Renie. Do you two know each other well enough to move all that way?" She got the cookies from the freezer; we always had frozen cookies dunked in hot tea after lunch. She placed the cookies on the table while removing my sandwich plate.

"Seems to me that he should come back here and if you are still serious, get married and then go to Seattle," My mother surmised emphatically. I dunked a cookie.

"In your generation that is just what people would do, but the world isn't like that anymore."

"Well, it should be like that, that's the problem, the world's going to hell in a hand basket just because of decisions like this."

"Mum, everything doesn't have to be set in stone, maybe that is also part of the problem with the world. Maybe we need to be allowed to make mistakes and change our minds."

"No, Renie, it's a sin. Remember, it's a sin to have sex before marriage!"

Then I got mad. "You know what I think is a sin, mum? A sin is dropping napalm on people. A sin is senators and presidents going to church one day, and the next day giving orders to bomb a country full of people living there, that's what sin is to me!" I put my head down on the table and wept. My mother, Mary Macalister, stood above me and rubbed my back in circles between my shoulder blades. Then she got a Kleenex from the bathroom and blew her nose. She was crying and said, "Yes, that is a sin but that is on their souls; I'm concerned with your soul, Renie. You've been through enough pain already; I don't want you to get hurt anymore."

I stood up and looked out the kitchen window at the snow-covered branches on "my" apple tree. She was beautiful and I pictured my little girl self, sitting high up in those branches, pretending the tree was my airplane. I looked my mother straight in the eyes and said calmly, "Mum, I've got to take this risk. I've got to get away, I can't bear for Paulie and me to stay around and watch Paul die a slow drug-addicted death, please just let me go."

I could see the determination drop from my mother's

face and there we stood, with the truth thick in the tea-scented air. I think she could sense the quicksand forming around my heels. I did in fact *have* to go; survival over-rode sin. We both sat down again at the kitchen table and poured more tea. I told her I was going to find out about the Montreal Express train that could take us from Montreal to Vancouver B.C. I watched her lovely green eyes pool with tears, but she quickly dabbed them dry. She put on her Scottish battlefield demeanor and said, "Let me know when you are sure about this and I will break it to your father." She gave me a big hug and then pushing me to arms length, said "Your father is going to want to know all the answers to the practical questions like, what about a job? Does Arthur have one? Will you ever go back to school and finish your education? So get some answers prepared Renie." and she pinched both my cheeks.

We walked to the front door and I put on my boots. We were changed. I knew what I needed to do next and my mother had become my ally. I put on my heavy wool pea coat and then cupped her sixty-eight year old face in my hands and comforted her by saying, "Don't worry, mum, I promise I'll always have my rosary in my pocket." I stepped out into the thickly falling snow. I started up my car and sat in it as it warmed up, looking at my mother waving to me through the storm door. We had lived in this house since I was four months old; it was my anchor, my Tara. If Seattle didn't work there would always be my apple tree rooted there for me. I smiled and waved back, and headed to Dora and Ed's; telling them would have to wait for another day, I was exhausted.

Chapter Twenty-Four

Desperately In Need Of A Stranger's Hand In A Desperate Land

—Jim Morrison

The same storm that brought me to my mother's table for lunch found Paul surviving the night huddled in the doorway of the Army Navy store in Central Square. Since Paul had left his parents' house in November out of compassion for them, he had been surviving by panhandling and crashing at other junkie's pads. At first he tried to stay at Danny's place but eventually his long time friend wanted him to admit himself into the VA hospital, and Paul just couldn't do that. "Fuck the government," Paul blasted at Danny. "The last time I was at the methadone clinic I heard the government wouldn't even admit that the Agent Orange they sprayed in Nam is responsible for vets being sick with cancer. Fuck the government, I'd rather die than trust those mother fuckers." He left Danny's, slamming the door on his way out.

Fortunately, the doorway Paul was taking shelter in was deep and had about eight feet of covered window space. Even though the wind was blowing, it was relatively calm in the back corner where Paul was huddled. He had a sleeping bag someone gave him from a shelter a couple of nights before, when they didn't have room to let him in, and he had a pack of cigarettes, so he figured he'd make it through the storm. Two other dudes joined him in his cove and when he found out they were both vets, he spread the sleeping bag down so they all could sit on it and he shared his smokes. One of the guys had a bottle of Jack Daniels and they passed that around until all three of them passed out against the window.

Suddenly a flashlight burned through their oblivion and into Paul's eyes. Paul pushed one guy off his shoulder and tried to sit up straight. The cop kicked the dude that was lying down asleep and said, "All three of you up, in the car."

"What the fuck for," Paul said angry to be aware of the cold again.

"There was a robbery down the street and we're gonna fingerprint you."

"Does it look like we're holding some precious shit here, officer?" Paul confronted the cop standing up and looking right into his eyes.

"Don't give me any crap, kid, or I'll cuff you and push you in the car." Paul surrendered, figuring it would be warmer in jail and they may even give him some coffee so all three of them got in the squad car. When they got to the station they were asked to produce ID's and then they were put in a group cell with about twenty other men. The cell wasn't too far from the front desk and Paul sat on the floor near the locked bars. He heard the police talking to each other. One of the cops said, "Fuck, you know all three of those guys I just brought in have military ID's on them. One's a Marine and two Army, one guy is Airborne." Paul always kept his old Screaming Eagles ID card in his wallet, it reminded him of Teddy; he didn't want to forget his friend.

"Was Airborne," the other cop said. "They ain't shit now."

"I'm calling the VA in the morning," the first cop said, "this shit ain't right, this is fucked up." Paul rested his head between his knees and tried to go back to sleep. At least that one cop is a little bit human, Paul thought, and then, mercifully, he fell back asleep.

"O'Connell," Paul heard his name and woke up. He stood and he almost saluted, then he saw his father standing beside the policeman, who proceeded to unlock his cell. Paul walked out and shook his dad's hand. "Sorry dad, bad way to start the day." They walked down the steep stairs out of the jail. Paul sat in the front seat of his dad's Chevy and watched the streets pass that he'd been panhandling on. His eyes stretched up Putnam Avenue to his crash pad. He watched as the street people took their coveted spots out of the weather and it all slipped behind him as his father silently drove down Massachusetts Avenue towards... towards what? Paul wondered. He leaned his head back and closed his eyes. Words to a song began to bubble up in him, then fear rushed in as he realized he'd need a fix within a few hours. But the song "Fire and Rain" by James Taylor kept playing in his head—"Won't you look down upon me, Jesus, and help me make a stand." Paul was lulled asleep by jumbled words that went very deep and he woke up when Ed jostled him saying, "We're home, Paul."

Irene Isobel Carver

When Paul and Ed walked into the living room, Paul's brother-in-law, Brian, was sitting in a straight-back chair, waiting. Brian put out his hand to shake Paul's and Paul reluctantly offered his. Paul looked over at his father, "What's up, dad?"

"Paul, sit down, I have something I need to tell you."

"Is mum okay?" Paul asked, his eyes darting around looking for his mother.

"Mum's okay, she's lying down. It's not about her, Paul, it's about you." Paul flopped onto the couch and asked his dad for a cigarette. They both lit one up in unison and Brian spoke up.

"Your parents and I had a talk with the counselors at the methadone clinic and then with the VA hospital. They have a bed for you at the hospital, Paul, and I am going to drive you over there and get you admitted after you go upstairs and take a shower." Paul crushed out his cigarette and stood up. He didn't have any energy or will to resist. As Paul climbed the stairs the words to "Fire and Rain" kept going through his brain ... "I've seen lonely times when I could not find a friend."

THE GROUNDHOG WAS WRONG

February and March were a blur of snowstorm after snowstorm. Shoveling all that snow kept the city's chiropractors affluent enough to buy condos in Florida. City road crews were making enough money in overtime to pay for their kids' college tuition. In submission, Bostonians just kept scarves wrapped around their faces, protecting the dreams of forsythia blooming in spring that lived in the marrow of their bones.

While serving martinis to my Saturday night regulars, I found myself telling many of them about my plans to start a new life in Seattle. Some would squeeze my hand and leave a bigger tip, while others would furrow their brows and say "be sure to cover your tracks honey, life can trick you." Each week, Arty would send me a postcard, so I was getting a general feel for where I was headed. Ferry boats, sunsets behind the Olympic Mountains, and Pike Place Market were the predominant pictures that stayed in my mind as I dreamed my way through the days.

When April arrived and the first crocuses dared to push through the soil, I was ready to plan a yard sale. Paulie helped me make a big sign on poster paper that said, "Moving Sale, Everything Must Go." I enlisted Paulie's excitement by giving him his own table and telling him that he could keep half of the money he made selling his toys so he could buy new toys when we get to Seattle. It turned out to be a beautiful spring day the morning of the sale and Donna decided to join us and set up her own table of stuff she was ready to let go of. Before I even had twenty-five dollars in my pocket, the phone rang, calling me inside. I anticipated someone calling from the ad with a question about the size of the bureau or something, but my excitement plummeted to the floor when I heard Paul's shaky voice. "Irene, it's me, I'm in the VA hospital and I was hoping you could come here and visit me," he blurted out. I was silent and Paul allowed it. Then with my head hanging as I muffled the phone, I stammered, "Paul, I … ah … I don't think I can handle this, Paul, I've got …" But Paul broke in with a stronger voice and said, "Irene, my counselor really thinks it is important for you to come and talk with me and him, please come." I felt as if I had to pull myself out of a dense

Irene Isobel Carver

fog as I said, "Okay, I guess I could come on a Sunday when I'm not working, is Sunday alright?"

"Yes, my counselor said he would be here anytime that works for you."

"Not tomorrow, the Sunday after, is one o'clock good?"

"Okay, thanks, Rene, I'll see you then."

I hung up the phone feeling nauseous, so I went to the bathroom. I looked into my eyes in the bathroom mirror and said out loud, "So what did you think Irene, you were just going to be able to slip out of town without Paul knowing?" I threw water on my face and ran a brush through my hair.

Dora flashed through my mind—the scene where I told her my plans to move to Seattle. Her right hand had gone directly to her heart and she said, "Oh, Irene, that's so far," and she collapsed into her rose upholstered chair. It was like I had stabbed her; I knelt before her and tried to explain. "Dora, I just have to take this chance of a new life, I can't bear for Paulie and me to watch Paul…" She grabbed my hand, stopping my words that were not to be said out loud. Then, like my mother had done, Dora's love for Paulie and for me caused her to be silent and let me go to my own destiny. None of us had the strength to fight anymore. As I walked back outside to my yard sale I realized that Dora and Ed must have told Paul of my plans to move, and I was petrified about the coming confrontation. I hoped that I could somehow avoid the pain of saying goodbye.

Paulie came bounding at me, "I sold my boxing men," he exploded as he held out a fist full of one dollar bills. Just then a wind swirled around us blowing the dollar bills every which way. Paulie and I laughed as we chased about, catching dollars and stuffing them in our pockets. "My life in a nutshell," I said to Donna, making light of how very messy I really felt on my knees, under folding tables that held bits and pieces of my life for sale.

SOME DAYS ARE HARDER THAN OTHERS

The hospital gave me explicit directions to Jamaica Plain but I felt so numb with fear that I had to stop twice at gas stations and admit I was completely lost. I don't think I was even in my body as I drove. I repeated over and over the mantra I had been studying in Autobiography of a Yogi, "Aum, blissful comforter, Holy Spirit, be with me, fill me. Aum blissful comforter, Holy Spirit, be with me, fill me." When I finally pulled into the hospital parking lot, I drove straight to an enormous oak tree and parked in her shade. I pushed the seat back and reclined, trying to get up the courage to actually get out of the car. I looked up through the branches of the tree. The leaves were just starting their spring bud, and I let their never-failing hope comfort my heart. "He just wants to say goodbye to me," I told myself. "His counselor probably told him that closure is important," I took a breath and sprung out of the car as if my gut had yelled, "ready, set, go!" I patted the hood of my trusty Mustang and said, "Don't worry, I'll be back…soon," as if trying to convince myself that the gigantic hospital wasn't going to engulf me.

I walked on the grass amidst sprawling trees until, forced from their protection, I had to follow the cement walkway and up the broad stairs to the hospital entrance. The lady at the front desk handed me a slip of paper with Paul's room number on it and a map to follow; a gerbils path through sterile halls to room 116. The door was open when I got there fifteen minutes late. I looked up from my paper right into Paul's piercing blue eyes. We smiled at each other and I noticed how close the counselor was sitting to Paul as if he was protecting him from something. The counselor stood and put out his hand to shake mine, introducing himself. "Hi, I'm Paul's counselor, Max Whitlow; have a seat." He was a middle-aged man and wore a white tee shirt with the VA emblem on its chest pocket. I took the seat that was set out for me at the foot of Paul's bed and I immediately began to feel pressure. The room was barely big enough for the three of us and there were no windows. I tried to take a deep breath to calm myself but the disinfectant in the air stopped me.

"Irene, Paul has something he'd like to say to you, which is why we have asked you to come today," the counselor stated calmly as he sat down, and passed the torch to Paul while he watched me. As I looked at Paul waiting for him to speak, I noticed that he was wearing a hospital johnny, which seemed odd. *Was he sick?* I thought.

"Irene," Paul finally began to speak slowly with each word separated, "I really feel ready to put down heroin for good this time but I think that I need you and Paulie in order to do this." My heart froze. Instead of seeing this physically weak and fragile man, I saw the Paul, who on the day after I came home from Portugal, told me he was in love with Natalie Rogers. I looked up at the clock on the wall, avoiding eye contact.

"Paul, a lot has changed since I saw you last October." I faced him squarely and with the courage of resurrected anger said, "I am about to move to Seattle."

"Yes, I know, my parents told me that." Paul's voice began to shake but he continued, "Which is why I thought I better tell you that a lot is changing for me also and I need…"

"Paul, I'm moving there to be with a man I met. I love him and I need to go, I need to get out of this city." I felt like a trapped mouse. The counselor reached over and held Paul's hand. I looked at both of them and holding back tears I said, "I need help too."

The counselor took this opportunity to try to convince me and said in a deeply empathetic tone, "Irene, you could come here for counseling with Paul and get help, too." That made me feel even more trapped so I stood up, every muscle in my body tense and on guard, as I looked firmly at Max Whitlow and said, "I just can't do this again. I have a five-year-old son to watch out for." I started to leave but stopped in the open doorway, not letting myself run. I couldn't, I had to say goodbye to Paul. I turned and looked directly at him. His lips were pure white, bloodless, like the night he told me President Johnson was sending the 82nd Airborne back to Vietnam. I whispered the words, "I'm sorry, Paul, I just can't, I have to go." I lifted my hand in a weak wave goodbye and walked down the long white halls as fast as I could without running to the exit.

I pushed open the heavy exit door and began running and I didn't stop until I got to the oak tree where my car was parked and I collapsed into her twisted and exposed roots. My body instinctively wrapped around her trunk; she became my weeping bowl, concealing me from the eyes of passersby. I tried to uncurl myself and stop my tears but instead I found a small stick and I began stabbing the earth over and over chanting, "Why, Why, Why?" The stick broke and I continued raging at the earth with my fingers, digging and clawing wildly. I thought I might vomit. My stomach clenched and I wanted to puke up this pain of being alive. But I heard voices behind me and I became self-conscious. I whispered to myself, "Stop it, Renie, stop it!" I found a Kleenex in my jeans pocket, which barely dried the bottled up tears that came pouring out of me. I pulled off my sneaker and took off my sock. First I wiped my eyes with my sock and then I blew my nose into it until I could breathe. I took off the other sock and began to clean the dirt from my aching fingers. I looked closely at my hand; it wasn't shaking. I felt dazed and dizzy but not broken.

After freaking out like that, I felt purged and almost light. I pulled myself upright and stood with my back on the tree and looked at my car. *Oh, thank God, I did make it back*, I thought as I slid into the protection of the car and locked the door. I adjusted the seat upright and gazed at the hospital entrance. I understood why this was set up. The counselor sat right next to Paul to help him cope with the possibility that he would lose Paulie and me; that it was in fact too late. I knew I should leave but I wasn't ready to drive and I didn't know where to go. I wasn't ready to pick up Paulie at my parents' house. I needed some time, I wanted to be with people who could bring me back to the life I had been living and growing in without Paul. I looked at the oak tree and the song "Country Girl" by Crosby, Stills, Nash, and Young began to play in my head—"Too late to keep the change … no time to stay the same." I started the car and immediately knew I would go to see my old friends Sheila and Fred. I could go there and hang out for a while.

As I drove, I was relieved that the fear of seeing Paul was behind me. I took the back roads to Sheila and Fred's Dorchester apartment. When Sheila opened the door there was a very surprised look on her face. "Hey, Irene, what brings you into town? It's been a long time since I've seen you, like a year or more." She led me to the living room where Fred was sitting on the couch with another couple. When he saw me he stood and said, " Shit, long time no see, want a cold one?" and he held up a Rolling Rock beer that he grabbed from the cooler next to him on the floor.

"Oh, no thanks, I really can't stay," I said realizing I had dropped in on a couples party.

"No, stay," he said as he pulled out a mirror from the bottom shelf of the coffee table that had four lines of cocaine on it.

"Here, I'll make another line, join us."

"No, really, thanks but I've got to pick Paulie up soon, I was just in the neighborhood so I took a chance, but…" I stammered. Sheila grabbed my arm helping me out of the awkward situation and said, "Yeah, that's cool, it would be more fun for me to meet you in Harvard Square some afternoon and we can shop and catch up." She hugged me at the front door and asked me how Paulie was doing. "He's five now, adorable and happy," I said opening the door, wanting to get out of there before she asked about his dad. I squeezed her hand and said, "Catch you later, have a fun party." Once again I collapsed into the privacy of my car, this time taking off immediately, feeling the need to escape. But I had lost my bearings, and the nooks and crannies of Boston's back roads confused me and I had to pull over to adjust. I put my head on the steering wheel and more tears began to flow. I was lost more than geographically. I felt dazed; lost between worlds, between identities.

I suddenly didn't know where I belonged. Paul was lying in a hospital bed fading away, friends were snorting cocaine in mid afternoon, and I couldn't figure out how to get out of Boston. The world seemed to be spinning into chaos and it frightened me. I had to get moving, so I drove around in a confused state for a while until I stumbled upon the entrance to Storrow Drive. I took a breath; I'd been saved. I felt like Alice crawling out of the rabbit hole, all shrunken and dirtied up by life.

I followed along the river until I got to the exit for Harvard Square. Some sanity returned with familiarity and I drove slowly to Mount Auburn Street, where I knew I could find beauty and privacy in Longfellow's Park. It was far enough from the Square that I immediately got a parking spot and walked across the expanse of manicured lawn to the bust of Longfellow. "You must have been one cool guy to have such coveted property memorialize you," I said to my long time friend, Longfellow. I started to feel like myself again. I thought, *Yeah, okay, I'll say it and get it over with,* "I'm a poet and I know it cause my feet are Longfellows," my voice mimicking my childhood self.

I lay down on the lawn and looked up through the towering trees to the clear spring sky. *You are Mary Adams's daughter, who loves history and poetry,* I told myself as I tried to stabilize my world. I flashed on Paul's face. *If you were Mary Adams's daughter, then you would be Catholic and if you were really Catholic you would honor your wedding vows of 'till death do you part.'* With that thought, I sat upright, shocked at my internal dialogue. I stood and began walking, no, pacing up and down the grass and ranting out loud to no one, like a crazy person. "I'm not Catholic, I declared. I haven't been to church on Sunday in years and I believe more in 'to thine own self be true' than to 'till death do you part,' by the way." I realized I was angry as I plunked myself down in a sunny spot off to the side as tourists milled about. "Till death," I said softly listening as my own truth bubbled up. "Till death," I repeated. I witnessed myself and how the Irene who had made that marriage vow at nineteen had been dying in bits and pieces ever since Paul rejected my pregnancy three years ago. I had wanted another child as a way to build our marriage and our family. I had been Catholic, but Paul discarded me then and many times since. That girl was dead, and we parted ways. I knew this was the truth and it was sad, but I had no more tears to add to the past that was melting away with each thought.

I flashed on the book, *Siddhartha,* and how he had stood right where I was, at the crossroads of his own consciousness. He couldn't stay with the traveling monks anymore, he couldn't follow the Buddha, and he couldn't go back to his father's house. I knew how he felt; it was the unknown. Many have stood where I was and it was terrifying and exciting at the same time.

FORKS IN THE ROAD, OR KNIVES!

Once I chose my road, which headed west, I did not allow myself to look back. If I looked over my shoulder to the events that happened in the last four years, it was just altogether too painful and confusing. I did not have the luxury of musing upon or remembering even the happy times. I had to keep my eyes firmly on each and every next step upon my new path.

I stopped reading *Autobiography of a Yogi*; I knew the Guru would always guide me. I began reading *Bury My Heart at Wounded Knee*, so I could be in tune with Arty when I got to Seattle. I studied the map in the front of the book, realizing I was heading into the sacred land of many of the Indian tribes of Washington State and I wanted to know their history. I learned the Davy Crockett version in elementary school, but this best-selling novel was written

Irene Isobel Carver

to uncover the true painful story of what the Native people experienced at the hands of my ancestors and through Manifest Destiny! My favorite picture in the book was of Juanita, the wife of the Navaho Chief, taken one hundred years earlier in 1874. When I looked into her eyes, they mirrored the pain in my own eyes, only one hundred times more. But I kept looking back at her; she was pulling me in. I read the quote on page one that asked, "Where are the Pequot?" I thought of the park in my town called Pequossette. "And where are the Narragansett?" The quote continued. I thought of the beer by that name. We took their names, not out of respect, I felt, but because we thought they were unique; another thing we could steal from them. God, I had hardly begun the book when I realized this was going to be very hard to read and yet I had to. It was somehow connected to the fact that I was choosing to move west into a new life and releasing the pain of my past. Maybe this was my version of manifesting my own destiny.

My days were kept busy with the details of tying up all the loose ends of my life. Making lists kept me from losing my mind. I would work on my lists at night and then look at it in the morning and get going on one thing every day. I worked at Plant Haven every day right up to the week before leaving, to keep the money flowing in. I made arrangements with my cousin to sell him back the Mustang. He said I could hold on to it and he'd come over the night before I left and pay me the exact amount I had paid for it. My dad said he would call and cancel the insurance for me as soon as I was really gone. I guess there was a part of him that felt like he'd believe it when he saw it. Gwen wanted to throw me a going away party but I told her absolutely not, that saying goodbye was very hard for me and I wanted only private one-on-one exchanges. She reluctantly agreed.

Before Donna and I moved out of our temple, on the last day of May, I set aside a private evening to pack the things I wanted to ship to Seattle in the trunk I bought at Lechmere Sales. The trunk measured two feet by two feet and was dark blue with fake brass trim, a solid lock, and a sturdy key. I took Paulie to Dora and Ed's house and they asked if they could keep him for a couple of days. It was sinking in for all of us that we were really moving, but we didn't talk about it, we couldn't; it made it too real, it was as if we all needed to allow a little illusion and detachment in order to bear it.

I had all the items to ship set aside and now was the time to prayerfully fill the trunk slowly, one thing at a time. I lit a candle and first lined the bottom of the trunk with my Indian print bedspread with little swirling shapes of red and purple on it. On top of that I placed a large white photo album labeled 1968-1973. I thought about leaving the photo album in my parents' attic, wanting to leave the past behind, but I realized that Paulie may need to see family pictures, with me taking him so far away. I placed it carefully in the center of the bedspread and wrapped the edges of the cotton material around it. Next, I spread out a small, cotton Swedish tablecloth Dora had embroidered with little boys and girls exchanging tulips. I wrapped my Fu Manchu tiki glass from the The Far East restaurant in it and placed it next to the photo album. I layered four of my most special tie-dyed diapers with jewelry and small delicate items cuddled inside of each one of them. I loved those diapers and they became even more precious since Paulie was about to turn six years old just before we would leave. *A baby no more*, I thought, but my heart held visions of another baby with Arty and I let hope fill me. I held up my Mateus wine bottle, which was layered thickly with many a night of dripping candle wax. I studied it and thought maybe I should leave it behind and begin a new candleholder for my new life, but I couldn't do it. I could see and feel a history of parties, people, and awakenings in the layers of wax. I flashed on the acid trip with Tim LaPasse and how we figured out who God was. It was like a rainbow of molded time; I had to have it, so I quickly wrapped it in my Red Sox beach towel before I could change my mind because the trunk was filling up fast.

Next, I layered in a small, framed picture of my dad, my sisters, and me all posing in red winter coats and each of us holding a pumpkin. We were ages five through thirteen and we were adorable. Next to that I placed my copy of *Autobiography of a Yogi*. I then wrapped all the tiny items from my altar in Dora's crocheted doilies, being especially careful with Ed's thumb-size leather copy of *Webster's Dictionary*. The trunk was very close to full now so I held up my last item—the blue velvet mandala wall hanging Teresa gave me for my birthday the year before. I held it closely to my heart, breathing in all the love it had absorbed at my Thayer Street home, where I had grown so much. I loved Teresa more than anyone in the world except for my Paulie and I wondered how she and Carlo were doing. We didn't connect much now that they were living together. I wiped away my tears of love with the fringe on the mandala cloth. Then I placed it carefully lengthwise on top of everything as a protective cover. I tried to close the lid of the trunk, but I couldn't. Each time I shut it, I pulled it right back open and stared at the mandala. I just wasn't ready to close off the present moment from the love of my past. I pushed the trunk into the corner of my room with the lid open.

I dashed out of the house and jumped in my Mustang, heading down Massachusetts Avenue. I had no idea what I was doing, but it felt like my last fling with my car and the city I was leaving. Energy was rushing through me, and it needed an outlet.

As I cruised into Inman Square, I saw a line of people waiting to go into a club, so I found a place to park and joined them. Once inside I ordered a Michelob beer and began dancing to the local band that were playing Bob Seger tunes. I had a moment's fright when I saw a guy with shoulder length strawberry blonde hair. My whole body tensed as I quickly thought, *Oh shit, he left the VA hospital and he's here.* When the guy turned around, I saw it wasn't Paul. *Thank God, I am leaving town, this could happen to me around every corner of life; I would never be free of the past.* Then a guy tapped me on the arm and nodded to the dance floor where I stayed until midnight. I told everyone I talked to that night, that I was moving to Seattle in two weeks, including the cute guy I had been dancing with. Most people reacted like I had, "Seattle, where's that, now?" Most had no comment about Seattle, but Seattle was real; I was making it real, and this was my own private goodbye party to Boston, and I was happy.

In the morning, to top off the evenings cool vibe, Arty woke me up with a phone call. He began to ramble excitedly about how he had just found a house to rent for us and he was moving in June first! I sat up in bed, willing myself awake to digest what he was saying.

"Landlords here are just grateful to have someone who wants to pay rent because so many places have been left vacant over the last couple of years," Arty explained. Then he started laughing as he called the house a "shack".

Irene Isobel Carver

"Yeah, it seems that back in the gold rush days a lot of ramshackle houses were thrown together and this is one of them, but it has two bedrooms and indoor plumbing," he joked, "and it is just up the alley from an elementary school for Paulie." There was a pause and when I didn't speak he said, "The rent is only $110 a month and no deposit is required."

"Guess we're ready to play house," I finally said as I lay back down. I could feel my heart relax into childhood memories of the game of "playing house" with my sisters.

"And I've been getting work," Arty continued when I didn't say more. "First, I painted an old lady's fence and then she told a friend, and that lady asked me to paint the trim in her kitchen, and I'm hoping..."Arty suddenly stopped talking.

"I know I'll be able to get a waitress job in September when Paulie starts first grade, and I have some money from selling all my stuff, so I can help out when I get there," I said, feeling hopeful. Another silence settled in as our dream took form as reality. "By the way, my phone gets disconnected today, so next time call me at my parents' number, okay?" I said softly.

"Will do, I'll call you on the tenth about eight o'clock your time." The tone of Arty's voice became subdued.

"Oh God Arty, just hearing that date made my stomach instantly nervous," I said as I got out of bed. "I've gotta go, I'll talk to you on the tenth," I said, needing to hang up.

It was hard to breathe after I put down the phone. My body, which had been dancing wildly the night before, now felt frozen. I was afraid. Everything suddenly felt way too real. My comfortable illusion bubble just popped as the finality of my decision to move settled on me like a heavy weight. I walked into the kitchen and smashed into a box of Donna's pans waiting to be moved. As I filled the percolator full of coffee, I realized what the fear was about—there could be no turning back now.

Irene Isobel Carver

Chapter Twenty-Five

The Transplanting Begins

Paulie and I moved into my parents' house while we waited for the twelfth of June to arrive. I bought us two tickets on the Montreal Express train, deciding on the middle priced seats that laid back into a bed. I figured it would be comfortable enough for three nights and it was affordable. Our train was scheduled to leave on June thirteenth, so I purchased airline tickets from Boston to Montreal on the twelfth, then made reservations in a hotel in Montreal that was near the train station. After all those purchases I had $1200 to begin my new life with. Everything was finally in order and I was stunned. There seemed to be a magnetic force pulling on just the logical side of my brain; no emotions were allowed.

I arranged for Gwen to drive us to the airport in order to avoid family goodbyes. We drove mostly in silence until we neared the terminal. Without looking at me Gwen asked, "Are you afraid?" I looked at Paulie sitting in the back seat already playing with his prepackaged toys for the plane ride. I answered quietly saying, "No, I'm not afraid, I'm actually really excited. Arty rented us a house and he said it is near an elementary school, so…" "What if you don't like Seattle? What if you and Arty don't like each other once you live together?" Gwen asked, not letting me finish my sentence. This time I had to cut her off, since all her fears seemed to be spewing out as she looked straight ahead at the road. "What if the sky falls in, Chicken Little?" I said squeezing her hand, trying to make light of her questions.

Gwen pulled her Volvo over in front of the United Terminal, where Paulie and I hopped out of the car and placed our backpacks on the sidewalk. Gwen got out of the car and stood next to me. I pulled her to my chest and gave her a deep hug while Paulie held onto my leg.

"I'm gonna miss you, my cooking mentor," I said as our hug broke apart. "Yeah, I bet they won't even have an Italian market out there in the Wild West." Gwen smiled, lightening up for my sake.

"I'll tell you what, if I need to run home, you'll be the first to know," I said, picking up my suitcase, signaling that the goodbyes were over. "Too painful, have to go," our body language said to one another. Gwen got back in her car, waved goodbye, and Paulie and I swung our packs on our backs and took our place in the line to Montreal.

Within a few hours Paulie and I were in our Montreal hotel room with our pajamas on, cuddled up next to each other in one double bed with the TV on. I set the room alarm for 5:00 a.m. and let the French-speaking people on TV lull us both to sleep. I dreamt of my high school French teacher, Sister Terese Martin. She was giving me a quiz and I woke up saying, Pourquoi?

Transplanted At Last

Paulie and I squeezed each other's hands as we walked down the long tunnel under Montreal that led to our train. We both had our backpacks on and mine was stuffed to the splitting point. I carried my white Samsonite suitcase,

Irene Isobel Carver

which was my high school graduation present. The tunnel was frightening in its inescapable-ness, and like a birth canal, there was just no other way out, so we kept moving forward in step with the dense crowd of fellow travelers. Each time I looked down at Paulie, he was looking up at me. I flashed on his book, *Where the Wild Things Are* and I wished I could whistle the song, "I Whistle a Happy Tune," which was my usual anti-fear tactic, but I felt too exposed. Instead, I pulled Paulie over to the side and knelt down. As I straightened his backpack on his shoulders I looked him right in the eyes and said, "I know the tunnel feels a little long and dark but they told us our train was down a little further at Berth 77 and we are at Berth 69 now, so we only have eight more to go." I tried to sound calmer than I felt. "See the numbers on the post?" I said pointing. He looked up, his face so white that his freckles seemed three dimensional on his face and I said, "So let's count as we walk and I bet that will help us get there faster." And it did, suddenly we were at Berth 77 and the train was marked with a large "E" matching our tickets. There were steps leading to the open door, our "birth canal." Paulie looked at me for permission to run up as I held onto his backpack, following him.

When I saw the red crushed velvet seats with bright light shining down on them, I almost cried with relief. I showed Paulie our tickets and together we looked for the ones marked with our seat numbers. "We made it," I said with incredible exuberance, as I flung my backpack onto the seat and then scooped Paulie into my arms and squeezed him. Paulie wiggled out of my arms, pulled off his backpack, and put it on his seat. He began pulling out his hot wheels and motorcycle men. His terror had passed and he moved right into the next phase of our journey. I was happy to see there was plenty of legroom in front of our seats and there was also a large luggage rack up above where pillows and blankets were stored. I pulled the pillows down and Paulie quickly turned the rack into his fort, standing up on the seat's armrest while I boosted him up. I decided I could let him have that space since my suitcase fit on the floor in front of my seat; it would give me easy access to my clothes. I showed Paulie how our seats folded back into beds and I tucked my pillow under my head. As I lay back, I noticed how much tension I had been holding in my neck. Paulie swung himself down and copied me, lying back on his seat. We lay there quietly for a couple of minutes, watching people walk down the aisle past us, finding their seats and settling in.

Paulie sat up abruptly when a little blonde-headed girl leaned over his seat and said hi. Her mother, who was sitting right behind me, introduced herself as Claudette. As we stood in the aisle talking and becoming friendly neighbors, telling each other where we were from and where we were going, we heard the porter yelling ALL ABOARD! We smiled at one another, happy to have someone to talk to on the train, as we took our seats. We heard doors slamming and locking and the train began to move in little jerky jolts. I pulled our seats upright and joined in the grand applause that broke out spontaneously. Everyone was obviously thrilled that our journey was beginning. The train itself seemed anxious to get out of the underground tunnel as the speed picked up rapidly and then, in one glorious whoosh, we left the dark tunnel and emerged into the light of a perfect June day. We were on our way! Paulie knelt at our closed window and I sat in his seat. Together we watched the city of Montreal move rapidly past us. "Off

Irene Isobel Carver

to the wild blue yonder!" I said. I heard Claudette and her four-year-old daughter, Hannah, chiming together, ready, set, let's go! Then I saw a little blonde head bopping up and down behind us.

I turned around in my seat and said, "Hey, Claudette, do you want to let the kids look out our window together and you and I can talk?" She stood right up with her little girl in tow and moved into our space for the next two hours. When I removed the armrest between the seats there was room enough for all of us. Canadian Claudette, as I soon was calling her, began telling me her life story. She was moving to Alberta to be with a man, so we had much in common. But in the middle of her story she said, "I feel sorry for you Americans with that stupid war you've been fighting." After she made that comment, I didn't hear any more of her words, because I realized I had never really talked to anyone about Vietnam who wasn't American, and her bluntness shocked me. I suddenly felt like a refugee myself fleeing from, yes, *that stupid American war*. I looked over the kids' heads and out the window as I batted back tears, and instead of the blur of towns and trees, I saw Paul lying in a hospital bed trying to stay alive. Those words began to haunt me and I was glad I had packed a pint of Jim Beam in my backpack in case I needed help sleeping.

I let Claudette ramble on until the train pulled into our first stop, Ottawa. The conductor walked through the train announcing that we would be at this station for a half hour and we could get off if we wanted but to be sure to be back on time, as the train waits for no one. Claudette and I both stood up and stretched. I pulled myself together and said, "Alright, Paulie, this is our first stop; let's go see if they sell Good 'n Plenty's in Canada. Claudette said, "Damn, Irene, you let me talk all the way. I need to hear about you when we get back on the train. I have some good weed, do you smoke?" "Yeah, sometimes, but I'm careful about it, as actually…" I hesitated then said, "My life has been seriously affected by the Vietnam War and I am trying hard to stay sane for my little sidekick here." I took Paulie's hand in mine and climbed down the stairs and into the brisk air of Ottawa.

Paulie and I stocked up on all the familiar treats that the train station store had. There were Juicy Fruits, Milk Duds, Wrigley's gum, and we each got a ginger ale. We headed back to our seats; I wanted us to eat the two peanut butter and jelly sandwiches that I had in my pack before we ate the candy. I spread out over both our seats so Claudette would take her own seat; I wasn't ready for any more conversation. As it turned out, she was one of the last ones back on the train and Paulie and I had already finished our sandwiches. When she came back, I scooted over and Hannah hopped into Paulie's seat with him, sharing her newly bought acrobatic toy. The whistle blew loudly three times. There was a lot of noise; doors slammed, and people hustled back to their seats. The train started chugging and off we went, first slowly, then quickly, picking up speed rapidly.

I looked out our window along with the kids, at rivers, lakes, and distant mountains, enjoying their excitement until Claudette nudged me and said, "Your turn, tell me about your life." "Well, first off, I'm trying to leave it," I said, and we both laughed. I knew I had to keep my story as light as I could to protect myself. Claudette let me gloss over the pain of war and move on to how I met Arty and what took him to Seattle. I think she could feel that I was hurting inside; we both knew we were on this train in hopes of leaving our pain behind.

"Will you stay here with the kids, while I go look for the bathroom?" I asked.

"Yeah, of course. There aren't any showers, by the way; they told us to bring wash cloths and our own soap and towels," Claudette said.

"Yeah, I got that info, too. I just want to see where they are, how big they are, and if there are lines to wait in before I bring Paulie with me."

"Take your time and when you come back, I'll go cruise for awhile." Claudette said with a mischievous smile.

Once I found the bathrooms, which were pretty large and had no line, I decided to take a little tour of the rest of the train while I had a bit of freedom. I stopped at the open space between my train car and the next, where I leaned against a swaying enclosure that was open at the top and had no window at all. I leaned out and let the fresh air whip my hair all around. I immediately felt so very free. Paulie was being watched and he had a friend to play with. I felt so grateful to have another mother to share the journey with and I allowed a huge sense of relief to flow through me. I breathed in deeply rejoicing in the sense of accomplishment I felt. I did it; I pulled off our move to Seattle. I felt a restrictive band of tension release from around my heart as I flung my arms wide open and took it all in. Then I stood in a Yogananda pose with hands in a steeple above my head, stretching up my spine and chanted, "Thank you, thank you, thank you."

I thought of the book I had in my pack, *Leaves of Grass* by Walt Whitman. Some of the words to my favorite poem, "Song of the Open Road" came to me: "You road I enter upon and look around, I believe you are not all that is here, I believe that much unseen is also here ..."

As I walked through the different train cars, I realized that life on a train was like a little society of different classes. We were in the middle class with our seats that folded into beds, and then there was the upper class that had sleeping berths with doors and their own bathrooms. The lower class just had rows of non-cushioned seats. Theirs was the party section where people gathered in many little groups to play guitar or cards, and where they passed around a pint of something to drink. I found the dining car last, where a young woman stood at the door with menus. She told me we needed to make reservations for meals if we wanted to eat there. So I decided on the spot to do just that; I would take Paulie out to dinner, just the two of us. She gave us the 6:30 p.m. time slot and I made my way back to my seat, my heart singing more of Walt's poetry to myself, "Afoot and light hearted I take to the open road, healthy, free the world before me …"

It was getting dark as Paulie and I ate our fancy dinner of creamed chicken with peas on toast. We had a salad, milk, and chocolate cake, too. I figured it was my one big splurge to celebrate. I told Paulie over dinner I was proud of him for being such a big boy to go on this adventure with me. He just smiled, with his mouth full of food, and I could see he felt safe in our new surroundings. When we got back to our seats, I gathered our washcloths, toothbrushes, and towels and we headed to the bathroom. This time there was a line but Paulie found another friend to play with and all the adults were sharing stories of their travels and plans, so the time moved along quite happily. Claudette and her daughter were already asleep in their reclined seats when we returned, so we made up our beds and I took out Paulie's favorite book, *Me And My Flying Machine*. We cuddled up and I read it two times, and then Paulie, who had it memorized, read it to me a third time.

When I woke up, after a deep and comfortable night's sleep, Claudette told me we had made a time change to central time and we would arrive in Winnipeg by mid afternoon. Paulie woke up happy and full of little boy energy. He wanted to go find the boy he had met in line the night before, so I helped him stuff a few of his hot wheels in his pockets. I took apples and rice crackers with us and off we went to the party car to see if he was there. I stopped at the open air spot between train cars, holding him in my arms, and we both hooped and hollered at the passing river. His friend was not in the party car but Paulie liked it there because the car was open and he could race his hot wheels right down the center of the uncarpeted floor. Of course the adult boys jumped right in and turned into six year olds and a full out game was on. I sat down in an open spot and listened to someone singing a Neil Young song, playing guitar and harmonica. It felt a bit depressing as he sang "See the lonely boy out on the weekend," and something like, "I can't relate to joy." The energy was sort of a downer, so I volunteered to go back to our seats and get Paulie's motorcycle men if these new friends would keep an eye on Paulie. I raced back through the cars on a toy mission. When I got to our berth I said to Claudette, "You guys should come back with me to the party train, we've got a game going and someone is playing depressing Neil Young songs." Claudette looked at me like I had slapped her and said, "Don't ever say anything bad about Neil Young, Irene, you're in Canada!" I burst out laughing at her seriousness, collected all of Paulie's motorcycle men and hot wheels, and with a wave I hurried back to party car.

Before we knew it, I heard an announcement that we were at the Winnipeg station. I was ready to get off and run around in circles. This stop was the halfway point between Montreal and Vancouver; one and a half days down, one and a half to go—we were loving it. "It was such a perfect idea to take the train," I said to Claudette as we came into the station. "I have gained new perspective as to the actual distance between places and the difference between where we were and where we are going, unlike traveling in an airplane, where you just watch a movie and after seven hours in the sky you end up in a new time zone. On the train we are living and experiencing geographical and cultural changes as clocks and scenery shift." Claudette said, "Well, get ready for another culture shift." She pointed out the window to the scene on the platform where many native people were panhandling, sleeping in rags in corners, and being arrested for disorderly behavior.

"Damn," I said, "I wanted to walk around a bit, but I don't think I want Paulie to see this sadness."

"Let's just go into the restaurant and get a burger," Claudette suggested.

"Good idea," I agreed, and we made our way to the exit. I bought Paulie a little tic-tac- toe game book to keep his attention on something while off the train.

"Man, the Indians are so sad in this area," Claudette said, "they just can't handle alcohol; their bodies are different somehow, but we French, we can drink!"

I didn't reply to her comment because I was thinking how naive I was about Indian people. In elementary school at Thanksgiving we learned of Pocahontas and we swam in the Merrimack River, named for a local tribe, but I had never actually met a Native Indian person and knew nothing of their problems with alcohol. When the whistle blew and we made our way back to our seats. Claudette said, "It's not just Canadian Indians, Irene; I've heard Seattle has a really big problem with Indians and alcohol too." I flashed on Arty telling me he had brought soup to Pioneer Square for the Indians at Thanksgiving but he never mentioned the alcohol part. I thought of the Jim Beam in my pack and was happy I hadn't even opened it. Then I remembered Claudette said she had weed and *that* I was ready for. Claudette was excited when I asked her if she would give me a joint.

"Great idea, you go first, go to the party car, get high, hang out, and I'll watch the kids. Then come back, read the kids to sleep, and I'll go party."

"Perfect," I said, taking the pencil thin joint and slipping it in my jeans pocket.

"Hey, Paulie," I said casually, " I'm gonna go to the train car where the people are playing guitar, and you stay here with Claudette and Hannah for a little while, okay?"

"Okay, ma," he answered without looking up from the Lego bridge he was building.

I slipped right into the scene on the party car and lit my joint. I felt super cool as the sweet smoke swirled around me. A cute guy with rolled up denim sleeves and a thick black beard reached out his hand and took the joint from me. "I like your style," he said as he pointed to my red tennis shoes with the rubber toes. "Keds" I said. I knew he wasn't American when he gave me a look like, "Huh?" He continued to flirt with me, saying that he had a private berth. I told him right away that I was on my way to Seattle to live with my guy and he handed me back my joint and moved on to the next cute girl. Now that I was nice and high I didn't really want to hang out in that scene. I went to the spot between cars and hung out with the night sky and my visions of Arty waiting for me in Vancouver.

Claudette was surprised when she saw me back so soon but she didn't waste a minute switching roles with me. She slid out of mama mode and ran a brush through her hair. Rummaging through her pack, she pulled out a spray bottle with an old fashioned rubber squeeze ball and spritzed herself with lavender scent and took off without saying goodnight to Hannah. I cuddled up with a kid on each side of me, both in their cozy Disney print pajamas and read them, *The Giving Tree* very slowly as their eyes fluttered shut. I let my mellow and stoned consciousness drift into a poem forming in my head.

Fierce energy to live to grow smashed open my suf-
focating pot
Heart tattered, yes torn
Roots vulnerable, exposed and hoping Seattle —
My new pot of fresh soil,
Arty my indirect sunlight Awaits

Sometime the next day Claudette and Hannah got off the train in Calgary. I knew I would never see them again and that was okay; it was all part of the journey of the train—a moment in time. We hugged goodbye and wished each other well with our dreams and our men and then the train engaged in its predictable chugging and jolting out of the station. I was glad to have a little alone time with Paulie before the next day when we would arrive in Vancouver. Then it would be our turn to collect our bags and memories and begin our new life. Neither of us slept very well our last night on the train, and I finally did resort to a swig of Jim Beam. Paulie awoke in the night with a nightmare.

Irene Isobel Carver

When daylight streamed in our window, we stretched and surrendered to the line for the bathroom. I decided we should splurge and go to the fancy dining car for French toast, which I heard they stuffed with bacon. Two hours later Paulie was having cocoa with his French toast and I was having a cup of wonderful French coffee; it was a real treat. As we ate, I told Paulie that the train would pull into Vancouver at three o'clock that afternoon and Arty would be there to pick us up.

"What do you remember about Arty?" I asked my little son.

"The time he tried on my superman cape and I didn't like it, it's not for big people, just me," Paulie pouted.

"Well, I'll make sure to tell him he can't touch your cape, because it's private, okay?" I answered feeling a little nervous.

"Where did dad go, ma?" Paulie asked not looking at me.

"He didn't go anywhere, he's in Boston, probably at Dora and Ed's house; we're the ones who went somewhere," I said surprised at his question. I always tried to avoid the pain of talking about Paul. We had been separated since Paulie was three, so I thought Paulie would feel distant from his father, but in that moment I realized that having a stepfather was going to bring everything to the surface.

The train was right on schedule and we pulled into Vancouver at 3:00 p.m. on a sunny June sixteenth. Arty said he would borrow his friend's 1962 Peugeot to drive the three hours to pick us up. He suggested I wear one of my bright red sweaters when I got off the train so he could easily spot me in the crowd. He said he didn't have any bright clothes, so to just look for the signature green turtleneck he usually wore. Three days had been the perfect amount of time to be on a train. Paulie and I were really ready to get off the train when we arrived. Leaving Boston had been one part of our adventure and now that I had to deal with arriving, I was scared, much like when we had entered the Montreal tunnel. Now I had to step into this new life that contained another person.

I held Paulie's hand tightly as we walked down the train steps, craning my neck looking through the crowd for Arty. Paulie didn't seem scared and asked, "Does our new house have a tub?" That shattered my fear and I burst out laughing, understanding that even a six-year-old knew how wonderful a bath was going to feel. "You know what, Paulie? I don't know; I forgot to ask Arty about that, but I'm sure it has a shower." We walked with the crowd towards the train station and I saw Arty walking towards us. He saw me as well, so I stopped moving and let him catch up to us. Arty reached right down and picked Paulie up and then put his other arm around me and we shared a long group hug. When Paulie didn't pull away before Arty and I did, I figured everything was going to be alright and we were going to be happy.

The first two hours driving from Vancouver B.C. to Seattle, the scenery was mostly rows of tall trees on either side of the road. It felt like we were in a tunnel again, which gave us time to talk. I sensed Arty's wisdom right away as he kept asking Paulie questions about the train ride and listening intently when Paulie described the hot wheels race. As Arty listened, he reached over and held my hand. I remembered that Arty was a Leo and that fatherhood is one of the natural qualities of that sign. Most twenty-four-year-old men would have been reluctant to take on parenting a six-year-old, but Arty rose up to meet the challenge from the day I met him. I

Irene Isobel Carver

looked over at the profile of this handsome man and realized I was for sure in love; I had made the right decision. Then the road opened up, and looming ahead in the sky like a giant hourglass, was the Space Needle. "Look, Paulie, remember I told you about the Space Needle; well, there it is." I let Paulie climb into the front seat with us and sit on my lap.

"Can we go up in that?" Paulie wanted to know.

"Yes, we sure can," answered Arty, "but not today. First I want to take you to our new house, and guess what? You can see the city from our house; not the Space Needle, but we can see that other tall building, it's called Smith Tower and it's the tallest building in Seattle."

Arty's enthusiasm for Seattle was spilling all over us and we were ready to receive it. "I'm taking the next exit that says 'West Seattle Bridge,' that's where we live." Arty took the exit and traffic began to slow down and soon stopped.

"Wow, look!" Paulie exclaimed, as we watched the suspension bridge open to let a large boat pass underneath.

"Yep, this is why we are all stopping. We can't drive over the bridge until it closes again after the boat has passed underneath it," Arty explained.

"This is so cool," Paulie yelled, kneeling at my window so he could watch all the action, causing me to scoot over close to Arty. While Paulie watched all the tugboat action going on, I stole my very first Seattle kiss, and yes, it was bliss; I blushed and Arty turned back into our tour guide.

"That's Puget Sound out there on that side of the bridge where the big ships come from, and on this side of the bridge is the Duwamish River."

"Duwamish sounds like an Indian name," I said.

"You've got that right; Duwamish is the name of a local tribe from this part of the city."

"I've been reading *Wounded Knee*" I said, "Have you read it yet?"

"Yeah, but I can barely stand it 'cause it makes me angry and I keep putting it down." The bridge was fully closed and after about twenty minutes traffic began to cross over the singing silver bridge and onto the peninsula of West Seattle.

"The city was named after Chief Sealth," Arty continued, "but they had to change it to Seattle because Indians do not want their name said after they go to the Spirit World."

"Spirit World," I repeated "I like that." I looked out the window as Arty drove along Alki Beach. By now Paulie was hanging out the window and excitedly asking Arty what each boat was for.

"Those are ferries filled with people coming and going from different islands," Arty explained. "Those huge ships are called container ships and they carry stuff from all over the world."

"Oh my God, Paulie, look, there's a mini Statue of Liberty. Arty, can you pull over and let me go see that?"

"Sure thing," Arty answered as he easily parked and shut off the engine. The three of us got out and stood at the statue listening to the slap of the waves on the rocky beach. The glorious Olympic Mountain range was the backdrop with their pointed peaks etched against the evening sky. When we got back in the car, I cuddled in under Arty's arm.

"I'm gonna drive you by the house where I painted the lady's white fence; it was my very first earned dollar in Seattle."

"I expected Seattle to be beautiful, after getting all your postcards, but I didn't know it would feel so …magical," I said placing my hand on Paulie's back as he leaned out the window. Arty pulled over and parked across the street from his "fence" and we all hopped out of the car again. Paulie watched seagulls dive for clams and smash them against rocks.

"Wow," he whooped, "I like Seattle, mum!"

"Good thing," Arty whispered in my ear, "'cause I'm never letting you two leave." We stood hugging and gently kissing as the breeze off Puget Sound welcomed us.

"Let's go," Arty yelled to Paulie who was chasing the seagulls down the sidewalk. We all got back in the car and Arty drove along Beach Drive until he came to a side street that wound us up a very steep and densely tree-covered hill, which ended up in a small shopping district.

"This is our neighborhood," Arty said as he stopped at a streetlight. "Paulie, look up the street right ahead of us, see the school?"

"Yeah," Paulie answered

"That's your new school." Arty was so excited. When the light turned green, he drove up the small hill and pulled into the alleyway next to the school. He drove past five houses and then pulled up in front the sixth house.

"This is it, we're home!" Arty shut the engine off and just about leapt out of the car. He came around to my door, opened it and took my hand, leading me out as if he was going to bow next.

"Madam, your castle." He reached for Paulie who was staring out the back window.

"Young sir, may I present your yard?"

"Well, you told me it was a shack, kind sir, but you didn't tell me it was a shack with a yard worthy of a mansion," I said play-acting at grandeur as Arty was.

"I know, it's an interesting city." We walked into the front yard that overlooked a group of buildings that was the Seattle skyline.

"I don't think people realize even the poorest areas have million-dollar views of Mt. Rainier and the Olympic range." I could see how much Arty loved it here.

"The skyline is so small compared to Boston," I said as Arty and I stood with our arms around each other's waists.

"Don't even bother to try to compare this to Boston; Seattle is just a baby, but they have managed something Boston never has." Arty bragged.

"Yeah, and what's that?" I asked, sneaking in kisses as we talked.

"They have all the streets numbered, in order, and marked North, South, East and West. It's amazing! We live on 42nd SW and there is a 42nd NE across town some-where."

"I never thought of that," I said, "but now that you mention it, I will probably find that handy as I learn my way around my new city."

"Yeah, and get this, there are schedules for the buses and they are even on time!"

Paulie let out a loud shriek, "Yuck, come here you guys, you've gotta see this weird creature." Arty and I joined him at the edge of the yard in an overgrown garden spot. There was a long, slimy thing with two pointy antennae, slithering over a leaf and leaving a silvery liquid trail of ooze behind it. "Oh, that's just a slug," said Arty. It's like an official hated pet around here. They eat your garden up if you aren't careful. I made the mistake of walking out here barefoot one night and it freaked me out when I stepped on one. I thought I had stepped on a snake; it was awful."

That was our signal to go in the house. We went back to the car and got my suitcase and our backpacks. Arty walked ahead of us and opened the door and we entered a tiny kitchen that was freshly painted royal blue. Paulie pushed right by us and ran through the house. "Ma," he yelled, "it has a bathtub!" I followed his voice and walked into the living room and was given yet another unexpected gift. There in the center of the room was my trunk! I walked up to it and stroked it lovingly, remembering the day I had shipped it. It made me feel a little off balance as I was immersed in my new life and the trunk looked out of place. For a second I wondered why had I shipped it. *Why didn't I just leave everything in my parents' attic?* Then I looked up at the wide-open windows and realized there weren't any curtains and at the very bottom of my trunk was my much-loved Indian print bedspread that would cover them perfectly. I pushed the trunk over to the wall. I wanted to be alone when I opened it, like I was when I packed it. I would light a candle and take my things out one by one.

"I'm hungry," I turned and said to my boys.

"I have a plan," answered Arty, "we're going to walk down to the junction and go to Skippers Fish and Chips for our first dinner 'cause the refrigerator is empty."

"It's pretty cool that it is still light out and it's eight o'clock," I said.

As the three of us walked down our little hill to the junction, the sun began to set behind the Olympic Mountains, turning the sky a deep pink with clouds of purple scattered about. I felt like I was in one of the postcards Arty sent to me. I took hold of Arty's hand. He squeezed my hand and said, "Now you know why I didn't come back to Boston, even when I was starving." I took a deep breath of the salty, moist dusk air and said silently to the mountains, *and now I know why I didn't let myself think of future fears. I just had to end up here.*

Chapter Twenty-Six

Fathers and Sons

ED CALLED THE VA HOSPITAL AND ASKED TO TALK to Paul's counselor. He wanted to ask for his support when he came to visit Paul that Sunday. Ed planned to tell Paul that Irene and Paulie had taken the train to Seattle and had arrived safely. Max Whitlow took Ed's call and told him he thought it was a good idea; Paul had recently asked him if he knew whether Irene had left.

"Do you want to wait until after Father's Day, Mr. O'Connell?" Max asked.

"Actually, no, I thought that might be just the right day to face this." Ed clutched his rosary beads.

"You're probably right, Mr. O'Connell. Paul needs to face the fact that Irene and Paulie have moved away if he is going to leave this hospital and live his own life again. I was mainly thinking of you and your day."

"Thank you, Mr. Whitlow, but I don't think I'll enjoy Father's Day at all if I don't get this off my chest," Ed said. He lit up a Tareyton cigarette and sucked the smoke in as deeply as he could.

"Okay, then agreed; do you want to come in early in the day or later like four o'clock?"

"I'd like to come at noon, if that is alright with you." Ed put out his cigarette half way down, saving the rest for later.

Ed hung up the phone feeling relieved that the first half of his difficult job was done. Max Whitlow hung up, realizing he had no idea what was best for Paul. He went back to his office and reviewed Paul's file. Paul was still fairly heavily medicated on Valium and Librium and had been sleeping fitfully and hallucinating since he saw Irene.

When Paul came to group therapy the week before, he told the group about a vision that he had. He had flown over Vietnam looking for a piece of his soul that had been lost there.

He captivated everyone by describing in detail what he had seen. First he flew over a muddy green river that was barely moving. There was a row of about twenty boats that looked like bananas all lying on their sides, tied together to make a barge. There were two children standing on top with bags of supplies. The mother was at one end of the barge steering and the father was at the other, standing and pushing them along with a large pole. "I floated above them and asked them if they knew where my soul was hiding. They shook their heads, no." Then Paul let himself cry.

After that group, Max Whitlow went to see the head counselor. He told him about Paul's hallucination and the counselor said, "I heard there has been some success using the drug Thorazine for this type of schizophrenia. Maybe we could look into that for this man." Somehow the young counselor didn't think that more drugs were really going to help Paul. He was more of a Freudian and thought Paul's vision was symbolic of Paul losing a part of himself in the war. Max Whitlow came to an even harder realization—no one in the VA had any idea how to help these Nam vets. What they were experiencing was much different than the shell shock of WWII vets.

When Sunday arrived Paul sensed the heaviness of his father's visit from the tone of his counselors voice when he said he would be around Sunday if Paul needed him. Ed came dressed in his plaid suit of soft blues with the matching vest under the jacket and a blue tie. When Paul and Ed walked to a sitting room to have a visit, Paul noticed how handsome his father was with his snow-white hair and bushy black eyebrows. They sat next to each other on a couch and Ed reached over and took his son's hand.

"How are you sleeping these days, Paul?" Ed asked, looking directly at his son.

"Not too good, dad; I wake up and then can't get back to sleep. I pace around, smoke and eventually sleep, how about you?"

"About the same," Ed smiled, glad to have common ground

"And how about mum?" Paul asked but was nervous to hear the answer as she had taught him to worry.

"Mum has never been a good sleeper. You know she's been having an affair with Larry Glick for about twenty years now." They both laughed at how the nighttime radio jockey was like Dear Abby to her.

"Paul, I wanted to let you know that Irene and Paulie left this week. They took a train across Canada and we heard that they arrived safely in Seattle." Ed lit a cigarette. Paul took one of Ed's Tareyton's and lit it with a shaking hand and said, "Dad …" then he started to cry. Ed squished out his cigarette and pulled Paul into his arms letting him cry into his chest. Paul was able to allow himself to cry deeply and for a long time—a good cry, while Ed stroked his head and said, "There, there," like he was stroking a child. Max Whitlow walked quietly into the room and put down a box of Kleenex and then left. With tears spent, Paul finally sat up, composed himself and said, "Dad, did I lose my son, my Paulie?" Ed, being the calm and gentle man that he was, just spoke from his heart and said, "No son, you may have lost Irene, but you can never lose your son. He is our blood, he has our name; your mother and I have talked about this." Ed handed Paul a Kleenex and Paul blew his nose and then lit another cigarette. "We decided that next summer, after Paulie finishes first grade, we will pay to fly him home to spend the summer with all of us. You can stay with us, too, if you want, and we'll go to Fenway and the Cape. We'll all be together, and then he can fly back to Irene when school is going to start." Ed lit another cigarette and poured a glass of water for each of them from the pitcher on the coffee table. Paul put his arm around his father's neck and hugged him, "Thank you, dad, thank you; now maybe I can bear this, thank you."

"It was actually your mother's idea. We love you Paul, let us help you okay? Do you need any money, son?"

"Actually, a twenty would be great for the vending machine and cigarettes."

Ed took a twenty from his wallet and said, "I think I better get going Paul, we're going to dinner at Charlotte and Brian's house."

"Well, say hi to them all from me, tell them I'll see them this summer and I won't be such a pain in the ass." Paul smiled and shook his dad's hand and pulled him into his chest for a hug saying, "Dad, you know I'm sorry, you are such a good man, you deserve better."

"You deserve better too, Paul; is your counselor helping you?"

"Yes, he's a real caring guy, I think he really gives a shit and that helps." Paul said as he walked his father to the parking lot and together they watched as a flock of crows flew between trees.

"See you soon, son." Ed got into his Chevy Impala.

"See ya, dad." Paul walked back through the hospital doors, thinking he may be ready to leave this place soon. Paul ran into Max Whitlow in the hallway.

"So how was your visit with your dad?" Max asked, still on standby if needed.

"He told me I may have lost Irene but I'll never lose my son, he gave me hope. Why didn't you think of that?" Paul jokingly asked.

"Because that's what fathers are for," Max said as he patted Paul on the back. "There's a movie on in the lounge if you want to join us," Max said.

"Nah, I've got some thinking to do. I feel like I may be able to leave here soon."

"Okay, we'll talk about that tomorrow in our session, sleep well, Paul."

"That would be nice," Paul said. The two men parted ways with Max thinking he had witnessed a real Father's Day.

Paul spent the month of July in the hospital trying to imagine how he would live and what he would do with himself once he left. Paul's counselor told him he should keep busy and he began to help Paul research job possibilities. They came up with Metropolitan State Hospital in Waltham, which was on the bus line from the O'Connell's house and they were taking applications. Max arranged for Paul to continue on his prescriptions of Librium in the daytime for anxiety and Valium at night for sleep. Max encouraged Paul and his parents that Paul was ready for this move. Paul had handled a very hard life change with Irene and Paulie leaving, without slipping backwards in the progress he made in counseling.

In early August when the news spread through the hospital that President Nixon was going to be impeached, Paul showed up at group counseling and announced to everyone that he thought he could give the world another try if the government was actually going to impeach that mother fucker! There was a big round of applause. Paul was disappointment the following week when Nixon was allowed to resign instead of the degrading impeachment they all felt he deserved. "Well at least he's out," Max said trying to keep everyone positive as the week moved on. On the fifteenth of August Ed arrived to pick Paul up from the hospital. Ed stood in the lobby with Paul while he said his farewells and hugged everyone. Paul looked back over his shoulder as they pulled away saying, "I'm gonna have to visit sometimes, I really care about all those guys." "Do you still have a driver's license, Paul? If you do, then next month if you're feeling up to it, you can take my car and come visit them." "Thanks for the confidence dad; I think my license is just expired. I don't have any tickets or warrants or anything," Paul answered feeling his father's love for him.

The following week Paul came home from applying at Met State, as everyone called it, with his schedule and job description. Over dinner he made light of the Hospital's intensity by saying he thought he'd feel right at home working with the mentally ill. Met State hired everyone who applied because the work was not pleasant and they only paid the minimum wage of $2.10 an hour. Paul's job description said he was to wash floors and bathrooms but to be prepared to help in any capacity when needed.

During Paul's first month on the job he had twice helped to hold down patients that needed a shot of Thorazine. Paul remembered he and Irene reading aloud the book, *One Flew Over the Cuckoo's Nest* and he felt this hospital was very similar; luckily, he was not a patient. Some days Paul wondered how long he could take the harshness of the job. He watched the lonely and medicated patients and wondered about their stories that led them to this end. But he kept showing up because it gave him a place to be of some use in the world, and it kept his mind off getting loaded. At night he was so physically exhausted that he slept well. His nightmares and flashbacks were at a level he could either hide or handle.

Many of the workers at Met State were immigrants from Haiti, and making $2.10 an hour was quite a luxury for them. Even though they were exhausted from the work, they always seemed happy and danced around, mopping to an internal reggae beat. Paul made friends with one twenty-year-old Haitian man named Raffe, who said he sent half of his pay check to Haiti each month to his wife to save, so she could eventually come to America as he had. "De land of opportunity, mon," he would say with a huge smile of strong, very white teeth. "We nah got dollars there, woman betta come soon," he would say when he stood in line to pick up his paycheck. Paul often took his lunch break with Raffe and they would share stories of their lives. When Paul realized where Raffe was from, that there was raw sewage in the streets, and his wife made $1.30 per day working in a factory, he could see why America still looked like the land of opportunity. Paul would try to let some of Raffe's optimism sink in, but he soon found himself telling Raffe how the American government sprayed the poison Agent Orange all over Vietnam causing much sickness, but the government would not take any responsibility for its effects. They both realized it would be best to just talk about music, which they both loved, so Paul brought a small transistor radio to work and left it in his locker. At lunch one day Paul put on WBCN saying, "Now I can turn you on to the cool music," and Raffe quickly said, "Day got Jimmy Cliff?" "Day sure do," Paul answered mimicking his slang. This became their routine and the hard days began to pass quicker.

On a mid November day, an Indian summer kind of day, when the sun was warm enough for Paul and Raffe to be sitting on the wall listening to music and eating sandwiches, an alarm went off. A patient had escaped. Paul almost missed the sounding alarm, as WBCN was playing The Doors' song, "Light my Fire," but he didn't miss the tall, wiry man dressed in hospital pajamas sprinting past him. Paul immediately responded. He dropped his food and began chasing the man through the woods that surrounded the hospital. He pushed through the trees, crushing the smaller maples with his speed. The New England woods had many diverse trees close together with no room for any of them to grow big. Inch-thick birches could whip you in the eyes if you let your arms down. Occasionally a tall fir grew out of the thicket and reached up into the light.

As Paul ran, his stored memories surfaced. He looked around. Where were the men who were supposed to flank him? He lost sight of his target, panicked, and fell to his stomach. *Lay low, miss the fire fight*, he told himself. Then he heard twigs crunching behind him. He rolled over looking for his rifle but he couldn't find it. He began to cover himself in leaves. *Hide, those gooks all have hand grenades*, he warned himself. One of the big Haitian orderlies knelt down next to him.

"Paul, it's me, Charles, be cool, it's okay, we got him."

Paul looked past the man and said, "Did you see that house with the pigs all underneath it?"

"There are no houses out here Paul, come on get up, let's get back in."

"Yeah, the A-frame house with the grass roof, it's up on stilts, you know the kind. There were two women carrying water jugs on their shoulders, and a little boy at the door." Paul stood, "Quick we gotta go help them, there's a plane coming in from the north."

"Okay, but first let's go back in for some supplies, we at least need water, right?" Charles said this calmly; he had been trained how to talk a person down by agreeing with them till he could get them to safety and get some assistance. They ran towards the hospital and as they got close, Paul started to see the familiar surroundings and began to come back to present reality. He saw the wall where he had been sitting and asked Charles, "Where's Raffe?" "Let's go in and find out," Charles said. As they walked into the front hall, Raffe came to Paul and handed him his radio. Paul took it from him, and sadness engulfed him. He sat down in a chair that was against the wall. His head collapsed into his hands and he shook with violent tears of fear. Charles and Raffe stayed with him until he quit crying and Raffe asked, "Where'd ya go, mon?" Paul explained his horrifying vision saying, "Back to a house that I saw bombed in Nam." Paul stood and walked up the long, wide hall and into the office. He said to the clerk at the desk, "Could you call a cab for me, I'm not well." Paul went back to the hall, found Charles and thanked him for bringing him back, then he found Raffe, shook his hand and said, "I won't be back man, you can keep the radio." He handed the little transistor to him and headed down the driveway to wait for the cab at the entrance.

When Paul walked in the house his mother said, "You're home early, everything okay?"

"I had an episode, I've gotta go lay down." He started climbing the stairs and said softly, "I've seen lonely days when I could not find a friend," as if the stairs themselves held the vibration of that song. Paul felt depleted and scared so he opened his bottle of Librium and took double his usual dosage. He flopped onto his bed, covered his head with the pillow and thought, *Oh shit and here come the holidays.*

1975

Paul mostly stayed in his room overmedicating himself until all the Christmas decorations were taken down and 1975 had been rung in. Occasionally he came downstairs to lie on the couch and watch "All in the Family" with his parents, but he would soon be annoyed by his mother's constant chatter during the show as she sipped on her small glass of whiskey. Then he would head back to the safety of his room with a bowl of popcorn and ginger ale.

February brought a hint of spring one afternoon. Paul opened his window and listened to the first courageous bird chirping in the maple tree. Soon a car drove down the street, its radio blasting a Pink Floyd song that Paul loved, "Dark Side of the Moon." It awakened something in Paul. He walked downstairs and sat at the kitchen table looking through the Boston Herald in the Help Wanted section. He saw a job pumping gas at a station in Bridgetown so he cut out the ad. He went upstairs and peeked in his parents room. His mother was lying on her bed reading a Norman Vincent Peale book.

"Hey mum, is dad working?"

"Hi Paul, yes, he'll be home by 5:30; can I help with anything?"

"Yeah, I think so. I am going to go apply for this job pumping gas and I could use a little bit of cash."

"I think dad has some in his top drawer, go look," Dora said surprised at the sudden change. Paul saw three twenty's folded in the corner of the drawer. He held up one and said, "This will be good, thanks." Dora sat up with a bunch of questions flowing in rapid succession.

"Are you sure you're ready? Did something happen? ....."

"Well… I'm not sure of anything actually, but I'm gonna give it a try and see what happens. Bridgetown sounds safe 'cause I won't have to run into high school friends, so what the heck." Paul walked over and touched his mothers shoulder, "Try not to worry, mum. What's that book you're reading, *Positive Thinking*, try using it on me; just think I'm gonna be okay." They both smiled as Paul went to take a shower.

When the manager of the station heard that Paul was a Nam vet he hired him on the spot. "My nephew was a Marine, killed in Danang two years ago," the station manager said with a bowed head, but he continued quickly, saying, "I'd like you to work the night shift, 5-11, alright with you?"

"Sounds good," Paul said with a bit of tension fluttering in his stomach.

"I need you five nights a week, Tuesday through Saturday. My guy just quit last week out of the blue, can you start tomorrow?"

"Yeah, sure," Paul answered as he looked around the garage and surroundings.

"Come an hour early tomorrow and I'll show you the ropes," said Mr. Garabedian, his new boss.

March brought the opposite of the old saying "In like a lion, out like a lamb." It came in like a lamb and went out like a lion! Paul kept a warm jacket at the gas station. He was happy to pump gas for the older clients like his parents. Occasionally changing a tire or windshield wipers kept the hours passing. His boss said to call him "Charlie." Paul and Charlie would drink coffee and smoke cigarettes when it was slow. Paul even caught himself looking at a girl here and there, which made him almost feel normal. Once, a car full of hippie kids came in to the station. As Paul pumped gas for the people across from them, he heard one kid say to the other, "Well, you can't fight a war without soldiers, so I don't know why they just didn't refuse to go to Nam?" Paul remembered the night he had contemplated the idea of going to Canada, but Irene was pregnant then and it had just been too much to handle. The casual way these kids talked about the war made him clench his jaw to hold down the rage and the pain that he wanted to spew on them. He finished pumping gas and the kids drove away.

Paul rushed past Charlie and into the bathroom that was around the side of the station. He pounded on the door. Damn, he needed the key. He bolted inside the station and knocked shoulders with Charlie. He didn't stop, just grabbed the key and hid in the small bathroom. It felt like he had a volcano of hot puss rising from his stomach. He began to punch the walls and yelled, kill-o, kill-o, kill, kill, over and over, punching till his knuckles bled. Charlie heard him and knocked on the door. "Paul, it's okay, you're gonna be alright, this will pass, take a breath..." he spoke slowly, "throw water on your face Paul, come out when you're ready, it's all gonna be okay." When he heard Paul crying, he knew the worst was over. Charlie walked away saying a prayer for Paul and remembering his nephew, Randy, and wondering what the fuck he had died for. Paul just about took a bath in the dirty sink, soaking his hair, trying to cool himself. *Rage is actually hot*, he thought as he soaked a paper towel and put it on his eyes. When he emerged, someone was waiting to use the bathroom and Paul handed him the key and walked into the office. "You can take the rest of the day off if you want to Paul, I got it covered, okay?" Charlie spoke with the wisdom of a fifty-year-old man. Paul grabbed his coat and decided to walk down Grove Street, which ran across Bridgetown and into Larchmont. He wanted to go to Donny and Teddy's graves and talk to them, they would understand.

Then There Was April

After Paul's rage incident, Ed took him to the VA hospital to have a counseling appointment with Max Whitlow and to say hello to some of the men he knew who were still there. It helped. Paul told Max what had happened at Met State Hospital. Max told Paul he did a good job managing his rage and that he was lucky to have a compassionate man for a boss who knew how to steady him. Max said he thought these incidents would go away with time but he really didn't know if that was true. He figured hope was more useful than truth at that moment. No one knew what was happening to all these Nam vets; they just kept streaming into hospitals, clinics, and morgues.

About one month later, Paul was on a break in the gas station office, listening to music on the transistor radio, which was always on. He was eating a Snickers bar when the six o'clock news began:

"Vietnam is in total chaos," the announcer said, "South Vietnam has surrendered to North Vietnam. Saigon is overrun with tanks. People are looting stores and others are storming the American Embassy trying to flee on helicopters."

Paul took his coat off the hook and walked out the door. When he passed Charlie at a pump he simply put up his hand in a wave and started walking down Mt. Auburn Street in a shocked state. He didn't feel anything. There was no rage, no "finally," no nothing, just a huge void. His body felt like a wasteland. Trolley cars passed him but he just kept staring straight ahead and walking. Then he had a vision that the world turned flat and he would just walk off the edge of it.

Paul came to Mt. Auburn Cemetery and walked through the huge iron gates. He went up a little windy hill called Iris Lane and found a bench to sit on. He looked around remembering the time he and Irene brought Paulie to this place. That thought stung deeply. He laid his coat on the grass, lay back and watched the clouds; dusk was coming on. He spoke out loud to the sky: "I lost Irene and Paulie because of Vietnam. I lost my mind. I'm totally lost because of the war, and now we lost that. Everything is fucking lost!" A service truck passed him and the driver leaned out the window and said, "We're locking the gates in fifteen minutes buddy, time to get a move on." *Who the fuck does that little creep think he's talking to?* "I'm not your buddy, asshole." Paul yelled to the passing truck. His sudden anger scared him, and he began running to the exit forgetting his coat on the grass.

Paul had no idea where he was but soon found himself along the Charles River. He slowed his pace and watched the water and it calmed him. He heard a car horn honk a few times and he looked up to see a car slowing down. The driver yelled out the window to a group of people, "THE WAR'S OVER" and they all flashed the peace sign at one another. Paul's head collapsed into his chest. All his anger dropped down and he said to no one, "This is fucked up, why don't they know how sad this is."

He walked in a daze until he found himself in Harvard Square. There were too many people, he became fearful. He darted into the alcove of the Harvard Coop to take cover but he wasn't alone. A young musician was using the alcove as an amphitheater, playing a portable synthesizer and singing. She began to play a rendition of Jefferson Airplane's, "Somebody to Love," which drew more people into the alcove. Paul moved to the back and sat down against the wall. He was surprised that such a passionate voice resounded from her petite body as she sang, "When the truth is found to be lies and all the joy within you dies ..." The intensity of her voice bounced around the alcove and pierced through Paul. After hearing those initial words, Paul held his breath, trying not to feel anything, but was jolted when the crowd burst into applause at the end. People threw quarters into the musician's hat and then moved on as the young girl began to fold up her equipment; it was getting dark out. Paul sat huddled in the back corner of the alcove. The truth of the words of the song continue to sting him. He couldn't make himself go numb again and the reality of the war being all lies, was suffocating him. *Yes, all the joy has died*, he told himself; *Irene and Paulie are gone, and I don't know how to live, how am I going to make it through this night?*

Paul looked in his wallet. He had forty-three dollars and he knew if he just kept walking to Central Square he could cop a bag of smack and that would end this painful reality. *Don't think*, he told himself, *just walk, don't think, don't care, just make it through this one night; tomorrow it won't hurt so bad.*

Chapter Twenty-Seven

Seattle

LIFE IN SEATTLE FELL INTO PLACE IN A GRACEFUL, kind way. Paulie started first grade in September and I applied for a waitressing job at the Space Needle. I was hired to work the lunch shift three days a week. That was perfect, I could be home at night with the boys and I wouldn't need a babysitter. Arty brought me home a catalogue from Seattle Central Community College where he was finishing the last year of his boat-building course. I was drawn immediately to the Acting 101 class. When I saw that I could fit that in around my work schedule, I signed up.

It was as if a piece of me got to slip back in time to the nineteen-year-old Irene at Boston State College, before the war had altered everything; I could explore avenues into who I might have been. In typical Seattle fashion, our class did our first skit about fog. The teacher narrated a poem: "The fog comes in like little cat feet..." Ten of us students dressed in grey tights and skin tight long sleeve shirts. We slithered into the room on our bellies from under a black velvet curtain, gradually standing up exposing a brilliant cardboard sun. The symbolism deeply moved me, making it apparent that I too was coming out from under something heavy.

I was happily leaving my acting class on the very last

Irene Isobel Carver

day of April and heading to Pike Place Market to catch the bus, I caught a glimpse of the headlines that were splashed on all the world newspapers lining the international newsstand on the corner of Pike and First Ave.

"U.S. EVACUATING! SOUTH VIETNAM SURRENDERS TO NORTH VIETNAM"

I stared at the words, my eyes roving from one city newspaper to the next. *The war is finally over and we lost,* I thought. The word "lost" brought up a mental list. We lost men, legs, arms, sanity, and families. We lost face as a nation. And that was only America; what had South Vietnam lost? They lost all of the above plus their land, their homes, and their children. Flashes of napalm ripped my mind open again to the horrors that we humans create.

There was no way I could get on a bus. I needed beauty to pull me out of the horror show in my mind. I walked into the Athenian Restaurant where I knew I could sit on a stool looking out at Puget Sound and not have to speak to anyone. I checked my purse for money and ordered three shucked oysters and a schooner of Rainier beer. After I sucked out the creamy oyster flesh I stared into the beautiful shell. In my mind I saw Paul putting on his parachute, preparing to jump from an airplane into Hue, into the death of his spirit, into the Tet Offensive. "Fuck President Johnson," I said as I gulped my beer. I wanted to throw the oyster shells on the floor and stomp on them as my rage erupted, but instead, I put my money on the counter and ran down the back streets to the waterfront. *There should be a ferry that goes to West Seattle,* I thought. I knew I had to stay close to the water to calm myself. There wasn't a ferry so I kept walking along Western Avenue, hugging the shore wherever I could between seafood stands, tourist shops, and docking fishing boats. As I walked, a guttural ache began to moan up and I threw up into a potted plant. Walking helped. The air was fresh and salty. I soon realized that I had almost walked all the way to West Seattle. I was under the suspension bridge and it felt good to be under the world a bit as I purged the depths of my psyche. I saw a restaurant with a payphone outside and knew that I should call home. Paulie answered with a "Where are you, mum?" sound in his voice.

"Paulie, I had to walk home today so it's going to take me about another hour, is Arty home yet?"

"No, I'm alone, and I'm hungry" he answered.

"Well, be a big boy and make a peanut butter and jelly sandwich and just watch cartoons until I get there." I instructed.

"Okay, but hurry up," he said and hung up.

I bought a Pepsi in the restaurant and took it to go and kept walking under the bridge until I came out on Alki beach. I sat down on an oily smelling log to rest and pull myself together. I stared into the lapping waves at the shore's edge. Looking at the evening sky inspired me to backtrack a bit and hike up Fauntleroy Hill to the junction. I just couldn't get on a bus; I didn't want to make eye contact with the world yet. By the time I got home I was sweating, but I felt calmer. Paulie ran to me, flung his arms around my waist and said, "Where were you, mummy, were you lost?"

"No, not really lost, but I've walked a long way and I'm starving, have you eaten?"

"Yes, Arty made us spaghetti," Paulie said, letting go of me but staying close to my side. Arty rounded the corner of the kitchen with a beer in his hand and a deep furrow on his brow.

Irene Isobel Carver

"Where the heck have you been?" he asked in an accusatory tone. "Been acting out with the guys in your acting class?" he added with a jeer. I looked up at the clock, it was almost seven and I didn't want Paulie around for this conversation so I side-stepped Arty and said to Paulie, "Hey, you want to take your bath now and we can have a salad together when you're done?" Luckily, Paulie always treated a bath like an extended play area with boats and GI Joe men diving in, so he headed to the bathroom.

After I ran the bath for him I went back into the kitchen and began chopping vegetables. Arty leaned against the kitchen counter and snapped open another beer. "Irene, I'm serious, where the hell have you been?" Part of me just wanted to weep into the colander but the other part of me decided to meet Arty's attitude with the volcano of rage that wanted to erupt in me. I slammed down the carrot I was washing and turned and looked Arty right in the eye and said, "Arthur, have you heard the news today?" As he shook his head no, I said, "Well, the fucking war has finally ended and we lost. South Vietnam surrendered, it was all for fucking nothing, and all you can think about is being jealous?" I picked up a cucumber and flung it across the room, meaning to smash it against the cabinet but Arty—without flinching and just like a little league catcher—lifted his arm to the side and caught it.

"Damn you, I wanted to see that splatter." Arty calmly walked over to me and taking my hand he walked me out the kitchen door. He stopped on the cement walkway, handed me the cucumber and said, "Go ahead, smash it." I lifted my hands above my head and did just that. I screamed, "Fucking war, I hate fucking war!" I looked at Arty and asked, "What else can I smash?" and we both laughed.

"Let's go to Chinatown and buy some fireworks," Arty said.

"You go," I answered, "I'm exhausted; and to answer your question, I walked home from Pike Place Market, that's where I've been."

"Sorry," Arty said. He hugged me and sang into my ear, "War, what is it good for?" Together we shouted: ABSO-LUTELY FUCKING NOTHING!" hoping the neighbors heard us.

Epilogue

FROM THAT DAY ON PAUL'S LIFE WAS LIKE A LINGER-
ing sunset—colors fading, energy draining, brightness
leaving, then briefly returning—until he reached his point
of no return and he could no longer bounce back from life's
painful blows. Day by day he walked towards the horizon
of his life, disappearing. Paul joined thousands of other
soldiers who had fallen between the cracks. A three year
crack between he last soldiers killed in Vietnam on April
29th, 1975 and 1978 when the Vietnam Veterans of America
was founded by activist veterans, who realized that the
government didn't know how to help them, and they had
better figure out how to help themselves.

Paul tried going to AA meetings a few times out of
desperation, but he always felt misunderstood there since
addiction was not his main problem. For him drugs and
alcohol were used to suppress the major problem of Post
Traumatic Stress, which was not even recognized as a syn-
drome meriting treatment or benefits until 1980.

*"In 1979, the Vietnam Vet's of America got congress to
approve non VA counseling. Twelve million dollars
was allotted for counseling centers throughout the
country. Depression and rage were huge problems for
Vietnam vets. It was not until 1984 that a class action
suit against chemical companies for Agent Orange was
settled and Veterans received 180 million dollars in
damages. Until then, veterans were ill and dying from
exposure to that chemical used to defoliate the jungle.
Veterans were dying of cancer and blood diseases and*

their children were being born with physical deformities.
All that time the US government would not own up to
the responsibility for any of it. No wonder our veterans
were medicating themselves. Along with the trauma
of war, they were disrespected and disregarded by the
government they had fought for. The VA hospitals were
overwhelmed with the problems of Vietnam veterans.
Some of the hospitals were like nursing homes for aging
WWII veterans. There was no policy and no structure
for how to help the thousands upon thousands of Viet-
nam vets that were either trying to commit suicide or
were committing crimes that landed them in jail or the
hospital. Either way they were experiencing some form
of psychological hell. The veterans seemed to be carry-
ing the guilt for the whole nation over a senseless war
we were ashamed of and we could not win."

—Quoted from WWW.vva.org)

The last time I talked to Paul was at the end of January 1977, when he called me in Seattle after hearing that President Carter had pardoned all draft dodgers. I remember Paul's voice being very low, not drugged or angry, but simply and completely defeated. All he said when I answered the phone was, "I wish we had run away to Canada. I'm sorry for everything, Irene, goodbye." He hung up not waiting for any response from me.

Paul lived another two years but we never talked again. He bounced in and out of the methadone program. Then some unbearable memory would send him back to the streets for heroin. He would make his way to his parents' house every few months and let them help him get somewhat back on his feet. He would ask to see a picture of

Paulie, put it in his wallet, and off he would go, not to be seen or heard from for months at a time. "He always hoped you would come back, Irene." Dora once told me. But there would be no going back for me. The little girl Leah, that Arty and I always felt would come to us, was born in March of 1976; we were content.

To Dora's great credit she called me herself on May 23, 1979 and told me the police had come to their house and brought Paul's wallet and his note. They said he was found at a friend's house in Cambridge. He had taken his own life with an overdose of pills and he left a note that said: "I don't care anymore, I do love you though, goodbye, Paul." I had just given birth to my second child with Arty, a son named Ben, born on April 28th, 1979. Paulie had just turned eleven and Leah was three years old.

I will never forget the pureness of the morning air that May day when Dora called with the sad news. I could feel its aliveness on my skin, or was it just that I was more alive in the presence of death? I don't know. When I hung up the phone with Dora, I walked out the back door in an altered state of consciousness, with my three-week-old baby at my breast. I crossed the lawn and stood next to my fig tree. I touched the tree with my free hand, aware of its special energy, and I knew that the tree was a gift at this intensely holy moment in my life. I sat down and leaned against her small trunk. A pair of sparrows landed on the tallest branch, drawing my eyes upward to a puffy cloud passing overhead. "Hi Paul," I said to the cloud. Leah came running up to me. I stroked the baby's tiny, soft cheek as he sucked milk from my breast.

New life was pulsating through me, yet I could feel my dear friend Dora experiencing the death of the son that was once at her breast. The truth of this filled me and I wondered if I could handle this much life? Then Leah looked up at the sky and said, "Look at the birdies, mummy," and she pointed up with her small finger. I joined her upward glance and watched as another large white cloud floated slowly by.

"Goodbye, Paul," I said to the sky, "I'll see you when it's my turn, you'll come meet me, right?" I hid my tears from Leah with the corner of the baby's blanket as memories floated through my mind like the clouds. I sat in the still morning air as a precious mini life review was given to me. I saw Paul and I carving pumpkins on my mother's front steps on our first date when I was fifteen. Then we were at Paul's senior prom dancing to Moon River, me in my long blue satin dress and Paul in a white tux. Soon we were driving to the Newport Jazz Festival on my twenty-first birthday in our new Toyota, laughing. Then we were at Woodstock, holding each other's hands as we stood looking down from the top of the hill into a sea of people, amazed. It felt as if Paul was looking down on me as he floated off to his new home, where his friends Teddy and Donny would greet him and he would know peace.

I was jolted out of my transcendental moment when Paulie yelled to me from the back door, "Hey, ma, where are you guys?" Leah jumped up and ran to her big brother and I shifted the baby to my shoulder. With my eyes still one with the sky, I said, "Mother Mary, please in the name of God show me how to tell a little boy that his father has died." Paulie and Leah ran up to me with a whoosh of energy and the tiny sparrows took flight.

THE END

Afterward

It is with great joy that I am able to tell my readers that I truly did watch my sister Teresa and Carlo step into their destiny that long ago night in downtown Boston. In 1977 they became free of addiction, finding help through a biofeedback program. They have been happily married for thirty-eight years and have three grown children. Teresa is still a nurse.

I am pleased to say that I have twenty-one years of sobriety as of this writing in 2015. If I had not become sober I would most likely be sitting somewhere with a glass of wine in hand saying, "You know I should write a book someday, I lived quite a story." But by the Grace of God that is not what happened. I did the challenging work of overcoming my genetically inherited disease and I used my sober energy to write this book. I offer it as a tribute to Paul and all the veterans of Vietnam whose names are not on the wall.

LET THIS BE MY WALL FOR PAUL,
Do I hear an amen!

48622668R00244

Made in the USA
Charleston, SC
08 November 2015